THE ORDNANCE SURVEY GUIDE TO
CASTLES
IN BRITAIN

D1040306

Edited by

Peter Furtado, Candida Geddes,

Nathaniel Harris, Hazel Harrison and Paul Pettit

ORDNANCE SURVEY
COUNTRY LIFE BOOKS

First published 1987 by
Ordnance Survey   and   Country Life Books
Romsey Road   an imprint of
Maybush   The Hamlyn Publishing Group Limited
Southampton   Bridge House, 69 London Road
SO9 4DH   Twickenham, Middlesex TW1 3SB

Regional maps on pages 18-19, 60-61, 88-89, 131, 147, 163, 203 by Thames Cartographic Services, © The Hamlyn Publishing Group Limited and Ordnance Survey 1987.

Hamlyn   Ordnance Survey
ISBN 0 600 35185 8 (softback) ISBN 0 319 00093 1 (softback)
ISBN 0 600 33387 6 (cased)   ISBN 0 319 00092 3 (cased)

Printed in Great Britain

Contents

How to use this guide

This guide is arranged regionally; a key map showing the area covered by each region is given on the opposite page. Within each region, the castles are listed alphabetically by county.

A detailed description is given of how to find the way to each castle from the nearest town, together with the sheet number of the Ordnance Survey Landranger map which covers the area and the National Grid reference of the castle site. Sections of Ordnance Survey maps are also included for over 70 of the castles.

The National Grid reference given for each castle consists of two letters and four numbers. This pinpoints the location to within one kilometre on Ordnance Survey maps. The following example identifies how these references are constructed:

Herstmonceux Castle, Hailsham, East Sussex has a grid reference TQ 6312.

TQ This identifies the 100 kilometre grid square in which the property lies and can be ignored from the point of view of locating the castles in this book.

63 Can be found in the top and bottom margins of the relevant Ordnance Survey Landranger map sheet (identified for each property). It is the reference number for one of the grid lines running North/South on the map.

12 Can be found in the left and right hand margins of the relevant Ordnance Survey Landranger map sheet. It is the reference number for one of the grid lines running East/West across the map.

These numbers together locate the bottom left hand corner of the one kilometre grid square in which Herstmonceux Castle appears.

When planning routes or driving to the areas of the properties included in this guide, the *Ordnance Survey Motoring Atlas of Great Britain* at 3 miles to 1 inch scale and the *Ordnance Survey Road Atlas of Great Britain* at 1:250 000 (approximately 4 miles to 1 inch) are ideal. For pinpointing the site once in the area use Ordnance Survey Landranger (1:50 000) or Pathfinder (1:25 000) maps. For London sites, the Ordnance Survey *ABC London Street Atlas* is a useful location guide.

Key to symbols

P	Car park	✿	Plant sales
WC	Toilets	⅍	Guide book on sale
⊖	Public transport	ⱦ	Guided tours
⬚	Access for the disabled	●	Restrictions on photography
⊟	Parties welcome	ⱦ	Playground
D	Dogs welcome	ⱦ	Nature trail
●	Refreshments available	NT	National Trust
⊓	Picnic area	EH	English Heritage
★	Free entry	WHM	Welsh Historic Monuments
◆	Shop		

M: Monday   T: Tuesday   W: Wednesday
Th: Thursday   F: Friday   S: Saturday   Su: Sunday

Map to regions

HIGHLAND

GRAMPIAN

Scotland

TAYSIDE

FIFE

CENTRAL

LOTHIAN

STRATHCLYDE

BORDERS

DUMFRIES AND GALLOWAY

NORTHUMBERLAND

1 Tyne and Wear

DURHAM

2

CUMBRIA

The North

NORTH YORKSHIRE

1 TYNE AND WEAR
2 CLEVELAND
3 WEST YORKSHIRE
4 SOUTH YORKSHIRE
5 GREATER MANCHESTER
6 MERSEYSIDE
7 WEST MIDLANDS
8 BEDFORDSHIRE
9 BERKSHIRE
10 WEST GLAMORGAN
11 MID GLAMORGAN
12 SOUTH GLAMORGAN

LANCASHIRE

HUMBERSIDE

3

6 5 4

GWYNEDD

CLWYD

CHESHIRE

DERBY-SHIRE

NOTTINGHAM-SHIRE

LINCOLNSHIRE

STAFFORD-SHIRE

LEICESTERSHIRE

NORFOLK

SHROPSHIRE

7

Central England

Eastern Counties

Wales and Western Counties

POWYS

HEREFORD AND WORCESTER

WARWICK-SHIRE

NORTHAMPTON-SHIRE

CAMBRIDGE-SHIRE

SUFFOLK

DYFED

GLOUCESTER-SHIRE

OXFORD-SHIRE

BUCKINGHAM-SHIRE

8

HERTFORD-SHIRE

ESSEX

GWENT

10

11

12

AVON

WILTSHIRE

9

GREATER LONDON

London and Southern England

SURREY

KENT

HAMPSHIRE

WEST SUSSEX

EAST SUSSEX

The West Country

SOMERSET

DORSET

DEVON

ISLE OF WIGHT

CORNWALL

5

Introduction

Human beings have long felt the need for security against attack by members of their own species, and from very early times natural defensive sites such as peninsulas and hilltops have been strengthened with ramparts, ditches and timbering. These sites served as places of refuge in times of danger, and in some instances developed into permanent settlements – at which point they might be classified as castles or even, if sufficiently populous, towns. The defining feature of the castle is that it is a fortified dwelling, habitable and defensible against a reasonably sustained onslaught, and therefore distinguishable from barracks, citadels and other more or less fortified places. Like all such definitions, this one is useful provided it is not insisted on too rigorously in the face of common sense and common usage.

Whether or not they should be defined as castles, the many fortified places, or duns, in Iron Age Scotland merit a place in any survey. While most Britons were still constructing earthworks for defensive purposes, people in the far north were already building in stone, partly at least because there was so little timber available in the region. As a result, the earliest British

A typical 13th-century castle: Rothesay Castle, on the Island of Bute.

dwellings to have survived are stone houses in the Orkney Islands; in the heavily forested south, only powerful religious impulses justified building in stone – as at Stonehenge – and both ordinary dwellings and any defensive works made of wood have simply rotted away.

The outstanding type of dun was the broch, a fortified round tower that is unique to western and northern Scotland. There are over four hundred known examples, the most striking being at Mousa on Shetland. Brochs stand up to about 40 feet high and have massive double walls that contain chambers and galleries, with a staircase leading to the top. Vulnerable points are reduced to a minimum: entry is by a single low door, and the inclined outer walls are windowless. These forbidding drystone buildings were evidently the residences of chiefs, and in many places the broch was the centre of a group of dwellings that were presumably occupied by his retainers or subjects; some were lean-to buildings, standing up against the sides of the broch, but there were also many examples of the distinctively Scottish wheel-house, a circular stone building with interior walls arranged like the spokes of a wheel.

Britons and Romans
Brochs were developed in about the 1st century BC, and continued to be used in Scotland during the early centuries of the Christian era. By that time, the southern British had become redoubtable warriors, had turned their hill-

forts into huge, formidable defensive structures – and had succumbed to the might of the Roman legions.

From 650 BC Britain was dominated by warlike Celtic tribes. In the 1st century BC they attracted the attention of the Romans by assisting their fellow Celts in France against Julius Caesar, whose two expeditions (55 and 54 BC) ended with a perfunctory British acknowledgement of Roman overlordship. In AD 43 the Roman commander Aulus Plautius landed on the Isle of Thanet with 40,000 men and began the conquest of Britain in earnest.

In the open field British spearmen, stone-slingers and charioteers could not stand up to the close-order discipline of the legions; and their hilltop forts proved equally vulnerable to Roman siege engines. The largest and most famous hill-fort, Maiden Castle in Dorset, was a vast enclosure which had been extended down from the hilltop until it covered no less than 45 acres. Its concentric ramparts and ditches represented a feat of careful planning and immense labour. The zig-zag approaches to the gateways show that the Britons realised this was the most vulnerable part of a fortress and made the approach to it as difficult as possible, thus anticipating the most sophisticated military thinking of medieval castle-builders. Nevertheless the east gate of Maiden Castle was stormed by the Legio II Augusta commanded by Vespasian; thousands of stones – ammunition for British slings – have been found on the site, and a mass grave near the east gate contains the bones of the losers.

The British proved stubborn enemies and mutinous subjects, but the Romans gradually strengthened their hold on the country in characteristic fashion, building forts and founding cities at strategic points and linking them with a network of well-made roads. Unless the site had some unusual features, the Romans followed a set plan in constructing a fort, whether it was to stand in Britain or in Bithynia. The rectangular walls, made of stone with a concrete core, were protected by a rampart and ditches. There were four gateways, each more or less centred in one of the walls, from which roads led to the headquarters, storehouse and other important buildings. Beyond the walls, even in remote places such as Hardknott in Cumbria, lay the indispensable luxury and symbol of Roman civilisation – the baths.

The Britons 'succumbed to the lure of Roman vices' (including the baths), in the view of the Roman historian Tacitus, and by the 2nd century AD villas – another symbol of Roman culture – had been built over much of England as far north as Yorkshire. Scotland remained unconquered despite sporadic Roman efforts, which culminated in the building of the Antonine Wall (actually a mainly earthen rampart) which for a few years after 143 kept 'barbarism' at bay along a line stretching from the Forth to the Clyde. Most of the time, however, the Romans relied on Hadrian's Wall, a more substantial stone structure, running from the Solway to the Tyne and equipped with an impressive system of forts, milecastles (fortlets) and signal towers at regular intervals.

Despite the intermittent political crises that shook the Roman Empire, life in Britain remained fairly secure until the late 3rd century, when Saxon marauders became a serious threat, plundering the south and east coasts. After Britain also became involved in a rebellion, the Emperor Constantius reorganised the administration, dividing authority between a number of officials. One of these, the Count of the Saxon Shore, was charged with erecting forts all along the coast from Norfolk to Hampshire. Unlike most Roman forts, these were not barracks or military headquarters but large, strong castles, built to withstand siege and assault. The walls were higher, the gateways fewer and smaller, and the towers now projected beyond the walls, providing platforms for the artillery-like ballistae, giant rock-flinging bows. The Romans' strategic grasp and engineering skills are illustrated by the fact that, centuries after their departure, Pevensey and Porchester Castles came back into use when the Normans built their own castle keeps within the old walls.

Saxons and Normans
Roman efforts to defend Britain remained vigorous until late in the 4th century. By this time barbarians were pouring into the Mediterranean heartlands of the Empire, and Britain was depleted of troops by a desperate imperial authority. The last legion left in 404, and it quickly became apparent that the British would have to defend themselves as best they could.

After the Romans' departure, their British province broke up into a number of kingdoms which for a time defended themselves with more or less success against the ravages of the Picts from the north and the Teutonic Saxons, Angles and Jutes from the Continent. The latter gradually turned from raiding to settlement, and over a long period drove back the Britons into Wales, Cornwall and the north-west. Eventually Anglo-Saxon England – Angle-land – emerged as a separate entity from the unconquered or in-completely absorbed 'Celtic fringe' to the west and north.

Not much now remains of the Anglo-Saxons' fortifications, though their history was turbulent and they were certainly capable of executing large-scale enterprises such as Offa's Dyke, the great earthwork built to guard middle-English Mercia from the unreconciled Britons of Wales. From the time of Alfred the Great the Saxons carefully fortified their *burhs* (towns) against Viking and other enemies; but this communal defence proved ineffective against the Normans. After the battle of Hastings, Anglo-Saxon resistance was sporadic, and it is probably significant that only one town withstood a long siege – Exeter, whose citizens were still protected by Roman walls. As one chronicler pointed out at the time, the battle of Hastings would have been only the beginning of a long campaign if the Saxons had had castles on the Norman model, lived in and commanded by individual lords.

This reflected a difference in social systems as much as military tech-nology. The Conquest swept away the Anglo-Saxon ruling class and replaced it with a tough band of Normans, Bretons and other aliens; and it also altered the relationships between rulers and ruled. The feudal system made the king the apex of a hierarchy of lords and vassals, and landlords and tenants, that included barons, knights and ecclesiastics. Most of the way down the hierarchy the lord–vassal relationship was personal, and involved military service in return for landholding. The greatest barons, or tenants-in-chief, held their lands directly from the king and were sworn to assist him with substantial contingents of knights, who in turn rendered military assistance to the tenants-in-chief in return for lands. Even if the Norman lords had not been unpopular aliens, they operated within a system that was essentially military in structure.

Nor was feudalism likely to reconcile the majority of Saxons to their conquerors, although it is impossible to be certain that they were actually worse off after 1066. Held down at the bottom of the social hierarchy, they became serfs, tied to the land and toiling on it to produce the food that supported the entire system. In theory, the lord justified his privileges by protecting his serfs; in practice, protection benefited the protector most, because, as the chronicler William of Malmesbury wrote of the Normans, 'they plunder their subjects, although they protect them from others'.

The Norman castle

In the years following the Conquest the Normans tried to ensure their security by building castles at strategic points all over England; from his castle the baron could dominate the surrounding countryside and overawe the villagers on his manor. In the first instance, almost all these castles were built of timber. The main reason for this was speed: the Normans needed adequately secure defences as quickly as possible. The use of stone demanded time, resources, skills and transport facilities; whereas the available Saxon labour force – accustomed to working with wood, and to banking and ditching – could build a timber motte-and-bailey castle in a remarkably short time.

The motte was simply a mound of earth raised in order to create a lofty defensive site suitable for the timber tower that was then erected on top of it. Some mottes were natural features that only needed to be levelled off at the top, but the overwhelming majority were artificial. In such cases the earth was packed round huge timbers that served as foundations for the tower; occasionally the builders exploited other local materials, such as the great blocks of local chalk used at Lewes Castle. The digging itself created a deep ditch that made any hostile approach to the motte even more difficult, while the tower above was protected by a timber palisade equipped with walkways for defence and observation. The tower on the motte was the refuge of last resort; in all but emergencies, most of the castle's activity was undertaken in a much larger area, the bailey, which was also banked and enclosed by a timber palisade. Motte and bailey were connected by a timber 'flying bridge' that could be put out of action if the bailey was captured during an attack. There was no watery 'moat' unless the surrounding ditch lay on low, marshy ground and filled up naturally through seepage.

Keeps and halls

For King William and his most powerful supporters, timber construction was at best a temporary expedient, and in some instances they dispensed with it altogether. The characteristic Norman stone castle was the keep, a generally square or rectangular tower whose chief defensive feature was its mighty walls, many feet thick; to build it involved quarrying substantial quantities of stone and transporting it to the site, often over long distances.

Most of the early keeps were located at points where a Norman military presence was of vital strategic importance. In 1078 William the Conqueror began replacing his earth-and-timber castle in the south-east corner of London with a stone keep tucked into the city walls. This, the White Tower, received its name from being regularly repainted in that colour, perhaps to remind Londoners of their master's might; it forms the earliest part of what is now the Tower of London. It was built for William by Gundulf, Bishop of Rochester, who later supervised the construction of the even bigger royal keep at Colchester. Even before Gundulf started the White Tower, the Breton earl, Alan the Red, had begun Richmond Castle to strengthen the Norman grip on the rebellious North; while other trusted lords built castles at Chepstow and Ludlow to hold the marches (borderlands) against the turbulent Welsh.

These and other early Norman keeps varied in shape and arrangement; but by the time Rochester Castle was built, in the second quarter of the 12th century, the tall tower keep had become the norm. Typically it was three or four storeys high. The walls were made of rubble – uncut stone laid out in rough lines – with dressed stone giving a more finished look to the corners and the door and window surrounds; in places such as London and Colchester the economical Normans embedded Roman tiles in the walls, often arranging them in the ancient herringbone pattern. The wooden roof was disguised and protected by a parapet that might well be crenellated – that is, provided with the familiar alteration of spaces and upright rectangular projections. Where the keep was sufficiently powerful the motte became redundant or impractical (an artificial mound might well collapse under the weight of stone), and the keep stood inside the bailey, which was protected by a stone wall (the curtain wall) that would eventually be equipped with a more or less formidable gatehouse and mural towers.

Life in early castles

Inside the bailey were living quarters, kitchens, workshops, stables, a smithy and all the other items needed to maintain a great household in both war and peace. But if necessary the lord and his retainers could withdraw into the keep itself and still be self-sufficient, although more austerely so. The entire ground floor was a storehouse, which also contained the most vital resource of all in times of siege – a well. The windows of the ground-floor storehouse were necessarily tiny, so that no enemy could squeeze through them into the keep. To make life harder for the attackers, the entrance to the keep was on the first floor, up a flight of stairs; from the 12th century the steps led to a drawbridge and an additional building (the forebuilding) which had to be captured before the besieging army could even reach the entrance to the main keep, protected by a formidable portcullis (the metal grid that slid down to seal off the entrance).

The most important room in the upper storeys was the hall, the large common living- and eating-room in which the lord, his family and his retainers spent most of their time. In essentials it differed little from the halls in which Homeric heroes, Viking chiefs and Teutonic war-lords had feasted over many centuries – or from the unfortified great hall, built by William II, which formed part of his Palace of Westminster. It was in fact a natural arrangement while master and followers retained something of the war-band mentality, and the hall, with the mentality it represented, long survived the end of the castle as a building seriously intended for military purposes.

Whether part of a manor house or keep, or a separate building within the castle walls, the hall was laid out in much the same way. Even in Norman times there was some physical separation between master and man. The lord and his family occupied a dais, raised a step or two above the rest of the hall, and had a separate private room (the solar) adjacent to the hall or just above it. At the other end of the hall a screen partitioned off the buttery (*bouteuillerie*, where the bottles were looked after by the butler) and the pantry (where the bread – *pain* – and other provisions were kept). The hall itself was a lofty place, usually two storeys high, if only to make sure that the inhabitants were not stifled by the smoke rising from the central hearth and lingering in the rafters; there was of course no chimney, and the fumes gradually seeped out through lateral holes or louvres in the roof. Windows in the hall were relatively large (but, in a keep, placed high up, out of reach of scaling ladders); except in fine weather, however, they were covered by wooden shutters, since glass had not yet come into general use.

The well-equipped keep contained all the necessities of Norman life, including at least one chapel and a garderobe or latrine. This last consisted of a stone seat above a shaft leading down to a cesspit; it was not unknown for a castle to be taken by soldiers intrepid enough to climb the shaft and risk the consequences.

Improvements in castle design

During the century following the Conquest large numbers of timber motte-and-bailey castles were converted to stone. Some of these consisted of a stone keep surrounded by a curtain wall, but there were also large numbers of shell keeps. This rather misleading term describes a powerful round or polygonal wall, built round the motte and serving as a keep though remaining open to the sky. The hall and other buildings inside were commonly built up against the wall. In most cases the shell keep replaced a palisade that had stood on the same spot, and the new structure therefore constituted a simple and economical substitution of stone for wood; doubts about the ability of the motte to bear the weight of a tower keep were probably another motive for constructing this sort of castle. Easily the most famous shell keep in Britain is the round tower of Windsor Castle, built for King Henry II.

Within his stone castle, a baron was not only more secure from resentful serfs and marauders: he was also able to contemplate defying his overlord, even if that overlord was the king himself. The Norman kings had always been aware of the potential danger offered by great lords ensconced in strong castles. William the Conqueror had shrewdly avoided granting large blocks of land to his followers except where it seemed essential to Norman interests; and he and his sons were sparing with the royal licences that a baron had to obtain before he could build himself a castle. But the fact that England was effectively an occupied country meant that they could hardly avoid creating powerful vassals, and putting up with the alarms and rebellions endemic to feudalism.

If the king's grip relaxed, matters grew far worse. 'They filled the land with castles' lamented a chronicler during the reign of King Stephen (1135-54), when England was wracked by the civil war between Stephen and the Empress Matilda. During this period, often called 'the Anarchy', central authority virtually disappeared. The royal combatants devoted all their energies to a seemingly endless succession of sieges, while the barons happily sold their services to the highest bidder or simply went their own ways.

Order was restored by Matilda's son Henry II (1154-89), the first Angevin king, who razed many castles that had been erected without the necessary royal licence; some were formidable strongholds, but most were timber motte-and-bailey structures, run up in a hurry to take advantage of the Anarchic good times. The next great wave of building, under Henry, was influenced by military lessons learned from the sieges of the previous reign, and also by ideas brought back from the sophisticated East by the Crusaders. Rectangular keeps continued to be built (including those in the royal castles at Scarborough, Peveril and Dover), but experiments began with other shapes. The corners of rectangular keeps created awkward blind spots for sentries or defenders, whereas polygonal and circular keeps allowed them to see almost everything that was happening below them, and to react appropriately. The new trend was represented by the royal castle at Orford in Suffolk, with its nearly circular (actually eighteen-faceted) tower and three tall turrets. Orford was under construction from 1165; the truly circular Conisbrough Castle, South Yorkshire, built by Henry's half-brother, followed in 1180-90.

The surviving curtain wall of Roger Bigod's castle at Framlingham, in Suffolk, provides a splendid early example of an even more important trend that was to dominate 13th-century military thinking. This was the tendency to substitute active defence based on the curtain wall for passive reliance on the strength of the keep, which was dispensed with altogether. Wall towers, hitherto rather haphazardly sited, were placed at regular intervals; the curtain wall at Framlingham is equipped with no less than thirteen. This arrangement was even more efficient than defence based on a single round keep, because projecting wall towers made it possible to scan the entire area round the base of the castle. And, no matter from what direction an attack was launched, the enemy could be caught in a devastating crossfire from two of the towers.

During the 13th century castle design increasingly favoured regular patterns, and by mid-century the most common plan for a new castle was a rectangle with four large, boldly projecting round corner towers. Defensive features became ever more elaborate and sophisticated. For example, it had long been realised that the most vulnerable point in a curtain wall was the entrance, so this was progressively strengthened. At first the gateway was driven through a tower, benefiting from its surrounding protection; then the still greater advantages of flanking towers were utilised. Eventually great twin-towered gatehouses not only controlled the entrances but constituted strongpoints akin to the keeps, habitable and able to function independently even when the rest of the castle had fallen into enemy hands. The gatehouse was further protected by a type of outworks known as a barbican, usually in the form of an outer gateway and passage that could be booby-trapped and – like the entrances to ancient Maiden Castle, 1200 years earlier – channelled the attackers along an oblique course towards the entrance, during which they would come under devastating flanking fire. A drawbridge and portcullis – or more likely several of each – protected the entrances to the courtyard and the gatehouse towers, while invaders who penetrated so far were liable to be dealt with by something shot or dropped through the aptly named 'murder holes' in the lobby ceilings.

Apart from battlements and arrow-slits, the castle walls were defended by machicolations, which were stone galleries on the outside of the walls. Spaces in the floors were masked with wooden panels until the defenders were ready to drop missiles or bucketfuls of water through them on to the besiegers. Cold water would be used to put out a fire, and scalding hot water to dampen the enemy's enthusiasm; 'boiling oil', which figures so largely in song and story, would have been too expensive and wasteful to use in ordinary circumstances. Even more active defence was possible by using the inconspicuous postern gate or sally port, through which surprise attacks could be launched against the besieging force, and which might also serve as an emergency exit when all was lost.

The arts of attack

Both besiegers and besieged had artillery of a sort, long before there was any question of using gunpowder. The Roman ballista, or arbalist, was still in service; this outsize crossbow could be adapted to fling bolts or rocks, and its compactness and mobility (it had wheels) made it particularly useful for defence. The mangonel, also used by the Romans, worked by torsion: its ropes were twisted as far as they would go, and then released to give a violent jerk to a catapult arm which flung huge rocks at the enemy. A third type of siege engine, the trébuchet, was a medieval innovation, considerably larger than the ballista and mangonel; it was worked by weights and counter-weights which could be adjusted to secure relatively accurate targeting. Some form of Greek fire was also used occasionally, though whether the English version was as potent as the Byzantine original is another matter; Greek fire – a flaming substance seemingly unaffected by water – was for centuries the Byzantines' secret weapon, and even now its exact constituents are a matter of speculation.

Stronger, better designed stone castles lessened the effectiveness of siege engines; and this was also true of direct physical assaults with battering rams, bores and belfries (wooden towers on wheels). Mining was probably always the greatest danger to a strong castle, and the relative ease with which corners could be undermined was a major reason for the 12th-century preference for rounded forms; Dover Castle was one of several notable rectangular keeps that was captured (in 1216) as a result of mining. The basic technique was to clear the soil beneath the foundations of a corner or some other vulnerable point, using props to avoid a premature collapse; usually this involved digging a tunnel all the way from the besiegers' territory to the castle. The space beneath the foundations was filled with brushwood or some other combustible material, which was lit and burned away the props; the resulting collapse of masonry allowed the besiegers to pour through the gap created. It is possible to appreciate the scope of such an enterprise at St Andrews Castle, where the visitor can still see the unsuccessful mine dug during the siege of 1546-47, and also the counter-mine dug by the defenders to intercept it.

The surest offensive weapons were always time and treachery. Even the strongest castles could eventually be starved out if no relief arrived, and on occasion the garrison and their besiegers made life easier for themselves by abandoning direct engagements and making a formal contract that stipulated the surrender of the castle if relief failed to appear by a given date. A surprising number of castles also fell to bluff, trickery or treachery – the threat to execute members of the garrison's families, for example; or attackers gaining entrance in the guise of a relief force; or sabotage by a heavily bribed inmate of the castle itself. The frequency with which such 'human error' factors is mentioned in historical records surely says a great deal for medieval military technology.

Apotheosis of the castle

Castle building reached a climax of magnificence, engineering skill and ruinous expenditure during the reign of Edward I (1272-1307). The earliest 'Edwardian' castle was the spectacular Caerphilly, built by a subject, Gilbert de Clare, who actually started it the year before Edward's accession. But in size and numbers there is nothing quite like the ring of massive fortresses constructed for the King to hold down north Wales, whose long history as a more or less independent principality was brought to an end by Edward's programme of conquest followed by castle building on an unprecedented scale. For once, incidentally, the name of the chief architect is known: he was a Savoyard whom the English called Master James of St George. Of course no such profession as 'architect' yet existed: James was simply a master mason, like the builders of the great medieval cathedrals, though King Edward paid him the high salary that professional men with special skills normally expect.

At Beaumaris, Caernarfon, Conwy, Harlech and the other Welsh royal castles the idea of actively defending the walls was taken to its logical conclusion. The mural towers became huge, turreted drums, and massive, elaborate gateways and barbicans proliferated, making the would-be be-sieger's task seem well-nigh hopeless. (The more gateways a castle possessed – provided that they could be adequately defended – the more difficulty a besieger experienced in blockading it without fatally dividing his own forces.) It was hard for an attacker even to get so far, as the castles were protected by earthworks and other outer fortifications, and also by more or less elaborate water defences – some, as at Caerphilly, representing considerable feats of engineering.

At Beaumaris and Harlech the builders copied de Clare's innovation at Caerphilly: instead of one curtain wall, two were raised, one inside the other; these structures are known as concentric castles. The bailey was now divided into two areas, called wards; the entire inner ward, defended by massive gatehouses, became the equivalent of the old Norman keep, housing suites of rooms, abundant stores and most other necessities and comforts of 13th-century life. The outer wall was always the lower of the two, so that archers on the inner wall could shoot over it at the enemy forces beyond it. Thus the besieger who breached the outer wall had the discouraging experience of finding life less rather than more pleasant inside it, as he was confined to a narrow strip of territory, trying to cross at a nasty angle towards the inner ward gatehouse while archers rained down arrows upon him.

Courtyards and comforts

The great castles of north Wales, breathtaking in their complexity, represent the apotheosis of medieval English military architecture. For a time the impulse to build seemed spent, and very few new castles were started between 1300 and 1360, though Dunstanburgh in Northumberland was a notable exception. However, many older castles were refurbished and brought up to date, most commonly by the addition of a twin-towered gatehouse, keep and barbican of the now standard and ubiquitous Edwardian type.

The revival of castle building during the latter part of Edward III's reign (1327-77) was probably stimulated by the French wars, which offered splendid opportunities for profit and advancement, and by the showy, self-consciously 'chivalric' outlook that was cultivated by the Court and society. All the same, there was an increasing concern for comfort and ostentation, even at the expense of military considerations. This tendency was fore-shadowed as early as the 1290s, in buildings such as Stokesay Castle in Shropshire, which was designed as a fortified house rather than a true castle – and, arguably, even the fortifications were a social-climbing afterthought, intended more for show than as a protection against the conquered Welsh. Similar qualifications can be made about even such an ambitious structure as Bodiam in East Sussex, built in 1385 to protect the south coast after the alarms caused by French raids; its large windows and other unmilitary amenities suggest that it was not seriously expected to withstand a prolonged assault.

Bodiam was one of the new breed of courtyard castles, which conformed in general terms to the Edwardian type but whose walls consisted of four ranges of buildings with ample accommodation and creature comforts. In the 15th century the use of bricks marked another stage in the domestication of castle architecture. Bricks were initially imported from the Low Countries, and were not used on any scale until the 15th century, when the brick houses that Englishmen saw while fighting in the French wars helped to make the new material fashionable. Two splendid brick castles, Herstomonceux in East Sussex and Tattershall in Lincolnshire, date from the 1430s and 1440s. As with other 15th-century castles-cum-mansions, their military role can scarcely have been primary; apart from any other consideration, brick is not the ideal material to choose as protection against siege engines or cannon.

The invention of gunpowder is often said to have rendered castles obsolete, and in the long run this was doubtless true. Yet most of the developments described above took place long before the cannon had become a reliable, let alone a decisive, factor in warfare. Impulses towards domestic comfort, peaceful enjoyment of wealth and competitive display were therefore making themselves felt before changes in military technique enforced them. Even more interesting is the fact that such impulses seem to have been largely unaffected by the late 15th-century Wars of the Roses, which loom large in histories of the period and must surely have added to the insecurity of existence. The principal antagonists in this civil war certainly had castle strongholds, but for the most part they were all too willing to leave them and risk everything on the outcome of a single battle; the loser then fled rather than shut himself up in one of his castles. This may have been a matter of the prevailing fashion in military behaviour, or perhaps a response to the volatile mood of the many uncommitted lords, squires and citizens, who seem to have quickly adhered to the more active and successful party – and to have become equally quickly disillusioned and ready to welcome back from abroad the exiles from the other party, whose derelictions had in the meantime been forgotten.

Castles had still less military significance after 1485, when the Wars of the Roses ended and the new Tudor dynasty created a more stable order. The Tudor age, culminating in the reign of Queen Elizabeth (1558-1603), was notable as a great age of building – but the buildings put up were not castles or churches but palaces, mansions and houses that advertised the security of English life. Comfort and ostentation had come completely into their own.

Pele houses and Scottish baronial castles
In the Border counties of England and Scotland the situation was different. Life was poorer and harsher, Scots and English were often at war, and at all times cross-border banditry was rife. In response to these conditions, both Scots and English built hundreds of pele towers – rectangular stone towers that might be characterised as poor relations of the Norman keep; dozens of them survive from the 13th and 14th centuries. The pele house was far less substantial than a keep, but sufficiently strong to hold out against fly-by-night raiders; the ground floor served as a store room in times of peace, but would be crowded with local people and their cattle in any emergency. One incontrovertible proof that, in England, better times arrived in the Elizabethan period is the conversion of pele towers into country houses at places such as Sizergh in Cumbria.

Scotland remained a much poorer and more turbulent country than England, and life there was harsh and dangerous for much longer; the pele tower continued to be the typical dwelling of most nobles right through to the 16th century. The chief outside influence was not England – the old enemy across the border – but France, Scotland's partner in 'the auld alliance'. As a result, when a surge of building activity did occur from the 1560s, the new residences had something of the character of expanded pele towers; in particular, the structure normally included a central tower with the main entrance at its base. An important practical consideration was the acute shortage of timber in Scotland, which restricted the span of the roof and so encouraged vertical rather than lateral expansion. Combined with the influence of French castle style, which in the Loire valley reached heights of fantasy undreamed-of in England, this produced what the Victorians named 'Scottish baronial' style – splendid storybook castles such as Craigievar in Grampian, rising several storeys from a relatively narrow base to a skyline enchantingly crowded with cupolas or conical turrets springing from the angles of the walls. The baronial style continued to flourish even when the Scots monarchs became domiciled in London as kings of England, and it was only after the Restoration of 1660 that Scotland was seriously invaded by classicism of the sort favoured by the English; Drumlanrig Castle in Dumfries (1675-89) represents virtually the last baronial fling.

Decline and fall

It would be churlish to deny the name 'castle' to one last group of buildings, since the ordinary person visits them in much the same spirit as he approaches true castles; and, besides, the coastal forts erected under Henry VIII are actually known as Deal Castle, Walmer Castle, and so on. Henry's foreign policy was generally tortuous, and was further complicated by the fact that he had broken with the Pope and set himself up as head of the Church of England. In 1539-40 the diplomatic situation looked particularly threatening, and there seemed a real possibility of a French, or even a joint Franco-Imperial, invasion to restore papal authority in England. A chain of artillery forts was constructed on Henry's orders, and represented a major defensive effort. Seen in plan (or in aerial photographs), these forts – essentially groupings of circular and part-circular gun platforms – comprise delightful clover-leaf-like patterns, worthy of the Renaissance passion for symmetry. Deal Castle is the best preserved example, with a moat and three sets of walls culminating in a central keep crowned with a lantern; the outer walls were made massively thick to withstand cannon fire, and gunports at every level gave the garrison command of a wide area. Though now deceptively medieval in appearance (crenellated parapets were added to the walls in the fanciful 18th century), Deal is not a true castle; like Henry's other forts, it had a small garrison but was never a family residence.

By the 17th century many castles had long before been abandoned, and were falling into decay. Then the English Civil War gave them an odd, impressive afterlife. Royalists and Parliamentarians all over England not only occupied castles but proved remarkably successful in defending them. This raises some interesting questions: if they stood up so well when battered by 17th-century artillery, why had they been abandoned so much earlier? Evidently not because they could not stand up to 15th- and 16th-century cannon. And why was so little use made of castles during the Wars of the Roses? Is it possible that fashion rather than realism can dictate the way wars are waged?

In the event, the very effectiveness of castles during the Civil War proved their undoing. A victorious Parliament ensured that they would never again pose a threat by ordering most of them to be slighted – that is, damaged sufficiently badly to make them useless for military purposes. The process of slow decay was resumed and, if used at all, castles became prisons; one curious result of this was that the French word for a keep, *donjon*, passed into English as the exclusively penal 'dungeon'.

Long after it had lost its martial function and its attraction as a residence, the castle kept a strong hold on the English imagination. An early Tudor palace such as Hampton Court was decked with ornamental battlements and other quasi-military features, and right down to 20th-century Edwardian times any imposing building was likely to have the prestigious word 'Castle' included in its title. Sham castles began to be built as early as the Jacobean period (Bolsover in Derbyshire), and later examples were adapted to suit a variety of moods from the thrill-seeking 'Gothick' to the Scottish baronial. The tradition was carried on in the 19th century and found its final expression in Sir Edwin Lutyens' huge 'Norman' Castle Drogo in Devon, built as recently as 1910-30. Obvious economic considerations make it unlikely that there will be another new British castle, whether real or sham; but one can never be sure.

London and Southern England

CAMBRIDGESHIRE

Ipswich

...FORDSHIRE

ESSEX

Harlow

...EATER

Southend

Tower of London

...ONDON

Upnor Castle

Eynsford Castle
Lullingstone Castle

Rochester Castle

Reculver

Richborough Castle

Canterbury

Allington Castle

Chilham Castle

Maidstone

Leeds Castle

Deal Castle

Walmer Castle

Chiddingstone Castle

KENT

Tonbridge Castle

Dover

Hever Castle

Dover Castle

Saltwood Castle

...EY

Crawley

Lympne Castle

EAST

Bodiam Castle

SUSSEX

Hastings

Lewes Castle

Herstmonceux Castle

Brighton

Pevensey Castle

Donnington Castle

Donnington, near Newbury, Berkshire

The licence to crenellate at Donnington was granted in 1385, the same year as that for Bodiam, and the castle's plan was of the same courtyard type, rectangular on three sides and semi-octagonal on the fourth. There were round towers on the four corners, central towers on the north and south sides and a fortified gatehouse on the east. The historian William Camden described it in 1586 as 'a small but very neat castle . . . having a fair prospect and windows in all sides being very lightsome.' Unfortunately, sixty years later, in the Civil War, it was reduced almost to its foundations, and only the great gatehouse now stands. This had been built on to an existing building by Richard Abberbury in 1386 as part of the programme of fortification that turned it from a manor house into a castle, and the architect may have been William de Wynford, known as the builder of the nave of Winchester Cathedral. Castles built at this time were in the main more fortified residences than pure military strongholds, and Donnington was no exception. It was seized without much difficulty from its owner at the start of the Civil War, and was then held for the King by John Boys, who set about building sophisticated outer earth defences in line with the latest military thinking. He clearly knew what he was about, and although the stone walls were flattened the earthworks proved their worth, and Boys and his men held out for nearly two years until 1646, earning the admiration of their enemies who at one stage allowed them to clean out their poisoned well.

1 m N of Newbury on B4494 turn W at Donnington

SU 4669 (OS 174)

Open daily throughout year at all reasonable times

⊖ 🅿 🅰 (limited access) 🚻 D (on lead, grounds only) ♣ ★ ♨ EH

Windsor Castle

Windsor, Berkshire

The castle stands on an isolated chalk hill above the river Thames. It began as a simple motte and bailey fortress, one of a ring built by William I to protect London, his capital. From an early date it became a royal residence as well as a fortress. From the central mound the spectacular Round Tower rises to dominate its surroundings. The original shell keep, built not long after the Conquest, was 15 foot high and of irregular shape. In the 12th century Henry II carried out large defensive works, building another wall within the original shell and rising 20 foot above it. During the reign of Edward III in the 14th century two-storey buildings were put up inside the keep, leaving an open courtyard in the centre. These are substantially the buildings seen today. The keep remained undisturbed for 350 years, until Sir Jeffrey Wyatville was employed to carry out reconstruction of the keep and the upper ward in the reign of George IV. The keep was heightened and given its buttresses, windows, battlements and machicolations. The state apartments on the north side of the upper ward were fitted out for Charles II, but were drastically reorganised by Wyatville. The rooms now exhibit a considerable collection of valuable arms and armour, statuary, tapestries, paintings, carvings and furnishings. The long continuity of royal use is unrivalled, and most of the kings and queens of England have left some reminder within the castle's walls.

☎ Windsor (0753) 868286

In centre of Windsor, on B3022

SU 9777 (OS 175)

Open varied times, subject to change at short notice; phone for details

⊖ 🅿 🅿 (by appt) 🚻 ♣ ◆ ⚲ (available in foreign languages) ● (not in house)

Hurst Castle

near Milford, Hampshire

This is fascinatingly situated, on a little spit of land running right out into the Solent, which the castle was designed to protect, and looking across at the Isle of Wight. To reach Hurst Castle the would-be visitor must take a boat from Keyhaven or walk a mile or so along the beach at low tide. It originated as one of the chain of forts built for Henry VIII when a French invasion seemed a distinct possibility, and dates from the early 1540s. It consisted essentially of a twelve-sided tower surrounded by a curtain wall from which three semi-circular bastions (gun platforms) projected. Hurst Castle was held for Parliament without incident during the Civil War, and Charles I was briefly a prisoner there in 1648, just before his trial and execution. The castle was surveyed soon fterwards, and as a result the garrison was strengthened. After the King's Restoration in 1660 it was proposed to dismantle Hurst, but this never happened (perhaps because the Anglo-Dutch wars revealed just how vulnerable the English coast was), and the castle remained operational; in the 1670s there were thirty guns mounted in the tower. Later, Hurst Castle continued to be periodically repaired and re-garrisoned during invasion scares, and it was much altered in the 19th century, when its military function continued to be taken very seriously (French invasions were still expected during the reigns of Napoleon I and Napoleon III). Hurst Castle, like other Henrican forts, was brought back out of retirement by the army during the Second World War.

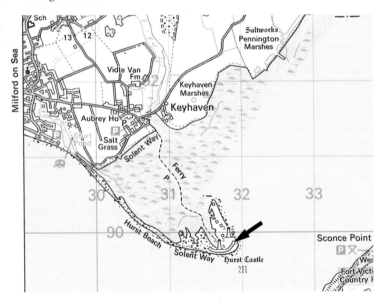

☎ Milford (059 069) 2344

3 m S of Lymington on A337, turn S (access by ferry or footpath)

SZ 3189 (OS 196)

Open daily am and pm (Oct to March Su pm only)

♿ WC 🚻 D (on lead, grounds only) ♣ 🍴 (Apr to Sept) ◆ ♨ EH

24

Portchester Castle

Portchester, Hampshire

Portchester is an extremely unusual castle for two reasons. It stands not on a hill but on a flat piece of land by Portsmouth harbour; and it is a Norman castle built inside a Roman fort, the walls of which still stand to their full height. The Roman fort was square in plan, with entrances on the east and west sides, which were destroyed to make the Norman entrances, rectangular towers with passageways. Most of the walls, however, were left intact, and the Norman castle was built in the north-west corner (about 1120), with a new curtain wall on the south and east meeting the Roman walls to form an enclosure. In 1133 an Augustinian priory was built in the south-east corner, and its chapel still remains. The castle seems to have been appropriated by Henry II at about this time, and it remained in royal hands thereafter. The keep was extended upwards in about 1170, possibly by Henry, making it four storeys high with the basement, and the battlements were added by Richard II (1377-99). Richard was also responsible for the two ranges between the keep and the gatehouse, known as Richard's Palace. These may have replaced earlier Norman buildings, and the main rooms were on the first floor, with the great chamber next to the keep and the great hall against the gatehouse wall. The castle was frequently garrisoned in the 14th century as a defence against French invasions, and in the 18th century it was used as a prison camp for French prisoners of war.

☎ Portsmouth (0705) 378291

4 m E of Fareham on A27 turn S to Portchester

SU 6204 (OS 196)

Open daily; Mar to Oct 0930-1830 (Su 1400-1830); Oct to Mar 0930-1600 (Su 1400-1600)

♿ 🅿 ♿ (limited access) 🚻 D (grounds only)
♣ ♦ ✵ (available in foreign languages) EH

Carisbrooke Castle

Carisbrooke, Isle of Wight

Carisbrooke Castle has been a Roman fort, a medieval castle and an Elizabethan fort, and remains are visible of all three phases of its life. Its general appearance, however, is medieval: the keep and curtain wall were completed by 1136, and the domestic buildings are mainly of the 13th century, with 16th-century additions. The dominating feature is the great gatehouse with drum towers, built partly in the 14th and partly in the 15th century. In the reign of Elizabeth I the castle was considerably altered to resist artillery, and an Italian engineer called Federigo Gianibelli was engaged to build the large earthworks surrounding the castle. This work was completed just bfore the end of the century, and no further alterations were made except minor internal modernisations. The castle, in spite of its long history and strategic position, has seen few major dramatic events, though Charles I was imprisoned here in 1647-48, having fled from the army at Hampton Court, and attempting to set sail for Jersey via Portsmouth he found himself conveyed to Carisbrooke instead. The castle became the home of the governors of the island, the last of whom was Princess Beatrice, daughter of Queen Victoria, who succeeded her husband as governor. An upstairs room contains the Isle of Wight Museum, and near the domestic buildings there is a well-house with a wheel still operated by donkeys. The chapel next to the main gate was rebuilt on old foundations in 1906.

☎ Newport (IOW) [0983] 522107

In SW outskirts of Newport off B3323

SZ 4887 (OS 196)

Open daily throughout year; Mar to Oct 0930-1830 Oct to Mar 0930-1600 (Su 1400-1600)

⊖ P WC 🖻 (limited access) 🚻 D (grounds only) ♣ ♥ (Apr to Sept) ◆ ✄ EH

Yarmouth Castle

Yarmouth, Isle of Wight, Hampshire

This castle was built by Henry VIII, though not as part of the well-known chain of forts he constructed to protect the English coast from about 1529. One of these, Hurst Castle, was situated on the other (Hampshire) side of the Solent and apparently gave adequate protection against naval intruders; but in July 1545 a large French fleet slipped past Hurst with no difficulty and landed troops on the Isle of Wight. Fortunately for the English, the French were raiding, not invading, and soon moved on; but Henry drew the appropriate conclusions. Within two years Yarmouth Castle was in service, though it may not have been fully equipped until later. Like other Henrican forts, it consisted essentially of a set of platforms (internal and external) on which guns could be mounted; but Yarmouth differed from the earlier structures in a number of important respects. The most obvious was that the high central tower was not cylindrical but square, with sides about 100 foot long. A still more unusual feature at the time was the bastion, which was also not round (like other Henrican examples), but shaped like an arrowhead so that it came to a point – a new-fangled Continental design with which Englishmen had only just become acquainted. To the north and west the guns of Yarmouth Castle covered the sea approaches; on the south and east sides it was protected by a wide moat (now filled in). The castle was undamaged during the Civil War; frequently repaired and altered, it remained in service until 1885.

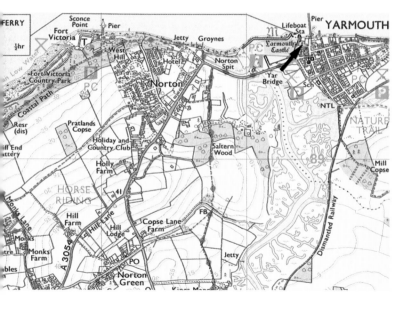

☎ Yarmouth (0983) 760678

In centre of Yarmouth

SZ 3589 (OS 196)

Open Apr to Sept daily am and pm, Su pm only

♿ WC 🚻 (limited access) 🅿 ◆ ⚒ EH

Allington Castle

near Maidstone, Kent

This small castle owes its present attractive skyline to Martin Conway, later Lord Conway. From 1905, when he bought Allington, Conway spent lavishly to have extensive restorations done, mainly under the direction of W. D. Caroe; these were sensitively in keeping with the medieval and Tudor remains while sensibly adapting the structure to modern habits. There were buildings on the site from at least the 12th century, but the earliest surviving remains are of the castle erected by Stephen de Penchester, who was granted a licence to crenellate in 1281. Allington was then typical of its period (the reign of Edward I), with its rectangular curtain walls, gatehouse and interval towers; one of these, Solomon's Tower, is still an impressive sight. By the early 16th century Allington had passed to Sir Henry Wyatt, who repaired it and put up a range of buildings that divided the courtyard into two unequal areas; the new buildings included a first-floor long gallery, possibly the earliest English example. Wyatt's son, Sir Thomas, was the first great English poet of the Renaissance period; his grandson, another Sir Thomas Wyatt, platted at Allington to raise the country against Queen Mary's marriage to Philip of Spain, and lost his head as a result. The subsequent history of the castle was mostly one of steady decline down to 1905. In 1951 it was bought by the Order of the Carmelites, who use it as a conference centre and retreat.

☎ Maidstone (0622) 54080

2 m NW of town centre on A20, turn NE

TQ 7557 (OS 188)

Open daily 1400-1600

🅿 WC ♿ (limited) ♨ (by appt) D

🍴 (pre-book) ◆ ※ 🏋 ●

29

Chiddingstone Castle

near Edenbridge, Kent

A solid Caroline house of 1679 replacing a medieval manor, dressed up in the 'castle style' early in the 19th century. Chiddingstone is most notable for the idiosyncratic collection formed by Denys Eyre Bower (1905-77). Bower was a Derbyshire bank employee who was deeply bitten by the collecting bug, and who on retiring in 1942 moved to London to conduct an antiques business. He bought Chiddingstone and opened it to the public in 1956 (long before country-house visiting had generally caught on) with the aim of displaying and sharing his treasures 'in the friendly atmosphere of a private home', as he put it. Three dominant passions informed Mr. Bower's collecting: enthusiasm for the Stuarts and the Jacobite tradition; the art of ancient Egypt, and the art of Japan. All the objects are still laid out in the way he wished. The great hall has a generally historical flavour, with paintings recalling the Streatfeild family which owned Chiddingstone for about three hundred years. Buddhist art from many parts of Asia is in the Buddha room on the ground floor. The 1st Stuart room and the 'white rose' room contain the main part of the collection to which the name refers, but documents elsewhere may be inspected by appointment. Japanese art is in the north Gothic hall and three other rooms designated Japanese. The collection in the Egyptian rooms extends from Pre-Dynastic to Ptolemaic times. Paintings and furniture which are apart from these three main themes are seen on the staircases and some other rooms.

☎ Penshurst (0892) 870347

10 m W of Tonbridge on B2027 take road to How Green and Hever

TQ 4945 (OS 188)

Open April S, Su, May to Sept W-S, also T mid June to mid-Sept, Oct S, Su, W 1400-1730; Su and Bank Hols 1130-1730

♿ (1 m) 🅿 WC 🏬 🍴 (by appt) ♣ 🐾 ♦ ⚘ ●

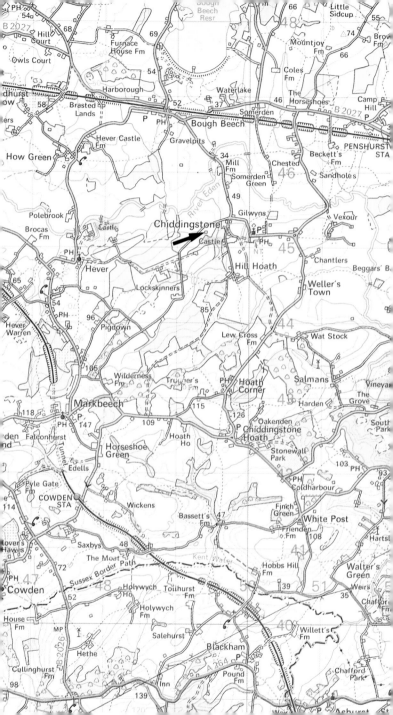

Chilham Castle

Chilham, Kent

Overlooking a bend in the river Stour, old Chilham occupied a strong defensive position; perched with its church and village on a small area of raised ground, it must once have typified the isolation and self-sufficiency of medieval settlements. There was an 11th-century stone hall on the spot; it was incorporated into the curtain wall when Henry II put up the castle in 1171-74. Inside the walls he erected a tall keep, which still stands on its motte to most of its original height. Its most distinctive feature was its octagonal plan (the only other octagonal keep in England is at Odiham in Hampshire, built a few years later under King John); such multi-faceted keeps were less easy for sappers to undermine than the conventional right-angled block, and represented the latest thing in military technology until superseded by round keeps. The present Chilham Castle stands between the medieval ruin and the village. It was built by James I's Master of the Rolls, Sir Dudley Digges, whose design suggests that he may have been inspired to emulate Henry II's edifice. At any rate the new Chilham was built around a courtyard as a hexagon, but with one side left open. It was finished in 1616 but – despite claims that are still sometimes advanced – not by Inigo Jones. The gardens at Chilham are enlivened by falconry displays, friendly animals and 'medieval' jousts.

☎ Canterbury (0227) 730319

8 m SW of Canterbury on A28, turn W on A252

TR 0653 (OS 189)

The castle is not open; gardens open Apr to Oct daily 1100-1700

⊖ P WC ☒ ☷ (by appt) D (on lead) ♣ ☕ ⛺ ◆ ☀

32

Deal Castle

Deal, Kent

Henry VIII's coastal fort at Deal owes its existence to the anchorage between the North and South Forelands of Kent, called The Downs, where whole fleets could ride out a storm, protected on the east by the Goodwin Sands. Deal Castle is among the last functional forts with a solely military purpose to be built in England, and was erected in answer to a threatened invasion in 1539 by the Catholic powers, France and the Holy Roman Empire. Its field of fire and the positioning of the large wide-angle gunports gave it a formidable sweep over any ships lying in The Downs. Thus it could help to defend an English fleet or bombard an enemy landing-force. With two others of similar type, at Sandown and Walmer in Kent, it was built as part of a defensive programme round the east and south coasts. The danger of invasion passed by 1540, and Deal saw action only once, in the Civil War in 1648, although the present battlements were added as late as 1732. The contractor for the building materials brought the fine Caen stone from the demolished Carmelite friary at Sandgate near Folkestone. The beautiful symmetry of this six-lobed gun-house is not as easily appreciated from the ground as it is in aerial photographs: the central tower, low in profile, is flanked by six smaller bastions at the return of the larger outer bastions, all elements being circular or arcs of a circle. The cross-cover for both artillery and small-arms fire is extremely close. Inside the keep there is a cunningly arranged double staircase.

☎ Deal (0304) 372762

In centre of Deal on coast

TR 3752 (OS 179)

Open daily throughout year; Mar to Oct 0930-1830, Oct to Mar 0930-1600 (Su 1400-1600)

♿ WC 🅿 (limited access) 🚌 ◆ ⚒ EH

Dover Castle

Dover, Kent

Dover's history is rich in episodes of invasion and defence, and the castle, high on the cliffs above the town, has been called the 'key of England'. It is one of the largest and best preserved castles in England, and has a long history: the main earthworks were almost certainly part of an Iron Age hill fort built before the Roman Conquest. The great keep was built in the 1180s by Henry II, and the surrounding curtain wall and outer fortifications were begun by him, continued by his son Richard, and completed by King John. In John's reign (1199-1216) the castle was besieged by Prince Louis of France, and the northern gateway successfully undermined, causing the collapse of the eastern tower. Clearly the castle was not impregnable after all, and in Henry III's reign a great deal of money was spent on rebuilding. The splendid 'constable's gate' was built about 1227, and by 1256 the castle had reached its maximum strength and size. During the Civil War of the 1640s it was taken by Cromwell's forces, and remained in their hands until the Restoration, thus escaping the usual slighting (destruction of defences), but it was drastically altered during the Napoleonic Wars, when the tops of many of the towers were cut off to provide artillery platforms. Most of the castle is open to the public, and within the walls is the Saxon church of St Mary in Castro with its free-standing bell-tower which was originally a Roman lighthouse. The roof of the keep, reached by the two great spiral staircases, provides an excellent view of the fortifications.

☎ Dover (0304) 201628

In E outskirts of Dover

TR 3241 (OS 179)

Open daily throughout year; Mar to Oct 0930-1830, Oct to Mar 0930-1600 (Su 1400-1600)

⊖ 🅿 WC 🍴 D (on lead, grounds only) ♣
🍽 (Apr to Sept) ◆ ♨ EH

Eynsford Castle

Eynsford, Kent

This is an interesting example of a Norman castle that never acquired a keep. The main surviving feature is the defensive wall, which is well preserved, standing almost to its original height of 30 foot; it is absolutely plain, with neither arrow-slits nor towers. It surrounds a large, unusually flattened motte, in the middle of which excavations have uncovered the remains of a timber watch-tower. The wall was built in about 1100 by William de Eynsford, who in 1135 decided to give up the world and become a monk. He or one of his 12th-century descendants – all Williams – built a stone hall on the motte; today only the undercroft (the ground-floor area below the first-floor hall and solar) remains in existence. The gatehouse and other buildings were also erected in the 12th century but are now visible only as foundations. The Eynsfords made an appearance from time to time in medieval English history; William III wrangled long and bitterly with Archbishop Thomas Becket, and William V took part in the civil wars as a rebel against King John. But the castle itself saw little action, and by the late 13th century it was falling into neglect. Matters were hardly improved in the early 14th century, when rival heirs disputed ownership of the property; one of the claimants, Nicholas de Criol, seems to have wrecked Eynsford, presumably doubting his chances of getting the castle for himself. After that, Eynsford sank steadily into decay until 1948, when it was taken over by the Ministry of Public Works.

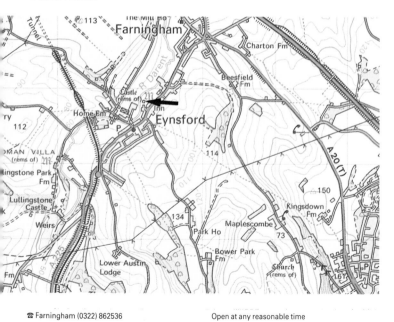

☎ Farningham (0322) 862536

9 m N of Sevenoaks on A225, turn W

TQ 5465 (OS 177)

Open at any reasonable time

🅿 ♿ 🚻 D (on lead, grounds only) ♣ ♨ EH

Hever Castle

Hever, Edenbridge, Kent

This compact stone castle in its rectangular moat was the home of Anne
Boleyn (c. 1507-36), who spent much of her childhood here and was courted
by Henry VIII within these walls. The castle dates to about 1270, when the
great gatehouse, outer walls and moat were built, and it was improved and
enlarged in the 15th and 16th centuries by the Bullen (Boleyn) family. But it
was not to remain a fine home for long – Anne's father died soon after her
own execution, new owners came and went through the centuries, and by
the end of the 19th century Hever had become a humble farmhouse. In 1903
the American millionaire William Waldorf Astor bought it and lavished a
fortune on restoring it, building the imitation 'Tudor village' just outside and
creating the spectacular gardens and lake. Mr. Astor was a man of taste, and
the restoration, carried out by the architect F. L. Pearson, was so careful and
meticulous that the outside of the building now looks almost exactly as it did
in Anne Boleyn's day. The interior still has some original panelling, but it
was almost entirely remade in a lavish pastiche of the Tudor style, with
carved woodwork, panelling and plaster ceilings far more elaborate than
anything Tudor craftsmen would have produced. The contents, collected
from all over Europe, reflect the tastes of this wealthy connoisseur: there are
superb tapestries and paintings, sculpture, an outstanding collection of
armour and some fine paintings, among them portraits of Anne Boleyn, her
sister Mary, Henry VIII and Anne's daughter Elizabeth I.

☎ Edenbridge (0732) 865224
11 m W of Tonbridge on B2027 at Bough Beech
take road to How Green and Hever
TQ 4745 (OS 188)

Open daily 1st Apr to 1st Nov 1100-1800 (last
admission 1700); reduced rates for parties

♿ 🅿 WC ♿ (limited access) 🍴 D ♦ ♥ ⌂ ◆
🐕 ⚘ 𝟀 (all year by appt) ● (not in castle) 🎋

Leeds Castle

Maidstone, Kent

The castle, situated in the middle of its large, lake-like moat, is one of England's oldest and most romantic buildings. But although it looks and feels medieval, and some parts are genuinely so, much rebuilding was done from 1822 by Fiennes Wykeham-Martin, who modernised many of the medieval rooms, cut down the encircling walls to provide a view of the lake, and restored the exterior, which had been given a Jacobean look by a previous owner. This careful restoration led Lord Conway to describe Leeds as 'the loveliest castle . . . in the whole world'. The walls of the gloriette where the royal apartments were, are medieval, but the interior was completely restored and redecorated by Lady Baillie, who bought the castle in 1926 and devoted much of her life to its restoration and care. A magnificent two-tier bridge connects the main building to the gloriette, and the visitor passes through rooms with beamed ceilings, furnished with carved wooden pieces and hung with tapestries, to a Gothic staircase which leads to the seminar room. When Lady Baillie left the castle to the nation she specified that it should be used for international medical meetings as well as for the public benefit, and this is one of the rooms used for meetings. It also contains a fine collection of Impressionist and later paintings. In the main house there are two fine 18th-century rooms, one of which has 17th-century panelling brought from another house. The Norman gate tower contains an unusual collection of medieval dog collars.

☎ Maidstone (0622) 65400

8 m E of Maidstone on A20 turn S

TQ 8353 (OS 188)

Open 1st Apr to 31st Oct daily 1100-1700; Nov to end Mar S and Su 1200-1600

⊖ (1 m) 🅿 WC ♿ (limited access)
🚻 ♣ 🍴 ⏸ ◆ ⚏ ⚶ ● (not in castle) 🐕 🚶

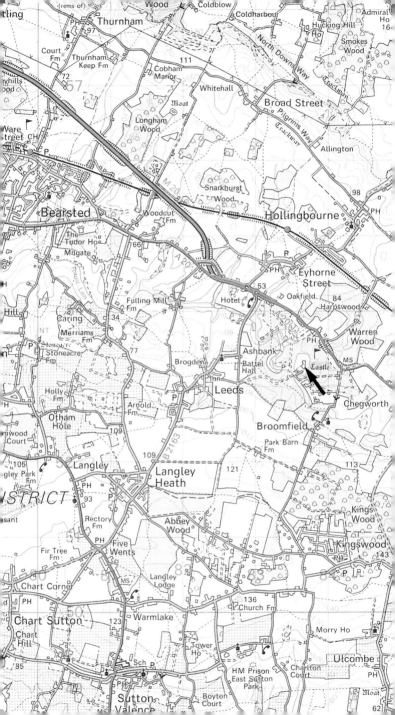

Lullingstone Castle

Eynsford, Kent

The original house was built in the reign of Henry VII by Sir John Peche. The great brick gatehouse of 1497 still survives, and to the west of it is a level area, the old jousting ground, a reminder of Sir John's prowess in the tournament. The house itself has an early 18th-century red-brick façade, but this is only skin-deep; the internal arrangement of the old Tudor house remains almost unchanged, though several of the rooms were panelled. These alterations were carried out for the new owner, Percival Hart, a Jacobite, and friend of Queen Anne who visited the house frequently. The front door opens straight into the great hall, where there is fine 18th-century panelling and a series of full-length family portraits as well as an interesting painting showing the house before the alterations. The dining room also has 18th-century panelling, and the staircase was built for Queen Anne herself, with specially shallow treads. This leads to the Tudor great chamber, known as the state drawing room, which has a lovely barrel-vaulted Tudor ceiling with plaster decoration and exceptional oak panelling. The room also contains some good paintings, and several interesting objects, among them a collection of fans. The state bedroom has an intricately carved four-poster bed, and the furniture throughout the house is varied and interesting. A small room leading off the state bedroom displays a set of fine needlework hangings, the work of the Hon. Mary Bell, maid of honour to Queen Alexandra.

☎ Farningham (0322) 862114

8 m N of Sevenoaks on A225 turn W

TQ 5364 (OS 188)

Open Apr to end Oct S, Su and Bank Hol M 1400-1800; parties by appt

⊖ (1 m) 🅿 WC 🔲 (limited access) 🔛 ♦ 🐾
🎌 🐾 ✗ (parties only) ● (not in house)

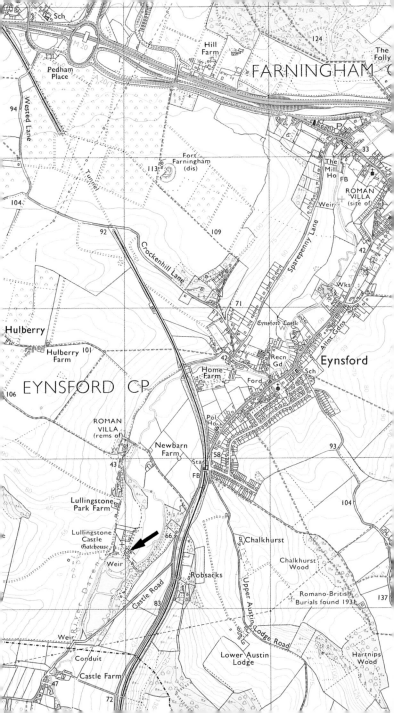

Lympne Castle

near Hythe, Kent

Lympne Castle, which has a spectacular setting on the edge of an escarpment bordering the Romney Marshes, was the home of the archdeacons of Canterbury, one of whom was Thomas à Becket before he became Archbishop. The castle we see today was the main residential block of a complex of buildings, and it has been adapted and altered over the centuries to meet the needs of successive owners. The oldest part is the northern part of the square tower next to the church, which dates from the 13th century. The main part of the building, the hall block, is 14th century, and about 1420 the castle was modernised, and the round part of the great tower, with its newel stairway, was built on. By the end of the 19th century the great hall had been turned into a house by the construction of a first floor, but the other parts were used only for storage, and by the beginning of this century the whole place had become dilapidated. It was saved from ruin by the Scottish architect Robert Lorimer, who in 1906 built on a new wing, restored the old buildings and turned the whole complex into a large house. Only the old parts are open to the public, and the rooms are purposely kept very bare to preserve their medieval atmosphere. The great hall, restored by Lorimer, who removed the first floor, made good the timbers above and fitted new tracery in the windows, is huge and very impressive. There is a toy museum in the west tower, and a fine view of the marshes can be gained from the Second World War observation post on the east tower.

☎ Hythe (0303) 67571

8 m W of Folkestone on A20 turn S onto B2068

TR 1134 (OS 179)

Open Easter to end Sept and Bank Hol weekends daily 1030-1800

♿ (½ mile) 🅿 WC ♿ (limited access) 🚏 D

♣ 🍴 (in village) ⛱ ◆ ⚘

Reculver Roman Fort

Reculver, Kent

These remains are of the Roman fort Regulbium, which stood on a mound overlooking the sea. It was one of the Saxon Shore forts, erected in the 3rd century AD to defend the British coast against increasingly active Germanic raiders. The site is even older, and may have been one of the bases used by the Romans for their invasion of Britain in AD 43. The Saxon Shore fort is an early one, dating from the first half of the 3rd century. It appears to have functioned until late in the century, to have been neglected for about forty years, and then to have been reoccupied for perhaps thirty years more before it was finally abandoned in about 370 by the rapidly shrinking imperial army. The northern third of Regulbium has been swept away by the action of the tides in eroding the cliffs. It was originally a large fort, covering more than seven acres, with thick towerless walls forming a rough square. Like other Roman sites, Reculver was well chosen, and continued to be used in later times. An Anglo-Saxon monastery was established there (the walls incorporating bands of Roman tiles), and its church survived until it was demolished in 1809. Only the 12th-century west front was left standing – and still stands – so that the towers might serve as a landmark for mariners.

☎ Herne Bay (022 73) 66444

2 m E of Herne Bay on A 299, turn N on road to Hillborough

TR 2269 (OS 179)

Open 28 Mar to 30 Sept M-S 0930-1830, Su 1400-1830

⊖ P WC ⓓ (limited access) 🚻 D (on lead, grounds only) ♣ ◆ ♨ EH

Richborough Castle

Sandwich, Kent

This Roman settlement – Rutupiae – was the site of a Saxon Shore fort, one of the chain set up in the 3rd and 4th centuries AD to protect the British coast. The history of the site goes back much further. The Romans probably first landed here when they embarked on the conquest of Britain in AD 43; at that time Richborough occupied a strategically important position on a peninsula by a little river, the Wantsum (now silted up), which separated the Isle of Thanet from the rest of Kent. Once their bridgehead was established, the Romans converted Richborough into a supply base. Then, in about AD 85, the timber buildings were dismantled and a huge monument or temple was erected; only the platform for the monument, and quantities of rubble, survive. In the mid-3rd century the settlement was fortified with a triple line of ditches, replaced in the 280s by the Saxon Shore fort. Most of the eastern side has been lost through erosion, but what remains is impressive – three sets of walls that still stand up to 30 foot high, protected by a double ditch. There were bastions for ballistae (giant crossbows) at each corner. Watling Street ran to the main gate, in the west wall. Richborough was occupied until the early 5th century, when the Roman armies were withdrawn from Britain for good. A Saxon church was built there, apparently in the 7th century, though only fragments survive. The site museum is excellent, with a very large number of excavated utensils, ornaments, weapons and coins.

☎ Deal (0304) 612013

1½ m N of Sandwich off A256

TR 3260 (OS 179)

Open 15 Mar to 15 Oct M-S 0930-1830, Su 1400-1830; Oct to Mar M-S 0930-1600, Su 1400-1600

⊖ 🅿 ⅏ 🚻 D (on lead, grounds only)

♣ ◆ ⅍ EH

Rochester Castle

Rochester, Kent

Although little remains standing except the great square keep, the ruins of Rochester, still one of the most impressive castles in England, dominate the town. The keep itself stands to its full height. In medieval times, barons and bishops both had need of castles, and this one was built by the Bishop of Rochester in about 1090. His building was probably not much more than a stone curtain wall and enclosure; the keep was built in the following century (1127) by the Archbishop of Canterbury, William de Corbeil, who was given the castle by Henry I. It is one of the largest in the country, and was one of the most luxurious. It is four storeys high, with a cross-wall, but the second and third storeys were merged to make the magnificent great hall, with the cross-wall becoming a pierced and columned arcade which divides the room into two. It is lit by a double row of large windows and, although all the floors have now gone, some fine decorative work can still be seen. Staircases in the thickness of the walls give access to the battlements and a close-up view of the four corner turrets, three square and one circular. In 1215 the castle was besieged by King John, whose men undermined the south tower and brought it down, so it had to be rebuilt under Henry III, by which time the circular style had replaced the square. The castle was damaged and repaired again in 1264, restored by Edward III and improved by Richard II, but its great days were over and it was thereafter allowed to decay.

☎ Medway (0634) 42852

In centre of Rochester facing Bridge Reach

TQ 7468 (OS 178)

Open daily throughout year; Mar to Oct 0930-1830, Oct to Mar 0930-1600 (Su 1400-1600)

♿ 🅿 ◆ ♨ EH

Saltwood Castle

Saltwood, Kent

The historical associations of this small castle are romantic, if a little vague. The land belonged to Lanfranc, the first Norman Archbishop of Canterbury after the Conquest, and later archbishops appear in the records frequently (but not always) as the owners of Saltwood. The castle was probably built by a layman, Henry of Essex, Warden of the Cinque Ports, in about 1160; a plausible legend has it that the four knights who murdered another Archbishop of Canterbury, Thomas Becket, stopped for the night at Saltwood on the way to Canterbury in December 1170. By the 14th century the inner bailey walls were much as they are today, lined with five towers and forming a rough oval flattened by a straight section on the south side. There was also a very wide, lake-like moat. Then in the 1380s another Archbishop of Canterbury, William Courtenay, added the triangular outer bailey, the massive gatehouse of the inner bailey, and a hall and other new domestic buildings. The gatehouse is inscribed with Courtenay's arms. His hall has been restored and in its present form is largely the work of a 20th-century architect, Philip Tilden; an earlier hall, dating from about 1300, is quite well preserved. Saltwood went into a decline after 1580, when an earthquake damaged it, but from 1885 Courtenay's gatehouse was restored and converted into a house which remains the residential part of the castle.

☎ Hythe (0303) 67190

2 m NW of Hythe

TR 1635 (OS 179)

Open M-F by appt, for parties only

⊖ P WC D (on lead, grounds only) ♣ ♥ (by appt) ✳ ⚒

Tonbridge Castle

Tonbridge, Kent

Tonbridge now surrounds this ruined castle, but in medieval times the castle stood between the town and a ford across the river Medway, and dominated both. There was a castle of some sort here as early as 1088, when it was held for the troublesome Earl of Kent, Odo of Bayeaux, who was half-brother to the Conqueror and in rebellion against his half-nephew, William Rufus (William II). The steep Norman motte is now occupied by the remains of a shell keep that probably dates from about 1200. Neither this nor the bailey wall has a great deal to offer, but the massive three-storey gatehouse is another matter. This was built in about 1300 and effectively superseded the shell keep, since it was provided with a hall on the second floor and formidable defences against attackers from any direction – even the interior of the bailey. Apart from the drawbridge in front of the entrance, invaders had to get past a set of murder holes, a portcullis, another set of murder holes, and folding gates; and similar obstacles faced the attacker who approached from the bailey. Even when he reached the guardrooms flanking the entrance, he had another choice of portcullises to batter away at. In emergencies, portcullises also shut off the gatehouse on both sides from the walkways, sealing off the gatehouse completely. Sadly, there are no moments of high drama associated with this elaborate example of military engineering. Like so many castles, Tonbridge was thoroughly dismantled by Parliament after the Civil War.

☎ West Malling (0732) 844522 ext 3432)
In town centre off High St
TQ 5846 (OS 188)

Phone in office hours for details of opening times

Upnor Castle

near Rochester, Kent

Upnor stands on the north bank of the river Medway, across the water from Chatham docks, where large numbers of English ships were laid up, and were therefore a sitting target for enemy warships. The castle – actually a fort – was designed by the leading Elizabethan military engineer, Sir Richard Lee, and built between 1559 and 1567. It consisted of a rectangular main block with a detached round tower on either side and, projecting dramatically from the base of the main block into the waters of the Medway, a triangular gun platform, the Water Bastion. In 1599-1601 Arthur Gregory linked the towers with the main block and extended the walls to enclose a courtyard; he also built the gatehouse in the west wall. This gave Upnor its present general appearance, apart from the heightening of the walls and gatehouse in 1653. The castle was briefly seized by Royalists during the uprising of 1648, but otherwise its history was uneventful until the Anglo-Dutch War of 1667. In that year the Dutch under de Ruyter made a surprise attack down the Medway, burned quantities of English shipping and triumphantly carried off the *Royal Charles*. This national humiliation, which Upnor had failed to prevent, effectively ended its role as a fighting unit. It became 'a place of stores and magazines' until 1827; it was then used as an ordnance laboratory, and formed part of the Magazine Establishment during the Second World War.

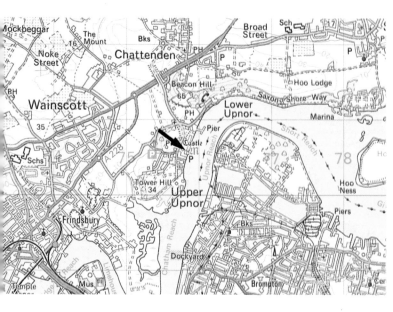

☎ Medway (0634) 78742

1½ m NE of Rochester on A228, turn SE to Lower Upnor

TQ 7570 (OS 189)

Open 28 Mar to 30 Sept M-S 0930-1830, Su 1400-1830

⊖ P 🅗 ◆ ♨ EH

Walmer Castle

Walmer, Kent

Walmer is the southernmost of three forts built by Henry VIII in 1539-40 along a short but vital stretch of the Kent coast. Deal was the grandest of the three and remains the best known. The other two, Walmer and Sandown, seem to have been very similar to each other in design, but whereas Sandown has almost entirely succumbed to tidal erosion and exists only as a fragment, Walmer is still in excellent condition. Essentially it consists of a circular central core or keep, which rises above four large surrounding drum towers; seen from above, Walmer thus presents the appearance of an elegant quatrefoil. Like other Henrican forts, it was designed for the effective deployment of artillery, and on the seaward side the gunports are very widely splayed so that their cannons could be realigned to remain in action for a long time against an enemy who was on the move. Walmer was also like the other forts in being intended for spartan regimental postings rather than prolonged residence, but alterations undertaken in the 18th and 19th centuries made it a much more comfortable place. It became the headquarters of the Lord Wardens of the Cinque Ports, of whom the most notable was the Duke of Wellington; he seems to have liked Walmer, visited it often, and died there in 1852. The first-floor rooms of the keep are furnished in 19th-century style, and there is a small collection of Wellingtoniana and other items associated with the Lord Wardens.

☎ Deal (0304) 364288

In town centre, 2 m S of Deal on B2057

TR 3750 (OS 179)

Open T-S and Bank Hol M am and pm, Su pm only; closed when the Lord Warden is in residence.

⊖ 🅿 WC 🔽 (gardens and courtyard only) 🚪 D (on lead, grounds only) ♣ ◆ ⚡ EH

Tower of London

Tower Hill, London EC3

The most visited castle in England, and one of the most important examples of medieval architecture. It was intended as a royal fortress, and at its core is the White Tower, the huge Norman keep built by William the Conqueror in about 1080. This was built within the Roman city walls, which probably formed part of the fortifications. By the 13th century the building had more or less the form it has today, with the White Tower encircled by two rings of massive walls with towers. Richard I and Henry II built the inner wall and Edward I the outer one, and although they have been much repaired and restored they remain substantially as built. The Tower has so many bloodthirsty associations that it is difficult to envisage it as a palace, but it was the home of royalty as well as a prison, and although the palace buildings were destroyed on the order of Oliver Cromwell, the Crown Jewels are a reminder of this function. The walls, particularly those of the Beauchamp Tower, are carved with inscriptions made by those awaiting trial or death, and the Bowyer Tower still contains the instruments of torture. State prisoners were usually admitted through the Traitor's Gate in St Stephen's Tower, and executions took place both inside the Tower itself and on Tower Hill. The White Tower is now the home of a magnificent collection of medieval arms and armour, including the famous suit of armour made for Henry VIII. St John's Chapel, built about 1080, was restored to its former Romanesque beauty by Prince Albert.

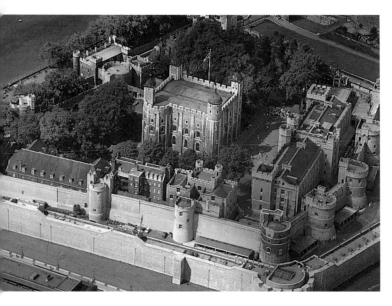

☎ (01) 709 0765

At N end of Tower Bridge off Tower Hill Road

TQ 3380 (OS 176)

Open Mar to end Oct M-S 0930-1700, Su 1400-1700; Nov to end Feb M-S 0930-1600

♿ P WC ♿ (limited access) 🚻 D ♦ ◆ ☂
🏃 ● (not in certain parts of Tower) EH

Farnham Castle

Farnham, Surrey

The land on which the castle stands belonged to the bishops of Winchester long before the town of Farnham existed, and the castle was their property right down to 1927, when it was taken over by the Ministry of Works. The earliest castle on the site was a rectangular keep built on a 30-foot-high motte by King Stephen's brother, Bishop Henry of Blois, in about 1138. It was pulled down (probably by Henry II in the 1150s) and replaced later in the 12th century by the present shell keep. This was built round the mound rather than on top of it, as was usual; the mound itself was levelled, burying the earlier keep, which was only rediscovered after excavations began in the 1950s. Farnham changed hands twice during the Civil War following the death of King John, but its existence was otherwise uneventful, and the new buildings inside the wall were mainly domestic in character. The surviving great hall, chapel and other rooms were built, rebuilt and altered over a period ranging from the 12th to the 19th century. The most spectacular feature is the brick tower built by Bishop Waynflete in 1470-75 on the south side of the castle. During the Civil War, Farnham was attacked and captured by Parliamentary forces and eventually slighted, but after the Restoration of 1660 it was refitted at great expense, and again served as the bishop's residence. There is much fine interior decoration dating from the 1670s.

☎ Farnham (0252) 713393

In town centre off A287

SU 8347 (OS 186)

Open am and pm (Su pm only)

⊖ 🅿 🅗 ◆ ♨ EH

Guildford Castle

Guildford, Surrey

This was once a royal castle controlling the strategically vital Guildford Gap. What now remains is the stern rectangular keep, 63 foot high and 47 foot square, built from about 1170 and standing on its very large 11th-century motte. As usual, the main entrance was on the first floor; the present entrance is modern. Interesting official documents from the reign of Henry III (1216-72) dispel something of the apparently gloomy atmosphere of the castle. They record the interior decoration to be undertaken on the King's orders – the marbling of its pillars and arches, the whitewashing of the great chamber, and the painting of its ceiling green with gold and silver spangles. In its rectilinearity Guildford, though built by Henry II, was more old-fashioned in design than more or less contemporary Henrican castles such as Orford and Dover; as little as a year or two evidently made all the difference to the royal plans, converting the King to a new idea – the polygonal keep – that had been brought back by Crusaders from the Muslim East. Guildford's fortifications were much extended at some time in the 13th century to create concentric defences, but the only remaining trace of the work is an arch from the outer gateway set up in Guildford's Quarry Street.

☎ Guildford (0483) 505050

To the S of town centre, off A281

SU 9949 (OS 186)

Grounds open daily sunrise to sunset, castle keep open Apr to Sept 1030-1800.

 ♨

Bodiam Castle

Bodiam, near Robertsbridge, East Sussex

In 1385 Sir Edward Dalyngrigge received orders from Richard II to 'strengthen and crenellate his manor house', the purpose being to defend the country from the French raids on the south coast (the river Rother was then navigable as far as Bodiam). But the castle was no sooner built than it became redundant, as by 1388 the English had regained control of the Channel, and for centuries the building was left to its slow decay. But in 1916 Lord Curzon bought it, restored the walls with great sensitivity and landscaped the surrounding land. Bodiam, although not large, is a perfect example of a 14th-century castle, and its strong, high, symmetrical walls and towers reflected in its broad moat present a lovely sight. Its plan is simple, with the curtain walls enclosing a rectangular inner courtyard, round towers at each corner, a square tower in the middle of each flank, a gate tower in front and a smaller one at the back. The idea of building a castle as a courtyard defended by the gatehouse, in which the main defences were concentrated, was then quite new, replacing the earlier notion of the keep, or central fortified tower. The great gatehouse at Bodiam is formed of two huge rectangular towers joined by a deep arch and parapet. The parapet is pierced with machicolations: the walls have gun 'loops' for the new weapon, the cannon; and there were originally no fewer than three portcullises, one of which could be closed against the interior, thus keeping the main gate secure from treachery within as well as foes without.

☎ Staplecross (058 083) 436

12 m N of Hastings on A229 turn E at High Wigsell to Bodiam

TQ 7825 (OS 188)

Open Apr to end Oct daily 1000-1800 (sunset if earlier); Nov to end Mar M-S 1000-sunset

P WC 🅰 (limited access) 🚻 D ♠ 🐕

🎪 ◆ ☈ NT

Herstmonceux Castle

Hailsham, East Sussex

Thanks to restoration and rebuilding in the 1910s and 1930s, Herstmonceux is in a splendid condition. In general appearance it is a medieval courtyard castle – a moated, rectangular edifice with four octagonal towers at its corners and three semi-octagonal towers on the north, west and east curtain walls. The entrance, on the south side, is protected by a mighty, twin-towered gatehouse equipped with a portcullis, two sets of battlements and neatly patterned rows of arrow slits. But despite its imposing appearance, Herstmonceux was not primarily built to provide security. It was constructed not with stone but with bricks, a fashionable new material that had been introduced to England from Flanders. Its numerous large windows would have been accounted military madness if gracious living had not been a more important consideration, as records of the original internal arrangements at Herstmonceux confirm. The castle was built by Sir Roger Fiennes in the 1440s, when life in southern England seemed to have become permanently peaceful and secure – that is, a decade or so before the Wars of the Roses showed that this was an illusion. Herstmonceux never saw military action, decaying quietly from the 18th century until its 20th-century resurrection. It became part of the Royal Observatory in 1948, and only the rooms with historic castle and Observatory exhibits are open to the public.

☎ Herstmonceux (0323) 833171 (ext 3320)

4 m E of Hailsham on A271

TQ 6312 (OS 199)

Grounds and exhibition rooms in castle open Easter to end Sept daily 1030-1730

P WC 🚻 (limited access) 🚏 (by appt) D (on lead, grounds only) ♣ 🍴 ⌂ ◆ ⚲ 🕭 NT

Lewes Castle

Lewes, East Sussex

After climbing up to the battlements of one of the towers of Lewes Castle, the visitor begins to appreciate the once critical importance of this site; it can be seen to command the valley of the Ouse, which creates a gap through the South Downs that a potential invader might well find inviting. Therefore, after the Norman Conquest King William gave the Rape of Lewes to one of his most trusted lieutenants, William de Warenne, who built the castle here in a relatively short time. This, like Lincoln Castle, has one very unusual feature: instead of a single motte, there are two within the bailey. Apparently a shell keep stood on each of them, one on the west side guarding the town and the other on the east overlooking the river. All that now remains of these is part of the west keep, with two octagonal towers that were added in the 13th century. Apart from the panoramic view from the top, the most impressive surviving part of Lewes Castle is the powerful double-towered barbican, which was a 14th-century addition, built in front of the original Norman gateway. The castle's history was uneventful, and by the early 17th century it was being plundered for building materials. It is now associated with the Castle and Barbican House Museum of Sussex Archaeology.

☎ Lewes (0273) 474379

In centre of Lewes

TQ 4110 (OS 198)

Throughout year M-S 1000-1730; Apr to Oct Su 1100-1730 also; closed 25 Dec

⊖ 🅿 WC 🔳 (limited access) 🚆 (by appt) D (grounds) ♣ ◆ ✻ 𝄢 (parties, by appt)

Pevensey Castle

Pevensey, East Sussex

Pevensey is a fascinating example of a site intermittently used for military purposes over a period of 1600 years: Roman, Norman and Second World War British defences coexist and even overlap there. Initially, Pevensey's appeal was that of a coastal peninsula, though silting has long since converted it to an inland site. Anderida, the Roman fort, dates from about AD 300 and was part of the chain of Saxon Shore forts; substantial areas of the wall survive. In 1066 William the Conqueror landed at Pevensey and immediately quartered his army in the south-west corner of the fort. After the Conquest, William's half-brother Robert de Mortain chose the same area for his keep and inner bailey. The keep was built into a section of Roman wall that was equipped with two D-shaped bastions, and the Normans took over the idea, placing five more bastions – also D-shaped – on the other sides of the keep. Pevensey was greatly strengthened in the early 13th century, when the present curtain wall was constructed around the inner bailey, with three three-storey D-shaped towers and a double-towered gatehouse. The castle has had a turbulent history, successfully withstanding sieges in 1264 and 1372; but from the 15th century it was allowed to fall into decay. During the Second World War it was refortified, and pill-boxes were placed on top of the keep and bastions, camouflaged to look like centuries-old masonry!

☎ Eastbourne (0323) 762604

6 m NE of Eastbourne on A259

TQ 6404 (OS 199)

Open daily am and pm (Su pm only)

⊖ 🅿 🔳 D (on lead, grounds only) ♣ ◆ ✻ EH

Arundel Castle

Arundel, West Sussex

The majestic keep and long walls of Arundel command the lower reach of the Arun between the South Downs and the sea. A large castle of motte and bailey type was erected not long after the Norman Conquest to guard the important gap carved by the river through the Downs. The motte is 70 foot high and the baileys extend north and south from it along a chalk spur. In the 12th century a battlemented shell keep was built on the motte, and curtain walls erected round the baileys. The walls of the keep are thick, supported externally by flat buttresses. A strong gate tower replaced the arched entrance in the wall in the 12th century, and was later heightened and strengthened by the addition of a two-towered barbican. At this time the castle was held by Richard Fitzalan, created Earl of Arundel in 1290; it passed through the female line to the Howard family in 1580. During the Civil War the castle was sacked by the Parliamentarians. In 1787 the 11th Duke of Norfolk began a substantial reconstruction of the castle; the library remains a monument to his taste. The 15th Duke restored the keep and barbican, and carried out a comprehensive rebuilding of the domestic blocks during 1870-90. The buildings today, though resting on 12th-century foundations, are mainly of this period.

☎ Arundel (0903) 883136

In centre of Arundel

TQ 0107 (OS 197)

Open Apr to end Oct daily exc S 1300-1700 (opens 1200 June to Aug); reduced rates for parties

 WC 🚻 🍴 ♿ 🍽 🎋 ◆ ⚞ 🏹 (by appt) ● (not in house)

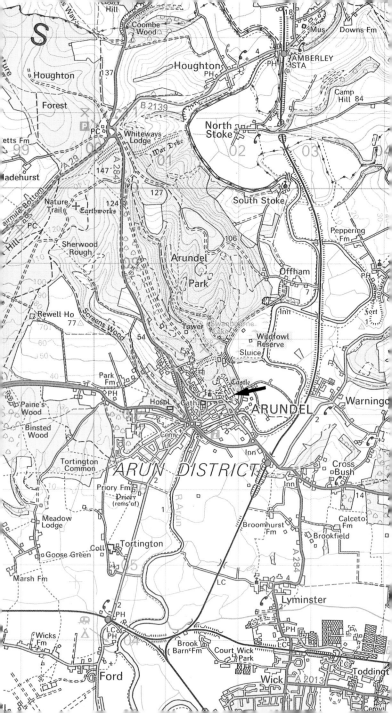

DYFED

WEST
GLAMORG

DE

Okehampton
Castle

Ca
D

Tintagel Castle

Lydford Castle

Launceston
Castle

CORNWALL

Berry Pomeroy C

Restormel Castle

Plymouth

Totnes Cas

St. Michael's
Mount

St Mawes Castle

Pendennis
Castle

Penzance

The West Country

POWYS

HEREFORD AND WORCESTER

Gloucester

GLOUCESTERSHIRE

OXFORDSHIRE

GWENT

MID GLAMORGAN

Swindon

SOUTH GLAMORGAN

Cardiff

Bristol

AVON

Bath

Farleigh Hungerford Castle

WILTSHIRE

Nunney Castle

Old Sarum

SOMERSET

Salisbury

Taunton

Wardour Old Castle

Tiverton Castle

Yeovil

Sherborne Castle

HAMPSHIRE

Bickleigh Castle

DORSET

N

Christchurch Castle

xeter

Bournemouth

Powderham Castle

Maiden Castle

Corfe Castle

ton Castle

rbay

Portland Castle

tmouth
stle

Launceston Castle

Launceston, Cornwall

This well-preserved ruin stands on a very steep motte in a public park that was once the castle bailey; the gateways and some remains of the bailey wall are still in place. There was a fort of some kind here before the Norman Conquest, and a wooden castle was put up by the Conqueror's brother, Robert of Mortain. Then, in 1200, a stone shell keep was erected on the motte. Further changes testified to the importance of the royal Earls of Cornwall, and of Launceston itself, which was the chief Cornish town throughout the Middle Ages. In the middle decades of the 13th century the buildings inside the shell keep were swept away by Richard, Earl of Cornwall, who built a much higher round tower within the walls. Though ruinous, both sets of walls are still standing, and it is possible to walk up an inside staircase to the top of the tower, which affords good views of Launceston and the surrounding countryside. The area between the inner and outer walls was originally roofed over, and the structure was further protected by a low outer wall which has entirely disappeared. The castle was already in a bad state early in the 14th century, but was repaired by the Black Prince. It fell into decay again, and the Royalists' attempt to defend it during the Civil War levelled most of it.

☎ Launceston (0566) 2365

Close to town centre on A388

SX 3284 (OS 201)

Open daily am and pm (may close in winter).

⊖ 🕀 D 🚻 🎡 ◆ ♨ EH

Pendennis Castle

Falmouth, Cornwall

This castle dates from the 16th century, when artillery had become a significant factor in warfare. It stands just south-west of Falmouth, guarding the western side of the entrance to Carrick Roads; with St Mawes Castle performing a similar function on the eastern side, it constituted a strong disincentive to would-be freebooters or invaders. Both castles were part of a chain built by Henry VIII along the east and south coasts of England. Henry's building at Pendennis – a three-storey circular tower and sixteen-sided curtain wall – was undertaken between about 1544 and 1546. The castle was greatly strengthened in the late Elizabethan period by the addition of an outer wall with bastions at the angles; the gatehouse was erected in the following century. Since guns could be stationed on the roof, in the ports or the tower, and on the walls, Pendennis was a formidable stronghold. Its moment of glory came in 1646, during the Civil War, when Parliamentary forces commanded by Sir Thomas Fairfax took over the area. St Mawes surrendered without a fight, but Pendennis, under its 70-year-old governor Colonel Arundell, held out for six months; even Arundell's opponents recognised his gallantry, and after surrender the garrison was allowed to march out with the full honours of war – colours flying and still bearing arms

☎ Falmouth (0326) 313388

Near town centre

SW 8231 (OS 204)

Open daily am and pm (exc Su am Oct-March)

⊖ (1 mile) 🅿 WC ♿ (limited access) 🕀 D (on lead, grounds only) 🚻 🍴 ◆ ♨ EH

Restormel Castle

Lostwithiel, Cornwall

This medieval castle, though ruinous, is very beautiful and excellently preserved in certain important respects. It is a shell keep, with battlemented circular walls that still stand at almost their original height (rather less than 30 foot); in diameter the circle measures 125 foot. Restormel is surrounded by a deep moat, and was built in a commanding position above the west bank of the river Fowey. It was protected by steep slopes except to the west, where an outer bailey is presumed to have stood, though no trace of it now remains. The first castle on the spot was erected by Baldwin Fitz Turstin in about 1100, and may well have been no more than a wooden stockade. Except for some 12th-century parts of the entrance, the present walls probably date from about 1200; everything else, including the chapel tower built into the wall, was the work of the Earls of Cornwall from the later 13th century. In particular, Edmund de Cornwall seems to have transformed the castle between 1271 and his death in 1300. Remains inside the walls indicate that by then Restormel had become an important and relatively sophisticated place, and this is confirmed by the fact that the Black Prince twice visited the castle, in 1354 and 1362. Soon afterwards it seems to have fallen quite rapidly into decay. It was said to be a complete ruin by the 17th century, but in 1646, during the Civil War, a Parliamentary force attempted (though without success) to hold the castle against the Royalist Sir Richard Grenville.

☎ Lostwithiel (0208) 872687
1 m N of Lostwithiel
SX 1061 (OS 200)

Open daily am and pm (Oct to March, Su pm only)
⊖ 🅿 WC 🄰 🖪 D ♣ ◆ ⚘ EH

St Mawes Castle

St Mawes, Cornwall

St Mawes guards the eastern side of the entrance to Carrick Roads, the estuary leading to Falmouth and on into the heart of Cornwall; the castle has a 'partner' on the other side of the estuary in Pendennis Castle. Both were links in a chain of castles built right along the east and south coasts of England by Henry VIII, who was diplomatically isolated in the late 1530s and fearful of a French invasion, since the great European powers were – for once – at peace. St Mawes was built in 1540-43 to a singularly elegant clover-leaf plan. It consists of a round central tower rising above three circular bastions on its seaward side. By English standards this design represented advanced military technology (probably applied on the advice of foreign experts), providing maximum sweep for the artillery that was installed in the castle's gunports. The royal arms are placed over the main entrance, and there are many other inscriptions and interesting decorative details. Below the castle stands a small Tudor blockhouse with three gunports. The history of St Mawes proved to be uneventful, since neither the French in the 1540s nor the Spaniards in the 1580s and 1590s attempted a landing. During the Civil War the castle surrendered without a shot being fired, apparently because the defenders were prepared only for a seaborne assault. In the 20th century St Mawes was still thought formidable enough to become part of the coastal defences during both the First and the Second World War.

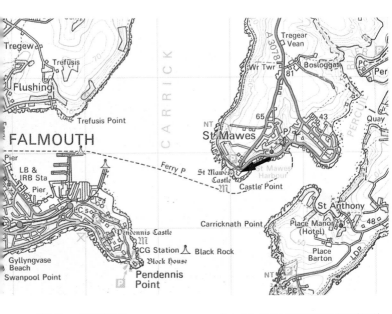

☎ St Mawes (0326) 270526

In town centre

SW 8432 (OS 203)

Open daily am and pm (exc Su am, Oct to March)

⊖ P WC ♿ (limited access) 🚻 D (on lead, grounds only) ♣ ◆ ♨ EH

St Michael's Mount

Marazion, near Penzance, Cornwall

St Michael's Mount, the conical-shaped island just off the coast of Cornwall, is the twin of Mont St Michel in France, and both are the home of monastic foundations. The fortified Benedictine priory in Cornwall was built by the Abbot of Mont St Michel in 1135 and remained attached to the French foundation for nearly 350 years, after which it passed into the hands of the convent of Syon. After the Dissolution in the 1530s the Mount was primarily used as a fortress, and was frequently garrisoned; it was held for the King in the Civil War. The St Aubyn family acquired it in 1657, but for some time it remained more or less unoccupied, until in the 18th century the family began to use it as a summer home. In 1875 it was transformed into a comfortable, usable country house, under the guidance of Piers St Aubyn, known as a church restorer. Today his restorations are generally deplored but St Michael's Mount is a remarkable achievement. He took great care not to alter the famous silhouette of rock-perched buildings. The finest rooms are the Chevy Chase Room, originally the monks' refectory, with its plaster hunting frieze, banners and coat-of-arms, and the two drawing rooms made from the Lady Chapel. These both have charming Rococo decoration and Chippendale chairs, and the larger one has a portrait of Sir John St Aubyn, a copy by Opie of an original by Reynolds. The little church is still basically the 14th-century building, although the seats and much of the decoration are modern, and it retains its serene monastic atmosphere.

☎ Marazion (0736) 710507

3 m E of Penzance on A30 turn E to Marazion

SW 5130 (OS 203)

Open Nov to end Mar M, W, F, guided tours only depending on tides etc; Apr to end May M, T, W, F; Jun to end Oct M-F 1030-1645

♿ WC ⊟ D ☂ (occasional) 🅿 ◆ ⚲ ⚔ ● NT

Tintagel Castle

Tintagel, Cornwall

Tintagel Castle is often referred to as 'King Arthur's Castle', but although the local tourist industry leans heavily on the Arthurian connection, there is no real evidence for it, as the earliest reference is in the fanciful and highly coloured *History of Britain* by the 12th-century monk Geoffrey of Monmouth. He was writing in about 1140 when the Norman castle was being built, and it was possibly the discovery of early monastic remains that gave him the idea of a much earlier castle on the site. This idea has appealed to the popular imagination ever since. Tintagel Castle is full of romance and atmosphere, particularly on a fine day, and its site, on a high, wave-lashed promontory, could not be more spectacular. The Norman castle and keep was built by Reginald, Earl of Cornwall, in the 12th century, and the Celtic monastery probably dates from before the 9th century. The original great hall, of which little more than foundations remain, was evidently built before the mid-13th-century curtain wall. The buildings were considerably extended by Earl Richard, younger brother of Henry III, who held Tintagel from 1236 to 1272, and the major part of the building on the mainland is his work (the castle is divided into two, with a narrow causeway between). During the 14th century it began to show signs of dilapidation, although it was used as a prison towards the end of the century. In 1377 the castle was made the property of the Black Prince, Duke of Cornwall, but from the 15th century onwards it was allowed to fall into disrepair.

☎ Camelford (0840) 770328

2 m N of Camelford on B3266 turn W onto B3263

SX 0588 (OS 200)

Open daily throughout year; 15 Mar to 15 Oct 0930-1830; 16 Oct to 14 Mar 0930-1600 (Su 1400-1600)

🅿 WC (¼ mile) 🚻 (by appt) D ♠ 🐶 🎋 ⚹ 🏌 (by appt) EH

Berry Pomeroy Castle

near Totnes, Devon

This is a very picturesque wooded ruin, comprising not one but two essentially separate structures: an early 14th-century castle and a late 16th-century mansion. The castle belonged to the de la Pomeroi family, and dates from about 1300. As the family came to England with William the Conqueror, there must have been at least one earlier castle on the site, but no trace of it (or them) remains. The existing building seems to have been a typical rectangular courtyard castle of the time of Edward I. Now only the southern curtain wall and part of the west wall survive, along with most of an imposing twin-towered gatehouse; at the far (south-east) end of the south wall stands St Margaret's Tower. The castle remained in the same hands right down to 1549, when Sir Thomas Pomeroy became one of the leaders of a rebellion against the new 'reformed religion' being introduced by the government of Edward Seymour, Duke of Somerset. After the failure of the rebellion, the Pomeroy lands were in fact bought by the Seymours, who in their turn kept theproperty for several hundred years – until 1930, when it passed into the public domain. Sir Edward Seymour (d. 1593) built a mansion on the northern and eastern sides of the old castle; it too is now in ruins, but the three-storey block on the east is relatively well preserved. Both the castle and the house were badly damaged during the Civil War, and were abandoned soon afterwards.

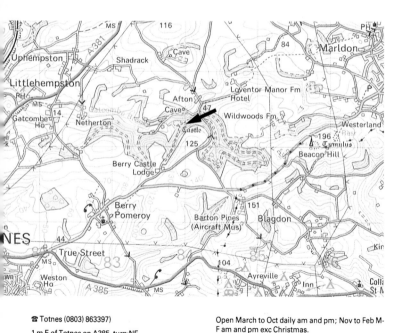

☎ Totnes (0803) 863397)

1 m E of Totnes on A385, turn NE

SX 8462 (OS 202)

Open March to Oct daily am and pm; Nov to Feb M-F am and pm exc Christmas.

🅿 WC 🚻 D 🍴 🍷 (summer only) 🎪 ◆ ☃

Bickleigh Castle

Bickleigh, near Tiverton, Devon

Bickleigh gives an excellent idea of how a lesser moated castle appeared in the late Middle Ages. It has been most fortunate in the loving care and restoration by its 20th-century owners, above all on its little Norman chapel, still with its sanctuary ring on the door. Believed to be the oldest complete building in Devon, dating from between 1090 and 1110, the chapel was used for worship until early in this century. It then served as a cattle byre until the 1920s, but has since been thoroughly repaired and rethatched. Thatch is a feature of the castle today and this helps recall the likely appearance of the place in Tudor times, as well as contributing to the sense of domesticity which is even more noticeable in the interiors. Early in the 15th century it came to the Courtenays who, as Earls of Devon, held a number of other castles and treated Bickleigh as a portion for younger sons. This gave rise to a romantic episode of importance for its later history: there being at one time no surviving younger son, the orphaned daughter of one, called Elizabeth, lived at Bickleigh in the guardianship of a Courtenay relative, William Carew, whose younger brother Thomas eloped with her. The ending was happy and heroic: Thomas fought at Flodden Field (1513) where, by saving the life of Lord Howard, the commander, he won his favour. The Courtenays approved the marriage and granted Bickleigh to Elizabeth as her dowry. The moat in front of the gatehouse has been made into an attractive water garden.

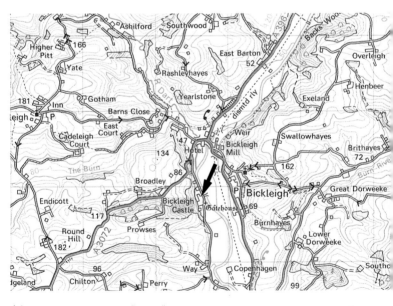

☎ Bickleigh (088 45) 363)

7 m S of Tiverton on A396 turn SW onto A3072

SS 9306 (OS 192)

Open Easter Week F-F and W, Su and Bank Hol M to end May; June to Oct daily (exc S) pm.

⊖ P WC ♿ (ground floor only) 🚻 (by appt) ♣ 🍴

Castle Drogo

Drewsteignton, Devon

This merits an entry because it will probably prove to be the last British example of a type of building with a long and interesting history: the sham castle, erected as an expression of nostalgia for a non-existent past. This massive granite house is superbly sited – granite on granite – at the edge of a bluff overlooking a gorge of the river Teign. It was conceived by Sir Julius Drewe, founder of the Home and Colonial Stores, who believed that his medieval ancestors were the Drogos or Drus, Norman barons who owned land in the area. He commissioned Edwin Lutyens, an architect with a flair for the grandiose that was to culminate in the creation of New Delhi, to design a fittingly monumental family home; and although Lutyens' designs (1910-13) were eventually scaled down, Castle Drogo was still so large that it took twenty years to finish (1910-30). Everything about it was handled with Lutyens' habitual care and assurance, and technically Castle Drogo is irreproachable. The sources of his style are many, but although he drew on Norman, Tudor and other precedents, his final design is quite personal, displaying his (and apparently his patron's) romantic passion for 'austerity' in the form of naked granite surfaces and unpainted woodwork, which would hardly have pleased those Norman ancestors who made a practice of painting their castles outside and in. Castle Drogo, with its forbidding exterior and coldly 'honest' interiors, is film-set medieval.

☎ Chagford (064 73) 3306)

12 m W of Exeter, 4 m NE of Chagford

SS 6788 (OS 191)

Open Apr to end Oct daily am and pm.

⊖ 🅿 WC ⬥ 🖪 (by appt) ♣ ♥ ☴ ◆ ◆ ● (no flash)

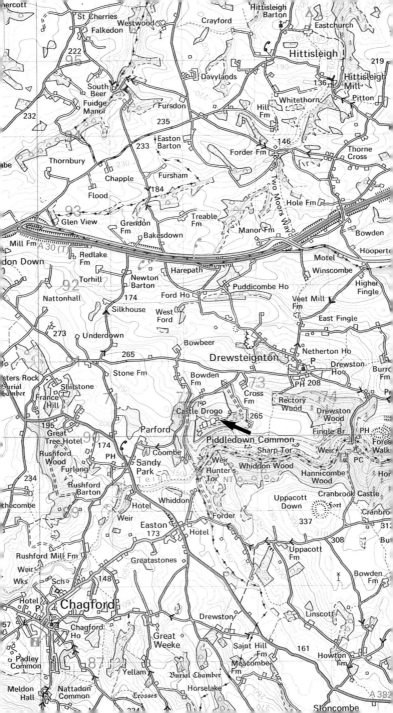

Compton Castle

near Paignton, Devon

This is not a true castle but a singularly spectacular fortified manor house. The tough façade, with its battlements, recesses and projections, buttresses, round archways and mullioned windows, makes the approach to Compton Castle an unforgettable experience. The 'medieval' atmosphere of the place is, however, misleading, since although it certainly originated as a 14th-century house, the façade was not added until the early Tudor period – a fact that explains the distinctly un-medieval neatness of the design. This was done by John Gilbert, who turned Compton into a fortress, presumably as a defence against French or other sea-raiders. There seem to have been Gilberts at Compton from the very beginning, and the family (which included Sir Humphry Gilbert, the mariner-explorer who tried to colonise Newfoundland) continued to own the house, with breaks, for hundreds of years – and it still does. Internally, Compton has been much altered, much damaged, and much restored over the centuries. The present great hall is a modern reconstruction, undertaken as part of a major rebuilding carried out over recent decades; but the withdrawing room to the west, the chapel and the south-west tower are authentically 15th century, and much of the east side dates from the same period as the façade.

☎ Kingkerswell (080 47) 2112)

2 m W of Torquay on A380, turn SW onto A3022 for 2 m, then NW

SX 8664 (OS 202)

Open Apr to end Oct M, W, Th 1000-1215, 1400-1700 (last admission 1145, 1630)

P WC (by appt) D (on lead in grounds) NT

Dartmouth Castle

Dartmouth, Devon

This historically important and visually exciting castle guards the entrance to the estuary of the river Dart – and therefore Dartmouth itself – from the west bank; the ruins of its 'partner', Kingswear Castle, lie on the opposite bank. From the late Middle Ages Dartmouth was a bustling little port with a large export trade. As such it was a natural target for raiders, and was in fact attacked by a sizeable French force in 1404. Various fortifications were built in the area, including a late 14th-century castle close to the present one. Work on Dartmouth Castle itself began in 1481 and continued for fourteen years. In an English context it was a revolutionary building – the first to be specifically designed for, and reliant upon, artillery. The main features of the castle are unchanged – that is, a massive round tower clumsily attached to a rectangular tower. Both were three storeys high. The rectangular tower was the heart of the castle; its basement, just above the water-line, was equipped with seven gunports splayed so that the guns could be moved laterally. The chain or boom across the estuary, which could be stretched tight to impede the progress of enemy ships up river, was controlled from the ground floor. The basement of the round tower was originally intended for musketeers, who fired through slits in the wall, but gunports were added later. The only significant actions at Dartmouth took place during the Civil War, when it changed hands twice; but it was not dismantled and remained of military significance right down to 1940.

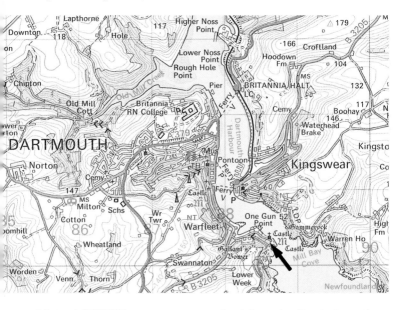

☎ Dartmouth (08043) 3588)

1 m SE of Dartmouth on B3205

SX 8850 (OS 202)

Open daily am and pm (Oct to Apr S pm only)

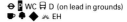

Lydford Castle

Lydford, near Okehampton, Devon

Lydford Castle itself is a rather stolid and forbidding keep, but it stands on a truly spectacular site – a spur of land surrounded on three sides by the deep gorge through which flow the river Lyd and one of its tributaries. A hill fort stood on the spur in Saxon times, and after the Conquest a small area was banked and ditched by the new rulers and, presumably, crowned with a now-vanished timber fortification. In the later 12th century a two-storey stone keep was built on level ground nearby. For reasons that are never likely to be discovered, the keep seems to have been (as we now say) 'condemned'; but it was not dismantled or abandoned. The top storey was removed, a ditch was dug round the site, and the surplus earth was packed all round the standing ground floor of the keep. When its interior had been filled up with rubble, the result was a motte for a new castle keep, which was duly erected. The tops of the old walls were built on directly, and the clearing out of the rubble has given present-day Lydford a 'basement' it never had during its active existence. The castle has almost always belong to the Crown or the Duchy of Cornwall. It was derelict by about 1700, but was repaired, and served as the Stannary Court of Devon down to the early 19th century.

8 m SW of Okehampton on A386, turn W

SX 5084 (OS 201)

Open at any reasonable time

(limited access) D (on lead, grounds only)

♠ ★ ⅍ EH

Okehampton Castle

Okehampton, Devon

This was one of the largest castles in Devon, and is still a very extensive ruin. The site is dramatic, a narrow, wooded spur looking down on the fast-flowing river Oakment. The first, timber castle was built by Baldwin Fitz Gilbert, whom William the Conqueror had appointed Sheriff of Devon, charged with holding down the rebellious south-west. There was probably a stone castle on the site by the time it passed to Sir Robert de Courtenay in 1172, and Okehampton waxed along with the fortunes of the Courtenay family. Hugh, 1st Earl of Devon, probably gave the castle its final form during the first half of the 14th century, extending the keep and putting up a range of residential and service buildings inside the bailey. Evidently comfort was already a prime consideration, though Okehampton remained formidable. It was entered through an outer gatehouse or barbican which led between narrow walls to a two-storey gatehouse giving on the wall bailey, which still contains roofless but substantial remains of buildings. Okehampton had risen, and also fell, with the Courtenays. Henry Courtenay did Henry VIII good service, but the King never overcame his suspicion of the old White Rose nobility, and in 1538 Courtenay, and many others, were the victims of a blood-purge. The castle was dismantled and never reoccupied; but there is still much to see.

☎ Okehampton (0837) 2844

½ m S of town centre on A30

SX 5894 (OS 191)

Open daily am and pm (Su pm only Oct to March)

⊖ P (limited access) ⊟ D ♠ ⊼ ◆ ⅍ EH

Powderham Castle

Kenton, Exeter, Devon

Powderham was a fortified manor house, the home of the Courtenay family since the 14th century. In medieval times the house stood on a dry knoll above the marshy ground of the Exe estuary, but in the 18th century the marsh was drained and reclaimed as parkland. The 14th-century house consisted of the centre building and six towers, one of which survives, as does the interior of the chapel and various bits and pieces of stonework. Several improvements were made in the 18th century, and many of the interiors are still of that time, with pretty Rococo plasterwork. There was another building campaign in the 19th century, and the entrance courtyard and banqueting hall, dating from about 1840, are the work of the architect Charles Fowler. The new hall is in the ornate Gothic style of the time, and chimneypiece, panelling and roof are resplendent with the heraldry of the Courtenays' illustrious descent. There is also a large painting of the 1st Viscount Courtenay by a local artist, Thomas Hudson, who preceded Reynolds as London's fashionable portrait painter. Of the 18th-century interior work by far the best is the staircase, which rises the entire height of the building and has an elaborately carved balustrade and walls which are a cornucopia of modelled plaster fruit and flowers. It is dated 1755 and was made by James Garrett and John Jenkins of Exeter. The elegant music room with its bow window and central dome was added by James Wyatt in the 1770s, and contains fine furniture and a marble chimneypiece.

☎ Starcross (0626) 890243

4 m S of Exeter on A379 turn E to Powderham

SX 9683 (OS 192)

Open late May to mid Sept Su-Th 1400-1730; parties at other times by appt

⊖ P WC 🔄 ♣ 🎒 🎍 ◆ 🎿 (available in foreign languages) 𝄃 (parties only)

Tiverton Castle

Tiverton, Devon

Tiverton Castle has been the seat of famous Devonshire families since
Norman times. Richard de Redvers built a castle here in 1106 which served as
a base for later members of his family, including Baldwin, Earl of Devon,
who was active as an opponent of King Stephen during the 12th-century
'Anarchy'. In the late 13th century Tiverton passed to the Courtenays, who
remained the dominant family in Devon until the 16th century, when they
were made to suffer for their nearness to the Crown (Henry, Marquis of
Exeter and Earl of Devon, was Henry VIII's cousin – and lost his head
because of his real or suspected ambitions). Another famous family, the
Carews, were among later owners of the castle. Inevitably, the present pink
sandstone remains of Tiverton cannot really do justice to such a rich
historical record. They comprise two towers (one round, the other square)
which are all that survive from a 13th-century rectangular 'Edwardian' castle;
and there is also a powerful-looking 14th-century gate-house, modified
during the Tudor period. A wing dating from 1588, and other even later
buildings, survive from the battering the castle received during the Civil
War, when it was besieged by Parliamentary forces commanded by Sir
Thomas Fairfax. The gatehouse is now the Joan of Arc Gallery. There are also
paintings, rugs, furniture and clocks on show.

☎ Tiverton (0884) 253200

On NW outskirts of Tiverton

SS 9513 (OS 181)

Open Easter to end Sept Su-Th 1430-1730

⊖ P WC ☒ (limited access) ☷ (by appt)
D (on lead indoors) ◆ ✻ 𝄡

Totnes Castle

Totnes, Devon

The remains of Totnes Castle lie on the northern edge of the town, on a hill
overlooking the river Dart. The site has a long history. There was an Anglo-
Saxon mint here before the Conquest, and soon after it the first wooden
castle was built by a Breton, Judhael, to whom King William had granted
Totnes; he rebelled against the Conqueror's son, William Rufus, and was
replaced by Roger de Nonant. A shell keep and curtain-walled bailey were
constructed by Reginald de Braose in the early 13th century, but they seem to
have become derelict within a few decades. The property eventually passed
to the de la Zouche family, who undertook a thorough rebuilding in the
1320s; everything of significance now to be seen on the site dates from this
period. The remains are limited but choice: a very large motte, and around it
a nearly circular shell keep in an excellent state of preservation. The
crenellations are virtually intact, and there is a rampart walk that can be
reached by two sets of steps built into the walls. Part of the curtain wall
around the bailey survives, but there is no trace of all the other buildings that
must once have stood here. Totnes passed into the public domain in 1947,
after being owned for four hundred years by the Dukes of Somerset.

☎ Totnes (0803) 864406

In town centre

SX 8060 (OS 202)

Open daily am and pm (Oct to March, Su pm only)

⊖ P ☷ D (on lead, grounds only) ♣ ◆ ✻ EH

Christchurch Castle

Christchurch, Dorset

In 1100 King Henry I granted the manor of Twineham to Richard de Redvers, who constructed a motte at Christchurch, close to the river Avon. The existing rectangular stone keep is later, but replaced an earlier building whose remains have been discovered below the present level of the motte. Christchurch Castle had an insignificant history until the Civil War, when the Parliamentary leader Sir William Waller pulled off a coup by surprising it and capturing an assembled group of Cavalier notables (1644); in the following year the newly intalled Roundhead garrison successfully held out against a Royalist attack. Now the chief point of interest is not the keep but the very well preserved hall in the castle bailey, which was built in about 1160. This is sometimes known as the Constable's House; the name is a plausible one, as Christchurch belonged to the Crown for a time, and the officer in charge of a royal castle was called a constable. The Constable's House conforms closely to type, with an upper floor divided into two residential rooms, the hall and the solar (private apartments) for the use of the lord or constable in charge. It is quite well lit, and although the fireplace has gone, the round Norman chimney still rises high above the walls. In the 13th century one of the chief amenities of civilised life arrived at Christchurch when a garderobe (lavatory) tower was added at the south-east corner, discharging into the mill stream beside the hall. The ground floor was probably used as a storeroom.

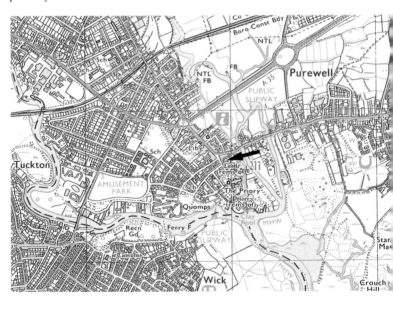

In town centre

SZ 1692 (OS 195)

Open at any reasonable time

♿ 🅿 ★ ♨ EH

Corfe Castle

Corfe, near Wareham, Dorset

Corfe Castle, standing on a steep isolated mound in the ridge of the Purbeck hills, was in its time one of the strongest castles in England. Excavation has found traces of a substantial pre-Conquest building, probably a royal house, but the building of the castle proper began in the 11th century and was basically completed by 1285. The early buildings are those near the top of the hill, with the remains of the keep, built during the early part of the 12th century, at the peak. The 'gloriette' (an unfortified house) was built for King John about 1200, while the outer bailey, a new south-west gatehouse and the outer gatehouse were the last to be constructed. From its construction by William the Conqueror to its destruction by Cromwell's forces in the Civil War, Corfe Castle has been a setting for many episodes in England's history. William I's son, Robert, Duke of Normandy, was imprisoned here; King John, whose favourite castle it was, imprisoned his wife here in 1212 and four years later hid his crown and treasures here, and Edward II, who improved and enlarged the castle, was himself imprisoned in it in 1326. Henry VII visited it in 1496, and in 1571 Elizabeth I sold it to Sir Christopher Hatton, whose widow later disposed of it to the Royalist Sir John Bankes. Sir John spent most of his time in attendance on the King, and when the Civil War broke out Lady Bankes was left to defend the castle on her own. She held out bravely, but was eventually defeated, and in 1646 the House of Commons voted to demolish the building.

☎ Corfe Castle (0929) 480442

6 m SW of Wareham on A351 in Corfe village

SY 9582 (OS 195)

Open Mar to Oct daily 1000-1800; Nov to Feb S and Su 1200-1600

♿ (limited) 🚻 D ♿ 🚻 ◆ (in village) ♨ NT

Maiden Castle

near Dorchester, Dorset

This hilltop site has been intermittently occupied for something like five thousand years, but it is above all famous as an Iron Age hill fort. In its present form it is enclosed by three high earth ramparts and their corresponding ditches; and it still makes a formidable impression. The earliest inhabitants were late Stone Age people of the Windmill Hill culture who settled at the eastern end of Maiden Castle. The Iron Age dwellers were present from about 350 BC and occupied a much larger area, eventually amounting to 45 acres. They progressively strengthened and elaborated their defences by enlarging and adding to the ramparts and ditches, and constructing winding, well-protected entrances of timber, stone and earth. However, Maiden Castle failed to withstand the invading Roman forces; in or around AD 43 it was stormed by the Legio II Augusta, commanded by Vespasian (later emperor of Rome) and supported by powerful siege 'artillery'. Archaeologists have uncovered the graves of the defenders, many of whose skeletons show damage inflicted by sword-cuts or the missiles hurled by Roman ballistae. Within a few years most of the surviving inhabitants had moved down to nearby Durnovaria (Dorchester).

2½ m S of Dorchester on A354, turn W to Winterborne Monkton

SY 6688 (OS 194)

Open daily throughout year at all reasonable times

🅿 🚻 ♠ ★ ⚲ EH

Portland Castle

Portland, Dorset

The exact date at which Portland was built is not known; it was probably begun during the great war-scare of 1539, when a Franco-Imperial invasion was believed to be imminent. In that year England was astir with musters, defence works were thrown up in many parts of south-east England, and Henry VIII launched a programme of fort-building that was to survive the scare. Within a few years the south coast and the Thames were lined with artillery forts, often arranged in pairs so that they could rake a vital stretch of water from two sides. Portland and Sandsfoot were one such pair, controlling Weymouth Bay. Sandsfoot has been seriously damaged by vandalism and erosion, but Portland is still in excellent condition. It is built of the local stone – even-textured, white Portland stone – and is simpler in design than most Henrican forts. In plan it is shaped like a fan with the rounded end – essentially a gun platform – facing Weymouth Bay; embrasures in the ground floor beneath the platform allowed more guns to be deployed, and still more could be positioned on top of the somewhat higher tower or keep at the back. This formidable battery was never tested in the Tudor period. During the Civil War it proved far from impregnable, but it had, after all, been designed to withstand assault from seaborne foreign attackers rather than the hostile natives from inland.

☎ Portland (0305) 820539

3 m S of Weymouth, off A354

SY 6874 (OS 194)

Open Apr to Sept M, Th, F, S am and pm (Su pm only).

⊖ 🅿 ♿ (limited access) 🚻 ♦ ⚲ EH

Sherborne Castle

New Road, Sherborne, Dorset

This is not one but two castles, standing on opposing hills and separated by a lake. The older castle, now a ruin, was owned by the Bishop of Salisbury and coveted by Sir Walter Raleigh. In 1592 Elizabeth I leased it to him, and when, two years later, he was banished from Court he built himself a new house, tall and square, with a picturesque skyline and walls rendered a pleasant yellow ochre. He called it 'The Lodge', and the name stuck until 1800, when it was rechristened, and in fact the name 'castle' describes it better, with its towers and pinnacles, heraldic beasts and forest of chimneys. Sir John Digby, later Earl of Bristol, whose descendants still own the castle, was granted the Sherborne estates in 1617, and added four long wings terminating in towers. The rooms inside contrast with the rather outlandish romanticism of the exterior, being quite small in scale and domestic in feeling. Much redecoration was done in the 19th century by P. C. Hardwicke in the 'Jacobean' style, and some of the plaster ceilings as well as the alabaster fireplace in the dining room are his work. One Georgian interior has survived – the delightful library in the Strawberry Hill 'Gothick' style – and the panelled Jacobean oak room has changed little since the early 17th century. There is some very good Georgian furniture, and there is also a large collection of porcelain. The family portraits, stretching in an unbroken line from the 17th century, include works by Van Dyck, Lely, Reynolds and Gainsborough.

☎ Sherborne (093 581) 3182

In the E outskirts of Sherborne, 5 m E of Yeovil off A30

ST 6416 (OS 183)

Open Easter S to end Sept Th, S, Su and Bank Hols 1400-1800

⊖ (1 m) 🅿 WC ♿ (limited access) 🚻 D (grounds only) ♣ 🍴 ⛱ ⚹ ● (not in castle) EH

Dunster Castle

Dunster, Somerset

In a tree-girt setting with superb views, Dunster is a picture-book castle with a romantic array of battlements, towers and turrets – essentially the creation of a medievalising Victorian architect. A Norman castle was built on the site soon after the Conquest, and from that time Dunster was owned by only two families: the Mohuns, who sold it in 1376, and its purchasers, the Luttrells, who presented it to the National Trust in 1976. The earliest surviving features are the 13th-century gateway and the imposing 15th-century gatehouse built over it by Sir Hugh Luttrell. In 1617 George Luttrell employed the builder of Montacute, William Arnold, to remodel Dunster into a Jacobean mansion standing inside the castle. During the Civil War the Luttrells were for Parliament, but Dunster was occupied by Royalist forces and held out for five months before surrendering to Parliamentary troops commanded by Robert Blake (later famous as an admiral). Three years later all its fortifications were demolished, leaving only the house itself and the gatehouse. In the 1680s Francis Luttrell made some excellent improvements, creating the present 17th-century staircase and dining room, with its woodcarving and plaster-work of very high quality. Dunster acquired its present aspect from 1867 when Anthony Salvin, an architect who specialised in medieval and Eliza-bethan work, remodelled many features and made other substantial additions.

☎ Dunster (0643) 821314)

3 m SE of Minehead on A39, turn S onto A396

SS 9943 (OS 181)

Open Apr to Sept S-W 1100-1700 (last admission 1630); Oct 1400-1600

⊖ ⓟ WC ⊟ (by appt) ♣ ☙ (in village) ◆ ⅍ ● (no video, tripods, ciné) NT

Farleigh Hungerford Castle

near Trowbridge, Somerset

Little now remains of Farleigh except two ruinous towers that stood at the south-west and south-east corners of the castle. In its time it was an imposing, ultra-modern building on the lines of Bodiam in East Sussex, but larger and slightly earlier in date. Farleigh was erected in the 1370s by Sir Thomas Hungerford, an able administrator who worked for the King's powerful brother, John of Gaunt, Duke of Lancaster, and became Speaker of the House of Commons in 1377; he evidently started building the castle without getting the appropriate royal licence, but presumably had no great difficulty in securing a formal pardon for his offence in 1383. Around an inner bailey Sir Thomas erected a rectangular curtain wall with round towers at each corner and a strong gatehouse in the middle of the south side, which was its most vulnerable point. Sir Thomas's son, Sir Walter Hungerford, extended and strengthened Farleigh in about 1425 by adding a barbican to the existing gatehouse and building a new outer bailey on to the south side of the castle. In doing so he enclosed the local parish church, St Leonard's, which henceforth became the family chapel. Farleigh Hungerford survived the Civil War, but by the end of the 17th century it was already a ruin.

☎ Trowbridge (022 14) 4026)

3 m W of Trowbridge, on A366

ST 8057 (OS 173)

Open mid-March to mid Oct daily 0930-1830 (Su 1400-1830); mid-Oct to mid-March M, W, F, and S 0930-1630, Th and Su 1400-1630.

ⓟ WC ⊟ D (on lead) ♣ ⊓ ◆ ⅍ ● EH

Nunney Castle

Nunney, Somerset

This sturdy, compact little castle is oddly sited: it stands in the village of Nunney, down at the bottom of a valley. It is really a fortified house rather than a true castle – a rectangular four-storey mansion with massive drum towers (about 30 foot across) at each corner. Since the house itself is only about 80 by 40 foot in plan, the big towers crowd in on it and on the shorter sides almost touch each other, giving Nunney its characteristically self-contained look. It is moated, and was further protected by three now-vanished bailey walls, with Nunney brook enclosing the fourth side. The castle's security function may well have been less important than its symbolic role; its style is very French (as was even more apparent when the towers were capped with conical roofs), proclaiming the fact that its builder, Sir John de la Mare, had served and made his fortune in the French wars. Although the de la Mares had owned the land for two centuries, Nunney dates from the 1370s; Sir John received his royal licence to crenellate in 1373. The only dramatic moment in the castle's existence came in September 1645, when it was held by Richard Prater for the King against the Parliamentary army under Sir Thomas Fairfax. The Royalist cause was failing fast, and the handful of defenders seem to have fought half-heartedly, surrendering after only two days. By that time, Roundhead artillery had severely damaged the north wall, which finally collapsed in 1910.

3 m SW of Frome on A361, turn NW

ST 7345 (OS 183)

Open at any reasonable time

(exterior only) D (grounds only, on lead)
★ ♠ ✿ EH

Old Sarum Castle

Salisbury, Wiltshire

The remains at Old Sarum are extensive but visually rather uninformative; all the same, the place is soaked in history and is popular with visitors. It was first used as an Iron Age hill fort, and the massive earthworks surrounding the castle site are still impressive. The Romans knew Old Sarum as Sorbiodunum, and its importance is indicated by the fact that four Roman roads (to Winchester, Dorchester, Bath and Silchester) converged in the area. The Saxon King Edgar held a great council at Old Sarum in the 10th century, but it was at its most important in the century and a half following the Norman Conquest. A castle was begun in about 1075, and was replaced by stone structures early in the 12th century, notably the strong curtain walls surrounding the outer and inner baileys. By this time Old Sarum was a cathedral town, and the buildings within the outer walls included the cathedral with cloisters and a bishop's palace. A decline set in from the 1220s, when the clergy moved to a new cathedral about a mile away at New Sarum, otherwise known as Salisbury. When Salisbury Cathedral was in need of repairs the old cathedral was plundered for materials, but the castle remained operational until the early 15th century. By 1500 the entire town was deserted. Old Sarum last figured in British history as a scandal: since the franchise remained unchanged for centuries, its insignificant population continued to return two MPs to Parliament – a classic example of the 'rotten boroughs' that were abolished in the Great Reform Bill in 1832.

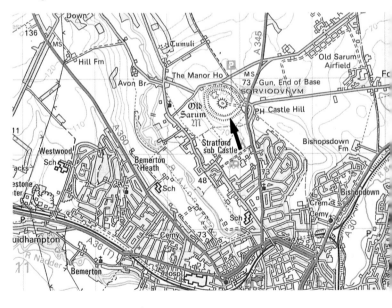

2 m N of Salisbury on A345

SU 1332 (OS 184)

Open 15 Mar to 15 Oct M-S 0930-1830, Su (28 Mar to 30 Sept) 1400-1830; 16 Oct to 14 Mar M-S 0930-1600, Su 1400-1600

⊕ P WC 🚻 (limited access) 🚻 ♠ ◆ ⚹ EH

Wardour Old Castle

Tisbury, Wiltshire

The castle was ruined in the Civil War after a prolonged siege, but it is a very romantic-looking ruin, its outer ward and grounds having been landscaped in the 'picturesque' manner in the 18th century. The castle was built in 1393 by John, 5th Lord Lovell, more for comfort and entertaining than as a serious fortification. It passed through various hands before Sir Matthew Arundell bought it in 1570. He and his architect Robert Smythson, who had previously worked at Longleat, began a major reconstruction, bringing the castle up to date decoratively, with a Classical main entrance and larger windows, without changing the actual plan. Unlike earlier castles, where there are usually several separate buildings including walls and towers, everything at Wardour is together under one roof. It is hexagonal in plan, with the great hall at first-floor level over the entrance and rising the full height of the building. Service rooms and kitchens were at one end and the lord's private rooms at the other, while the remaining sides of the hexagon were 'lodgings' for the use of guests. After the Civil War damage the Arundells built themselves a small house on the south side of the outer ward, and although there was a scheme for rebuilding the castle it came to nothing, and the new house (Wardour Castle) was built instead. The landscaping was done at this time, and the pretty 'Gothick' banqueting house or pavilion was built on what may have been an old gatehouse. The elaborate stone, brick and plaster grotto was made in 1792 by Josiah Lane.

☎ Tisbury (0747) 870487

19 m SW of Salisbury on A30, turn N

ST 9326 (OS 184)

Open daily Apr to Sept am and pm (Su pm only);
Oct to March S am and pm, Su pm only

🅿 WC ⊟ D (on lead, grounds only) ♣ ◆ ✻ EH

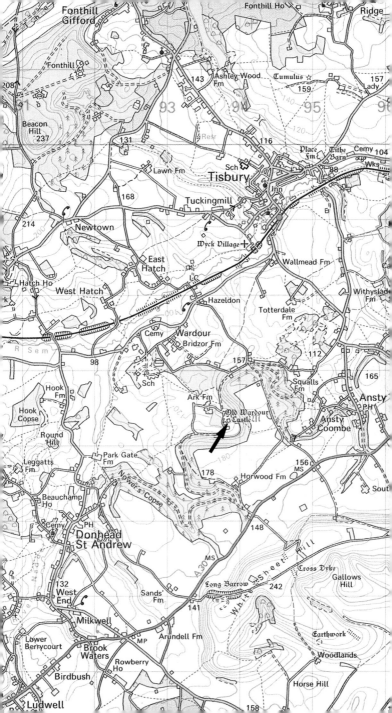

Beaumaris Castle 🏰
Bangor
Conwy Castle 🏰
Rhuddlan Castle 🏰
Penrhyn Castle 🏰
Denbigh Castle
Caernarfon Castle 🏰
🏰 Dolbadarn Castle
C
GWYNEDD
🏰 Criccieth Castle
🏰 Harlech Castle
○ Aberystwyth
P O W
Llandrind
Wells
🏰 Cilgerran Castle
D Y F E D
Carmarthen ○
🏰 Carreg Cennen
Llanstephan Castle 🏰
🏰 Kidwelly Castle
🏰 Carew Castle
Pembroke Castle 🏰
🏰 Manorbier Castle
WEST
GLAMORGAN
Swansea
MID
🏰 Weobley Castle
GLAMORG
Coity Castle 🏰
SOU
GLAMO

Wales and Western Counties

ERSEY-
SIDE

Liverpool

Manchester

Sheffield

Flint
Castle

Ewloe
Castle

Chester

C H E S H I R E

DERBYSHIRE

Beeston Castle

Stoke-on-Trent

Y D

Wrexham

Nottingha

k Castle

Derby

STAFFORDSHIRE

Shrewsbury

Telford

Leicester

Powis Castle

SHROPSHIRE

LEICESTERSHIRE

WEST
MIDLANDS

Stokesay Castle

Ludlow Castle

Birmingham

Coventry

HEREFORD

&

WORCESTER

Worcester

WARWICKSHIRE

Hereford

Eastnor
Castle

Grosmont
Castle

Sudeley Castle

ower
astle

Skenfrith Castle

Goodrich
Castle

White
Castle

Gloucester

OXFORDSHIRE

GLOUCESTERSHIRE

Raglan
Castle

Oxford

G W E N T

Chepstow
Castle

Berkeley Castle

aerphilly Castle

Penhow
Castle

astell Coch

Cardiff

Cardiff Castle

A V O N

Swindon

Bristol

WILTSHIRE

BERKSHIRE

Beeston Castle

Beeston, Cheshire

A very large castle that must once have seemed utterly impregnable, Beeston rises 500 foot above the Cheshire plain, on the very top of a hill with cliff faces falling away on two sides. It was built by Ranulf de Blundeville, Earl of Chester, in the 1220s, but soon passed to the Crown. Edward I strengthened it, and Richard II is said to have buried a great treasure somewhere within its walls before meeting his doom at the hands of the usurper Henry Bolingbroke. The outermost defences of Beeston consisted of cliffs on two sides (north and west) and a wide, rock-cut ditch that ran along the south and east sides. Behind these lay the outer bailey, protected by a curtain wall with seven towers and a gatehouse. Not much of this survives, but the inner bailey on the heights is still very impressive. The immense twin-towered gatehouse in the south wall is flanked by two more towers, and another tower defends the east side. The north and west sides were evidently felt to be safe enough with a plain curtain wall standing above the cliffs – but during the Civil War Beeston did fall, to a handful of intrepid Royalists who climbed up the cliff face and over the north wall. Parliament had its revenge at the end of the war, when Beeston was slighted. On the skyline medieval Beeston Castle is nicely juxtaposed with nearby 'medieval' Peckforton, designed by the Victorian architect Anthony Salvin.

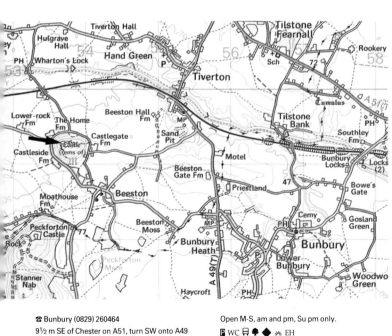

☎ Bunbury (0829) 260464

9½ m SE of Chester on A51, turn SW onto A49
for 2 m then W

SJ 5359 (OS 117)

Open M-S, am and pm, Su pm only.

🅿 WC 🚻 ♣ ◆ ⚒ EH

90

Chirk Castle

Chirk, Clwyd

The Welsh name for the castle is Castell y Waun, which means 'meadow castle'. The rather grim-looking building was built as one of the great Marcher (border) castles by Roger Mortimer, one of Edward I's generals (completed 1310). In 1595 it was bought by the merchant adventurer Sir Thomas Myddleton, who began to convert it into a country house. The Myddletons still live in the castle, which has examples of decoration from the 16th to the 19th centuries, though the exterior has been little changed, and the dungeon, portcullis gate, and stone steps leading to the watch tower remain exactly as originally built. Considerable interior remodelling was done in the 19th century by A. W. N. Pugin, and the entrance hall, in the Victorian Gothic style, is his work. The great staircase next to it, formed inside one of the towers, was designed by Joseph Turner in 1777, and the first-floor state rooms, with their elegant Adam-style decorations, are of the same period. They contain good furniture, portraits and tapestries, and both the saloon and the drawing room have delightful blue-and-gold coffered ceilings. The long gallery, with its boldly carved panelling and mullioned windows, was built about a century earlier. The garden has seen many changes since it was first laid out, but in the 1870s part of the original formal garden was recreated, with topiary work and a charming rose garden. The park, entered from the town, has superb wrought-iron gates made in 1721 by the Davies brothers.

☎ Chirk (0691) 777701

6 m N of Oswestry on A483 turn W onto B4500 for 2 m

SJ 2638 (OS 126)

Open Easter to end Sept Su, T-F and Bank Hol M; Oct S and Su 1200-1700

⊖ P WC ⬧ ▤ ♣ ⬤ ⊼ ◆ ✳ ● NT

Denbigh Castle

Denbigh, Clwyd

Now thoroughly ruined, the castle stands at the highest point of a limestone bluff with the town of Denbigh placed on the north slope immediately below it. The site was chosen by Henry de Lacey, Earl of Lincoln, to whom Edward I gave the lordship of the area in 1282. Following Edward's policy (designed to hold down newly conquered Wales), de Lacey turned Denbigh into a walled town on the English model and then built the castle inside the walls, in the south-west corner. On the south and west sides the relatively thin town walls and small towers were protected by a mantlet (a secondary defensive screen) above the cliffs; on the north and east sides, adjacent to the town, the wall was much more powerful and its octagonal towers were much larger. The gatehouse is still an impressive sight. Like that at Caernarfon, it consisted of two flanking towers with a third tower set back and linked by walls to the others; the effect was to create an octagonal area, exposed to fire from three towers, that an attacker had to cross before passing through into the main courtyard. Denbigh Castle had a colourful history, and its lords included Roger Mortimer (Queen Isabella's paramour), 'Harry Hotspur', and Queen Elizabeth's favourite, the Earl of Leicester. It changed hands several times during the Wars of the Roses, and in the Civil War period was held for the King until a respectably late date. In the later 17th century it was deserted and badly damaged by an explosion.

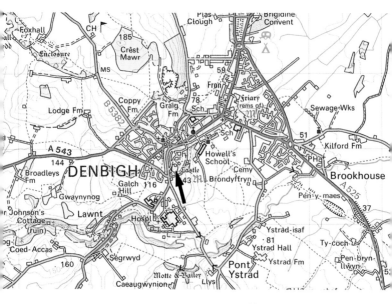

To the S of Denbigh on B4501

SJ 0565 (OS 116)

Open daily am and pm (mid Oct to mid March Su pm only)

♿ P WC ⏸ (by appt) ⚒ WHM

Ewloe Castle

Ewloe, Clwyd

The ruins of Ewloe Castle stand on a pleasantly wooded site not far from Flint; and indeed the building of the much more powerful Flint Castle from 1277 ended Ewloe's military importance and 'froze' the structure in its 13th-century state. The advantages of the site – at the bottom of a valley – are not immediately apparent, but it may be that an ability to lie concealed down among the oaks was regarded as more valuable than the defensive benefits of a hilltop position. This seems all the more likely in terms of Anglo-Welsh political geography: situated in the borderlands of the north-east, Ewloe was disputed territory, and was only strongly held by the Welsh from the mid-12th century. The earliest stone building at Ewloe is the so-called Welsh Tower, actually a small (two-storeyed) keep, D-shaped and dating from soon after 1200. The north-east briefly passed into English hands until Llywelyn ap Gruffydd, the last Prince of Wales, began to assert himself; in about 1257 he strengthened Ewloe, creating two wards by building walls round the motte and also further down the slope; he put up the round West Tower to protect the far end. Edward I's campaigns of 1277 and 1282-83 culminated in the death of Llywelyn and the subjection of Wales to English rule; the earth bank above Ewloe (providing a splendid view of the place) may well be a platform built for the deployment of English siege engines against the castle.

/2 m NW of Ewloe on A55

SJ 3066 (OS 117)

Open daily throughout year exc 24-26th Dec and 1st Jan

⊖ (½ mile) 🚌 D ♣ ★ WHM

Flint Castle

Flint, Clwyd

Edward I's master mason, James of St George, began building Flint Castle in the summer of 1277, even before the King had finished his successful campaign against Llywelyn, Prince of Wales. It was the first of the new 'Edwardian' castles with which English authority was stamped on the conquered nation, and was sited on the estuary of the river Dee, from which it could be supplied by sea; though it is now silted up, in the 13th century the Flint' was a rocky promontory on the west bank of the estuary. The outer bailey of the castle has largely disappeared, but the rest, though ruinous, is interesting and impressive. It consists of the four towers and some sections of the wall of the square inner bailey. Three of the towers were placed at the corners, projecting for most of their circumference beyond the wall. The fourth tower, a huge circular edifice with walls up to 23 foot thick, was built just beyond the angle of the walls and surrounded by its own moat; it could only be reached from the inner bailey, and was in effect a keep, furnished with the full complement of residential and service quarters. In 1282 part of Flint Castle was captured by the Welsh under Llywelyn ap Gruffydd before their revolt was crushed. In legend it is the place where the deposed and deserted Richard II came face to face with Henry Bolingbroke.

In town centre, 10 m NW of Chester

SJ 2473 (OS 117)

Open daily am and pm

⊖ 🅿 ★

Rhuddlan Castle

Rhuddlan, Clwyd

Controlling the lowest crossing of the river Clwyd, this site has a long military history. Welsh princes and Saxon kings fought over it before the Conquest, and the Normans seized it and put up a motte-and-bailey castle as early as 1073; the earthworks can still be seen at a little distance from the present stone ruins of Edward I's castle. This, like Flint Castle, was in progress even before Llewelyn ap Gruffydd surrendered to the English king in October 1277; the work was directed by Edward's expert, Master James of St George. Edward was determined to hold down Wales, and (given the mountainous nature of the interior) that meant building castles and being prepared to supply them by sea; in the case of Rhuddlan, 1800 ditches were employed to divert the Clwyd into a canal that ran down one side of the castle. A moat covered the other three sides. Rhuddlan was a concentric castle; the outer curtain wall has virtually disappeared, but the inner wall is still a striking sight. The castle's defences remained unbreached when the Welsh rebelled in 1382, and Rhuddlan held out again in 1400 when Owain Glyndŵr attacked the town. During the Civil War it was held for the King until 1646, and afterwards thoroughly slighted by Parliament.

SW of Rhuddlan on A547

SJ 0277 (OS 116)

Mid Mar to mid Oct daily 0930-1830; mid Oct to mid Mar M-F at any reasonable time, S 0930-1600, Su 1400-1600

⊖ P WC 🅰 (limited access) 🚻 D ♣ ◆ ⁕ WHM

Carreg Cennen Castle

Dyfed

The dramatic ruins of this castle stand at the edge of the Black Mountains, on a crag 300 foot above the river Cennen. In the 12th century there was a Welsh stronghold here, perhaps built by Rhys ap Gruffydd, which changed hands several times during wars between the Welsh princes. When Edward I of England attacked Wales in 1277 the castle quickly fell. It was given to John Giffard; between the 1280s and about 1310 he and his son John the younger effectively built a new castle on the spot, an orthodox courtyard castle protected naturally on three sides by the cliffs. The defences of the rectangular inner courtyard were concentrated on the fourth side – the north – which was given two corner towers and a typically powerful twin-towered gatehouse. Then a barbican was added; this is well preserved and one of the most interesting features of Carreg Cennen – a long uphill passage which makes two right-angled turns, is barred by drawbridges and gates, and is booby-trapped with five pits before confronting the attacker with the strongly fortified gatehouse. Finally, the Giffards added an outer curtain wall across the north side. Carreg Cennen should have been impregnable, but was not: Owain Glyndŵer seems to have captured it in 1403-4. It was held for Lancaster during the Wars of the Roses, but surrendered in 1462 after the Yorkist victory and was thoroughly slighted.

☎ Llandeilo (0558) 822291

3 m N of Ammonford on A483, turn E at Llandybie

SN 6619 (OS 159)

Open throughout year at any reasonable time; in winter keys available at farm

P WC 🚻 D 🐾 (by appt in winter) ◆ ⁕ WHM

Carew Castle

Carew, Dyfed

This castle, on the estuary of the river Carew (pronounced 'cary' to rhyme with 'Mary'), is exceptionally rich in Anglo–Welsh historical associations. In its present form, Carew consists of a number of Tudor structures grouped round the courtyard of a late 13th-century castle and built into its ruins. Some of the masonry may date back even earlier, for there was a princely castle here in the 11th century, when Rhys ap Twdwr ruled South Wales. When his daughter Nest married the Norman Earl of Pembroke, Gerald de Windsor, Rhys gave them Carew; the marriage was promoted by Henry I of England, by whom Nest – famous in her time as 'the Helen of Wales' – already had a son. Gerald's son took the name Carew, and the castle was held by his descendants for almost five hundred years. It was bought by Sir Rhys ap Thomas, who in 1485 rallied South Wales to Henry Tudor when the latter landed on the Pembroke coast and marched against Richard III; Henry was victorious at the battle of Bosworth (thereby becoming King Henry VII) and Rhys was knighted on the battlefield and favoured ever afterwards. He enlarged Carew Castle, building the present great hall in a style appropriate to the uncrowned king of South Wales. Further building (notably the north wing) and alterations were carried out in the Elizabethan period by Sir John Perrot, supposedly one of Henry VIII's bastards. The later history of the castle was uneventful.

☎ Carew (064 67) 782

6 m NE of Pembroke on A4075 at Carew

SN 0403 (OS 158)

Easter to end Oct daily exc S 1000-1700

⊖ P ⧖ (by appt) ⊟ D ⊓ ◆ ✗ ⅍

Cilgerran Castle

Cilgerran, Dyfed

This picturesque ruin, long a favourite subject for painters, stands on a rocky outcrop looking down the steep, wooded banks of the river Teifi. There was a castle at Cilgerran in the 12th century that was regularly fought over by the Normans and the Welsh, changing hands quite often until 1223, when it was captured from Llywelyn the Great by William Marshal, son of the famous Earl of Pembroke. All the significant remains at Cilgerran date from Marshal's time or later. He was certainly responsible for the features that give the place its present character – the two massive round towers, the rectangular inner gatehouse and the stretches of curtain wall that link them together. All these were part of the inner bailey defences; the rest of the fortifications are very broken down, though it is clear that the late 14th-century tower at the end of the promontory was once a powerful defensive structure. After a long period of neglect the castle was repaired by Edward III, only to be captured by Owain Glyndŵr and badly damaged as a consequence. It was nonetheless occupied by the Vaughans until the early 17th century, but evidently fell into decay soon afterwards.

☎ Cardigan (0239) 614249

3 m S of Cardigan on A478, turn E

SN 1943 (OS 145)

Open daily am and pm (Su pm only)

⧖ (limited access) ⊟ D ◆ 🖤
◆ (summer only) ⅍ WHM

Kidwelly Castle

Kidwelly, Dyfed

A substantial and well-preserved ruin, Kidwelly Castle stands at the mouth of the river Gwendraeth, on the south-west coast of Wales. Bishop Roger of Salisbury put up a Norman castle on the site at the beginning of the 12th century; the remains of its earthworks still form a low mound outside the main gate of the present castle. It changed hands many times during the Anglo–Welsh wars, and eventually passed to Payn de Chaworth. He built a 'modern' defensive structure at Kidwelly in about 1275 – a square curtain wall with strong round towers projecting from each corner. In 1291 the Chaworth heiress married Edward I's nephew, Henry of Lancaster, who put up a range of domestic buildings on the east (river) side of the courtyard, including a chapel tower that rises dramatically from a scarp thrusting out over the river. Early in the 14th century Kidwelly was even more thoroughly modernised by its conversion into a concentric castle. A semi-circular curtain wall was thrown round the inner bailey (as the earlier courtyard now became); the straight side was formed by linking the ends of the semicircle with the east wall of the inner bailey, so that it followed the line of the river. The outer wall was furnished with four round towers and two gatehouses – the main (southern) gatehouse being a typically powerful Edwardian building that in an emergency was capable of functioning quite independently, like a keep. There were some further, mainly domestic improvements in the Tudor period.

In town centre, 7 m W of Llanelli

SN 4007 (OS 159)

Open daily am and pm (mid Oct to mid March Su pm only)

♿ P WC ♿ (limited access) 🍴 ♿ ◆ ♿ ⚑ (in summer, groups only) ♿ WHM

Llanstephan Castle

Llanstephan, Dyfed

The ruins of Llanstephan Castle stand on a bluff overlooking the Tywi estuary, a superb position that offers wonderful views to the visitor. An ancient bank and ditch on the vulnerable western side of the site may well be the remains of an Iron Age fort. The first certain reference to a castle on the spot occurs in 1146, when the Welsh princes Cadell, Rhys and Maredud briefly captured it from the English. At this time it was evidently a timber-and-earth structure divided into two wards. Towards the end of the 12th century William de Camville became the owner by marriage, and it was probably he who built a stone curtain wall round the nucleus of Llanstephan, the upper ward; a square three-storey gatehouse was added in about 1225. The de Camvilles lost control of Llanstephan at least twice; and after the second William de Camville was again dispossessed and reinstated (1257), he brought the castle's defences right up to date. The lower ward was surrounded by a strong curtain wall with a tower on the north and west sides and a bastion – a kind of pseudo-tower made by expanding the curtain wall – on the east. In about 1280 a great two-towered gatehouse, copied from Caerphilly Castle, was installed. The hall (now quite vanished) stood against the north tower, which was larger than its western equivalent and probably served as the lord's private apartments. Llanstephan was captured by Owain Glyndŵr's men, but after that it had a peaceful existence.

10 m SW of Carmarthen on B4312, S of Llanstephan

SN 3510 (OS 159)

Open daily throughout year at all reasonable times

P ☒ ⊟ D ♣ ★ ✺

Manorbier Castle

near Pembroke, Dyfed

This small castle is a perfect model of a medieval nobleman's seat, although partly in ruins. It is best known as the birthplace and home of Gerald de Barry (Giraldus Cambrensis) who wrote vivid accounts of life in 12th-century Wales and Ireland. Gerald was also well known in his day for his unsuccessful struggle with Henry II to make the See of St David's independent from Canterbury, and his brothers played a prominent part in Henry's conquest of Ireland. The de Barrys held Manorbier from about 1130 until the mid-14th century, and nearly all the buildings and fortifications had been put up by 1300, with only minor alterations made since. In 1403 the castle was ordered to be put into a state of defence against Owain Glyndŵr, and during the Civil War it was held by the Royalists but captured by Cromwell's forces in 1646. The castle had a large outer ward, and the main feature of the inner ward was the stone-built hall block, with the hall itself at first-floor level and rising through two storeys. It was divided by a wall from the buttery, which was also on the first floor, though it once had another room above it – the solar, or withdrawing room. This structure and the gatehouse date from about 1140, while the defences, which would originally have been earth and timber, were rebuilt in stone about 1230, and the chapel was added about 1260. These buildings are all now ruined, but the castle is still occupied (some of the domestic buildings have been altered recently), and the inner ward has a very attractive flower garden.

☎ Manorbier (083 482) 421
5½ m SW of Tenby on A4139 turn E onto B4585 to Manorbier
SS 0697 (OS 158)

Open Easter week and mid May to end Sept daily 1030-1730
♿ 🅿 (limited) 🚻 D (on lead) ♠ ⛱ ◆ 🌼

Pembroke Castle

Pembroke, Dyfed

Pembroke Castle was one of the mightiest fortresses ever built in Britain, and even more extraordinary when compared with other Welsh castles dating from before Edward I's late 13th-century masterworks. The site is superb – a mass of rock jutting out into the Pembroke river, with steep cliffs descending on three sides into the waters below; running away to the south-east, like a long body attached to the 'head' (the castle), is the old town of Pembroke, whose walls are still almost completely intact. The first Norman conqueror of Pembroke was Arnulph de Montgomery, who in 1093 erected 'a slender fortress with stakes and turf'. Then, about a century later, William Marshal, Earl of Pembroke, put up a keep and built a curtain wall across the promontory, creating a roughly triangular courtyard. This became the inner bailey when, from about 1250, a new and powerful curtain wall greatly extended the area of the castle. The keep is a marvel – a great round tower some 80 foot high and with walls approaching 20 foot thick at the base. The outer curtain wall is protected by five projecting round angle towers and a gatehouse and barbican that were at one time equipped with an astonishing series of portcullises, machicolations, and other defensive devices. Nevertheless, Pembroke Castle had a remarkably uneventful career. During the Civil War it was held for Parliament by the mayor, John Poyer; but when he joined the Royalist revolt of 1648, Oliver Cromwell invested the castle, captured it after a six-week siege, and then slighted it.

☎ Pembroke (0646) 684585
To NW of town centre
SM 9801 (OS 158)

Open daily am and pm (exc Su, Oct to Easter)
♿ WC ⊟ D (on lead) ◆ ⚹

Caerphilly Castle

Caerphilly, Mid Glamorgan

Caerphilly is the largest castle in Wales, in a splendid state of preservation, and with enough of its artificial moats and lakes still in place to give a fair idea of its original majestic complexity. Among its other distinctions, Caerphilly was the first concentric castle, antedating Edward I's famous strongholds. In characteristic 'Edwardian' style, the heart of the castle consists of two roughly rectangular curtain walls; the outer is protected by two twin-towered gateways, and the inner is even stronger, with two more gateways and four massive drum towers at the corners. But few attackers could hope to get so far. The mighty concentric castle was protected by an outer defensive system that was, if anything, more formidable still. Beyond the outer curtain lay the lakes and moats, with a strong outwork to the west and, to the east, a notable piece of engineering – a 1000-foot-long screen or barrage that served both as a dam and as a crenellated stronghold, consisting of defensive platforms, gatehouses and walls bristling with towers. Caerphilly Castle was the creation of Gilbert de Clare, Earl of Gloucester, who began a castle in 1268 that was destroyed by Llywelyn, Prince of Wales. Gilbert started again in 1271. Edward's conquests removed the main Welsh threat, but Caerphilly was besieged twice during the troubled reign of Edward II (surrendering once) and was occupied for a time by Owain Glyndŵr in the early 1400s.

☎ Caerphilly (0222) 883143

In centre of Caerphilly

ST 1587 (OS 171)

Open daily throughout year; Mar to Oct 0930-1830, Oct to Mar 0930-1600 (Su 1400-1600)

♿ 🅿 WC ♿ (limited access) 🚌 ♠ 🛆 ◆ 𝕏 (by appt) WHM

Coity Castle

Coity, Mid Glamorgan

According to contemporary records there was a castle at Coity in about 1100, but this was probably a timber structure on top of a mound and ditch. The earliest masonry on the site is that of the ruined 12th-century rectangular keep and part of the circular curtain wall that enclosed the inner bailey. The keep stood to the north-west and the rectangular gatehouse tower to the north-east. A high round tower, added in the 13th century, provided a strongpoint on the undefended south side and made it possible to catch attackers from the west in a devastating crossfire; an interesting feature of the tower is that the entire block was designed for peacetime use as a WC. A rectangular outer bailey was added in the 14th century, when a number of repairs and additions were carried out, and some new building was done as late as the Tudor period. The earliest Norman occupants were the Turbervilles, and according to legend Payn de Turberville became Lord of Coity early in the 12th century by marrying into the family of a Welsh chieftain. The Turbervilles died out in the 14th century. In the 15th and 16th centuries the Gamage family owned Coity, and in 1404 Sir William Gamage was besieged in the castle by Owain Glyndŵr, leader of the Welsh national revolt. In 1584 Sir Robert Sidney (brother of the more famous Sir Philip) married the Gamage heiress, Barbara. The Sidneys owned Coity down to the 18th century, but it had fallen into decay long before then.

☎ Bridgend (0656) 59335

1½ m N of Bridgend on A4061, turn E

SS 9281 (OS 170)

Open mid Mar to mid Oct daily at all reasonable times; mid Oct to mid Mar by appt only

♿ 🅿 (limited access) 🚻 D ♠ ♨ ☫ WHM

Cardiff Castle

Cardiff, South Glamorgan

The Romans were the first to occupy the site of Cardiff Castle, erecting several forts on the site. Six centuries after their departure the Normans took over the remains of their fort, throwing up a 40-foot mound surrounded by a ditch in the north-west corner and dividing the rest into an inner and an outer bailey. They broadened and deepened the silted up ditch round the fort, covering the remains of the Roman walls with excavated soil and building a wall on top so that they lay hidden for nearly eight centuries. Early in the 12th century the 12-sided shell keep was built on the mound, the walls 30 foot high and with an entrance on the south side. The octagonal tower in front of the entrance is a later – probably 15th-century – addition. The medieval domestic quarters were established against the western curtain, and some of their foundations are incorporated in the existing range of buildings. The present towers and apartments along the western curtain are mainly the result of reconstruction work carried out in the second half of the 19th century for the 3rd Marquis of Bute by William Burges. Their extravagant ideas were translated into reality by the superb skills of Victorian craftsmen in the banqueting hall, Gothick chapel and several towers that form an exciting skyline – the clock tower where a Roman bastion once stood, the Guest and Bute towers; even the octagon tower, the one medieval tower to survive apart from those on the south wall and the Norman mound, was given a timber spire.

☎ Cardiff (0222) 822000

In centre of Cardiff

ST 1876 (OS 171)

Open daily: Mar, Apr, Oct 1000-1700; May to end Sept 1000-1800; Nov to end Feb 1000-1600

♿ WC ⊟ ☕ (limited opening) ✳ ◆ ⚲
● (not in castle)

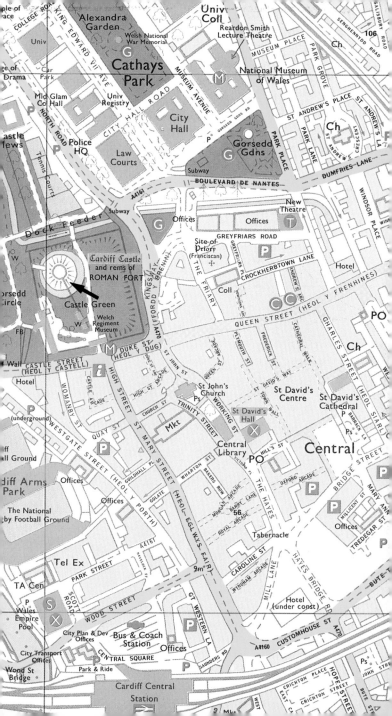

Castell Coch

Tongwynlais, South Glamorgan

Castell Coch is unique, a medieval fantasy created by the Victorian revivalist architect William Burges for John Crichton-Stuart, 3rd Marquis of Bute. Little is known of the original castle except that it was built of red sandstone (*coch*=red) and was probably destroyed in the 15th century, but its ruins prompted the rich, energetic and scholarly Marquis to commission his '13th-century' retreat. Work began in 1875, and Burges treated the commission extremely seriously, producing a building that could easily be a real medieval fortress. Its bold, round towers are 10 feet thick at the base, there is a dry moat, portcullis and drawbridge with winding mechanism, the walls are battlemented and the arrow slits fully operational. Inside, the castle is quite small, with the four main rooms, which Burges called the castellan rooms, grouped round a galleried courtyard. These rooms are wonderfully decorated with paintings and carvings in Burges's own 'medieval' style. The great fireplaces have almost life-size carved figures, while walls and ceilings are covered in murals, resembling one of the richer medieval manuscripts. The most lavishly decorated of all is the octagonal vaulted room in the keep, two storeys high, which has delicate flower paintings in panels round the lower part and illustrations from Aesop's *Fables* above. Birds and butterflies mingle with Aesop's creatures, and the ribs of the dome are decorated with more butterflies, carved in wood and painted in different colours. The furniture was also designed by Burges.

☎ Cardiff (0222) 810101

8 m NW of Cardiff on A470 turn SW onto B4262 and at roundabout turn NE under A470

ST 1382 (OS 171)

Open throughout year; M-S mid Mar to mid Oct 0930-1830, Su 1400-1830; mid Oct to mid Mar 0930-1600, Su 1400-1600

⊖ P WC 🍴 ♿ 🎌 ◆ ♨ WHM

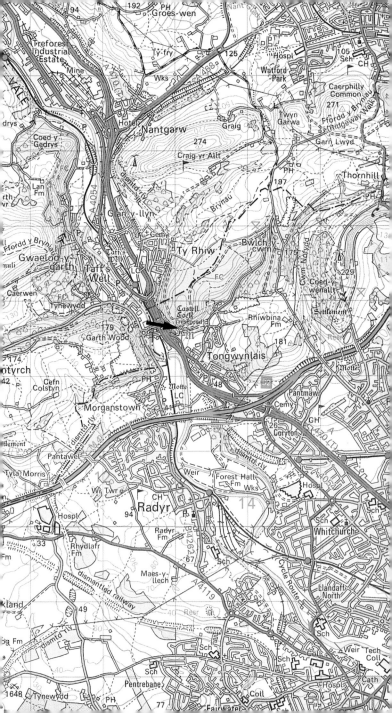

Weobley Castle

Llanrhidian, West Glamorgan

Weobley, on the north coast of the Gower peninsula, is not so much a castle as a fortified manor house; and its defensive arrangements in fact seem more than a little half-hearted. It was begun in the late 13th century and finished in the early 14th, though additions were made from time to time. The buildings are grouped round a courtyard which is entered through the gatehouse; their outer sides form the 'castle walls', since there is no curtain wall to protect them, and they are primarily residential in interest – and all the more strongly so for being well preserved and giving an unusually vivid insight into medieval domestic arrangements. The hall and solar are on the first floor, over the kitchen, 'cellar' (so called because, although on the ground floor, it was unlit), and guest-house; the spaciousness of the guests' accommodation is a good indication of a prosperous and increasingly civilised society. The chapel was beyond the square south-west tower, which was presumably intended to be the chief place of refuge or defensive action. It is now a ruin, which conceals the fact that it was never completed, and was abandoned altogether at quite an early date. Money may have run out at a critical moment, or the owner may have concluded that elaborate fortifications had become unnecessary in 'pacified' Wales. Weobley was certainly left untroubled until the early 15th century, when it was attacked and evidently damaged by Owain Glyndŵr's men.

6 m W of Swansea on A4118, turn onto B4271 for 9 m then turn W

SS 4792 (OS 159)

Open daily am and pm (Su pm only)

🅿 ♠ 🍽 ◆ ♨ 🏛 WHM

Berkeley Castle

Berkeley, Gloucestershire

A couple of miles inland from where the Severn begins to broaden out above Chepstow, Berkeley Castle hides the secret of King Edward II's murder on the orders of his Queen Isabella and her lover Roger Mortimer in 1327. 'Hides' because within some twenty years or so of that horrific crime, the whole castle had been gutted and rebuilt (1340-50) inside its old walls. Many of the buildings in the inner courtyard date from that time. The cost of such extensive works may well have been put against the price of total discretion on the part of the then Lord Berkeley and his family. The castle was started very soon after the Conquest by William FitzOsbern, one of William's closest supporters, who was rewarded with the earldom of Hereford. It continued to be extended, with masonry replacing timber, and in 1153 passed to a supporter of Henry II, Robert Fitzharding, in whose line it has remained to the present day. The chapel has a timber roof painted with 14th-century texts translated from the Book of Revelations. There are stone fireplaces and doorways in various positions which were acquired in France by the 8th Earl (died 1942). The gem of the rebuilding in 1340-50 is the great hall, with its fine saddle-beam timber roof and five-sided 'Berkeley arches', which was raised on the foundations of the old hall. The inner keep, one of the oldest parts of the castle, is unusual, being a circular wall over 60 feet high and empty inside, like a hollow stone drum (a 'shell keep'). The breach was made by the Parliamentarians after the siege of 1645 to prevent its further use for warfare.

☎ Dursley (0453) 810332

19 m SW of Gloucester on A38 turn W onto B4066 to Berkeley

ST 6899 (OS 162)

Open Good Fri to end Apr, Sept, daily exc M 1400-1700; May to Aug daily exc M 1100-1700 (Su 1400-1700); Oct Su only 1400-1630

⊖ 🅿 WC 🎑 ♣ 🍴 🎪 ◆ ⚒ 🏹 ●

Sudeley Castle

Winchcombe, Gloucestershire

Sudeley Castle, perched on its lofty hill, was largely built in 1442 by Ralph Boteler. In 1469 he was forced to sell to the future Yorkist king, Richard III, who rebuilt the east side as a sumptuous state apartment. The castle remained royal for nearly eighty years, but in 1547 it was granted to Sir Thomas Seymour, who married Henry VIII's ex-wife Catherine Parr. She died the following year and was buried in the chapel, but Seymour's ambitions led him to the Tower. The castle was then granted by Queen Mary to Lord Chandos, who rebuilt the outer courtyard about 1572 (Elizabeth I was entertained here several times). The 6th Lord Chandos, a Royalist, held the castle for Charles I during the Civil War, and although he later changed sides, the order to slight the castle was not revoked. The building became more or less a ruin, and remained so until 1837, when it was bought and restored by the brothers Dent, wealthy glovemakers from Worcester. This restoration was carried out with a care and attention to detail unusual at the time, and the exterior work is hard to tell from the original fabric. The rooms open to visitors are those on one side of the outer courtyard, and they are almost entirely 19th-century, though Catherine Parr's room has a 15th-century window. There are many excellent paintings including works by Rubens, Van Dyck, Poussin, Turner and Constable; a collection of lace is shown in the first-floor corridor, and the great dungeon tower contains one of the largest collections of dolls and toys in the country.

☎ Winchcombe (0242) 602308
9 m NE of Cheltenham on A46 turn SE at Winchcombe
SP 0327 (OS 163)

Open Apr to end Oct daily 1200-1900
⊖ P WC ♿ (limited access) 日 ♠ ♥ 戸
◆ ⊛ ☂ ⚔ (by appt) ● (not in house) ⌖
Falconry display T-Th, May to end Aug

Chepstow Castle

Chepstow, Gwent

The ruins of Chepstow Castle occupy a long, narrow east–west ridge above the river Wye; the site was of immense strategic value, controlling the lowest crossing-point of the river and serving as a base for forays into Wales. The latter was certainly its main purpose as far as William Fitz Osbern, Earl of Hereford, was concerned: he continued to extend Norman power westward even while he was building Chepstow Castle in about 1067-71. He erected a two-storey hall or keep that stretched almost all the way across the ridge, leaving only a narrow area connecting the two walled baileys on either side. In 1115 Chepstow Castle passed to the Clare family. In 1189 the famous soldier–statesman William Marshal married the Clare heiress and strengthened Chepstow; his sons, and later the Bigod Earls of Norfolk, carried the process further and created the castle whose ruins we now see. The keep was heightened with a tall third storey; the upper bailey at the west end was strengthened by the addition of a barbican; and the bailey on the other side now became the middle bailey with the addition of a new lower bailey containing a range of residential buildings and a strong D-shaped tower, and protected by a double-towered gatehouse. Chepstow Castle was twice besieged and captured during the Civil War period; luckily it was not slighted, but was garrisoned by the victors.

☎ Chepstow (029 12) 4065

15 m E of Newport, on A48

ST 5394 (OS 172)

Open daily am and pm (mid Oct to mid March Su pm only).

⊖ 🅿 🚌 ♣ ◆ ⋇ 𝕂 (for parties in summer) 🕈 WHM

Grosmont Castle

Grosmont, Gwent

This is the most ruinous of the 'Three Castles' (Grosmont, Skenfrith, White Castle) built by the Normans to hold down the Abergavenny area and check Welsh raids on the English lowlands. Grosmont stands on a hill above the Monnow Valley, and was certainly in existence during the 12th century. In 1201 King John granted the Three Castles to Hubert de Burgh, who built the long two-storey hall that still fills the straight side of Grosmont's D-shaped layout. In 1233 the castle was attacked by the Welsh, and although they failed to capture it, this probably led to the strengthening of its defences that followed; the timber fortifications were dismantled and replaced by a stone curtain wall with three towers and a twin-towered gatehouse. In the early 14th century further alterations were made; one of the wall towers was virtually demolished in order to make way for the new buildings. Grosmont experienced two moments of high drama: in 1233, when Llywelyn the Great attacked the castle while Henry III of England was actually in residence; and in 1405, when it was besieged by Owain Glyndŵr until a relieving force arrived under the leadership of the young Prince Henry, later King Henry V.

12 m NW of Monmouth, on B4347

SO 4024 (OS 161)

Open daily am and pm

⊖ 🅿 ★

Penhow Castle

Penhow, near Newport, Gwent

Penhow was one of a ring of Norman castles surrounding the great stronghold of Chepstow, seat of the Marcher lords. It was the seat of the St Maur family, who came from France in the wake of the Conqueror and founded the illustrious Seymour line. Sir Roger, who moved away from Penhow to Somerset in the 14th century, was the ancestor of the Dukes of Somerset and Marquesses of Hertford. The castle, which unlike most Welsh castles is still inhabited, is quite small, with the buildings grouped round a courtyard. The square stone battlemented keep was built in the 12th century, the curtain wall in the 13th, and the hall block, built in the 14th century, was enlarged in the 15th, when it was remodelled to make two halls, the one below for retainers, and the other, more splendid one above with a screen and minstrels' gallery, for the lord of the castle. Gradually the keep fell into disuse, and various additions and alterations continued to be made, including the building, in the Tudor period, of another hall wing. This was modernised in the late 17th century, and contains a delightful Restoration-style dining room and a fine oak staircase. In 1709 the castle was let as a farmhouse and only the Tudor wing occupied. It became derelict, and remained so until the present owner, Mr Stephen Weeks, bought it in 1973. He is now restoring it as his home. Excavations have shown that the present buildings are only the castle's inner bailey; most of the outer bailey has disappeared, but the outer defences included a moat.

☎ Penhow (0633) 400800

10 m SW of Chepstow on A48 at Penhow

ST 4290 (OS 172)

Open Good Fri to end Sept W-Su and Bank Hols 1000-1715; parties at other times by appt

⊖ 🅿 WC 🏠 ♣ ♥ 🎋 (by appt) ◆ ❀
✗ (evening candlelit tours by appt) ☂

Raglan Castle

Raglan, Gwent

Probably the last castle of the medieval type to be erected in Britain, Raglan is ruinous but still magnificent. It was both a formidable stronghold and an almost palatial family residence. The earliest surviving structure is also the most impressive – the big keep built from about 1435 by Sir William ap Thomas. It was hexagonal in shape, but in other respects conformed to the centuries-old keep pattern, being entered at first-floor level and furnished with a hall, private apartments, bedrooms and a kitchen. The surrounding hexagonal wall with angle-towers, and the wet moat, emphasised the isolation and self-sufficiency of this, the 'Yellow Tower of Gwent'. Beyond it, to the north and north-west, lay the rest of the castle, which eventually consisted of a range of buildings laid out on a roughly rectangular plan, with the hall and chapel block across the middle, dividing the area into two courtyards. The fountain court, and much else, was the work of ap Thomas's son, Sir William Herbert, later Earl of Pembroke. Raglan passed by marriage to the Earls of Worcester, and the third Earl built a large and splendid long gallery (now virtually invisible) and the pitched stone court in its present form. During the Civil War the castle withstood a long siege before surrendering to Sir Thomas Fairfax's Parliamentary troops, and as a consequence was heavily slighted. A few years later it was abandoned for good.

☎ Raglan (0291) 680228

9 m SW of Monmouth on A40

SO 4108 (OS 161)

Open daily am and pm (mid Oct to mid March, Su pm only).

♿ 🅿 WC 🦽 (limited access) 🚽 ♦ 🏓 ♦ ⚘
🏃 (for groups in summer) WHM

Skenfrith Castle

Skenfrith, Gwent

The river Monnow runs close to the east side of Skenfrith Castle, and this largely accounts for its siting: it guarded the bridge across the river, which also fed the other three sides of the castle's wide moat. In 1201 King John gave Skenfrith, Grosmont Castle and White Castle to Hubert de Burgh, and the 'Three Castles' were generally owned by the same lord throughout their active history, since they formed a defensive/offensive triangle on the marches of Gwent. Skenfrith is the smallest and simplest of the three, but interesting because it exemplifies castle-building techniques at a moment of transition. A timber motte-and-bailey castle stood on the site for about a century until rebuilding in stone began (presumably under Hubert) in the early years of the 13th century. The new castle consisted of a round three-storey keep, to which the builders added a feature that was beginning to replace keeps – strongly fortified curtain walls, which in this case meant roughly rectangular walls with four boldly projecting corner towers. Parts of three towers and stretches of wall survive, but the keep, though also ruinous, is now the main feature. It was not built directly onto the motte, which might not have been strong enough to bear the weight: the mound was hollowed out and foundations were sunk in the ground, with the area immediately above ground level constituting a basement. Within the walls there are also the foundations of residential buildings.

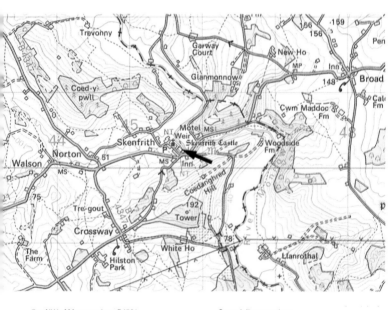

7 m NW of Monmouth on B4521

SO 4520 (OS 161)

Open daily am and pm

⊖ 🅿 ★

White Castle

near Abergavenny, Gwent

This is the best-preserved and most elaborate of the 'Three Castles' (White, Grosmont and Skenfrith) with which the Normans guarded the Gwent borderlands against attacks by the Welsh. It was originally known as Llantilio Castle, but had acquired its present name by the 13th century, thanks to the coating of white plaster covering the outside. Like Grosmont and Skenfrith it was originally a timber fortification, but its subsequent building history was out of phase with theirs. The first stone structures – a keep and an enclosing wall – were put up earlier than at Grosmont and Skenfrith, and date from about the mid-12th century; linked moats (still pleasantly duck-haunted) surrounded this bailey and the timber outworks to the south of it. Also unlike the other two castles, White Castle was not materially altered when the entire group was given to Hubert de Burgh in 1201; but later in the century, as relations with the Welsh became increasingly strained, it was thoroughly rebuilt in line with the latest military theories. The keep was demolished and the curtain wall strengthened with six round towers; the northernmost two form the present mighty gatehouse. To the north, access to the gatehouse was covered by a large new outer bailey or ward, which was protected by a four-towered curtain wall and a dry moat. In the event, Edward I's subjugation of Wales made White Castle's role more or less obsolete, and it had been abandoned by the 16th century.

☎ Llantilio (060 085) 380

9½ m NE of Abergavenny on B4521, turn S

SO 3816 (OS 161)

Open mid Mar to mid Oct M-S 0930-1830
(Su 1400-1830); mid Oct to mid Mar M-S 0930-1600
(Su 1400-1600)

🅿 ♿ (limited access) 🍴 D ♣ ♨ WHM

Beaumaris Castle

Beaumaris, Anglesey, Gwynedd

Beaumaris, strategically situated in flat, once-marshy land on the south side of Anglesey, was the last of the great Welsh castles built by Edward I in the early 14th century. It was designed by Edward's military engineer Master James of St George, and the flat land allowed him to build a castle which is almost perfectly symmetrical. It consists of two concentric rings of walls, an inner and an outer. The smaller and lower outer wall had sixteen towers defended by a broad moat, whose waters were fed by the Menai Strait, while the square inner ward, whose walls are some 16 feet thick, has cylindrical towers on the corners and two gatehouses. Beaumaris was never completed – even though the building took over thirty-five years and at one time 3,500 people were working on it – and the southern gatehouse lacks its rear portions. Both gatehouses contained suites of rooms for royalty, and other residential buildings once stood against the walls. By the 1330s the castle was as complete as it ever was to be, and it was considered impregnable. The southern gatehouse was protected by a barbican, and both rings of walls had arrow slits all round, providing maximum cover in the event of attack from any quarter. But the castle's defences were never put to the test, and within twenty years of the last building operations the stonework was apparently deteriorating and the timber rotting. One gatehouse and the walls now survive, and visitors can walk round the walls, through the passages and into the attractive chapel.

☎ Beaumaris (0248) 810361

5 m NE of Menai Bridge on A545 in Beaumaris

SH 6076 (OS 115)

Open daily throughout year; Mar to Oct 0930-1830 mid Oct to mid Mar 0930-1600 (Su 1400-1600)

⊖ P WC 🖾 🗄 ♠ 🖝 🛱 ◆ ☇ 大 WHM

Caernarfon Castle

Caernarfon, Gwynedd

The castle at Caernarfon is one of the greatest examples of medieval military architecture. It stands on the southern end of the Menai Strait, on a site first used by the Normans, who in about 1090 constructed a motte-and-bailey castle here. The present castle consists of two baileys that narrow at their junction to form an hour-glass plan; the Norman motte controlled the shape of the eastern bailey, while the long, straight walls of the lower or western bailey enclose a five-sided space. Work on the castle was begun immediately after the fall of the northern Welsh castles to Edward I in 1283. Its distinction lies in the bulk and height of the curtain walls, the thirteen multi-angular towers astride them and the elaborate defensive devices – twin-towered fortress gates, drawbridges and portcullises, shooting galleries and murder holes. The towers all differ in size and design. The castle has no keep, but the great Eagle Tower at the western end of the curtain is a remarkable early example of the tower house, with its basement giving access to the waterside and its three upper storeys designed for domestic comfort as well as security. At the same time as the castle took shape, walls were built out from it to enclose the town, one of the few examples in Britain of a 'bastide'. Edward I chose to administer Wales from Caernarfon, as both the Romans and its Welsh rulers had done; it remained an administrative centre for 250 years.

☎ Caernarfon (0286) 3096

In centre of Caernarfon

SH 4762 (OS 115)

Open daily: mid Mar to mid Oct 0930-1830; mid Oct to mid Mar 0930-1600 (Su 1400-1600)

⊖ 🅿 WC 🚻 ◆ ♨ ⚔ WHM Royal Welsh Fusiliers Museum

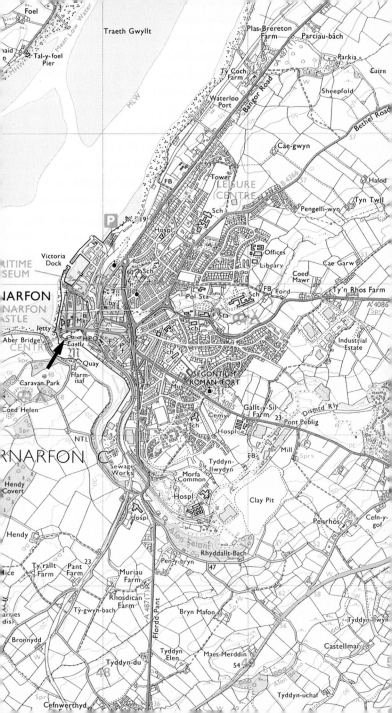

Conwy Castle

Conwy, Gwynedd

Conwy Castle, together with the great town wall with its twenty-one towers, forms one of the most impressive medieval fortifications in the British Isles, and it was completed in the astonishingly short time of five years, from 1283 to 1288. It is one of Edward I's castles, and was built under the supervision of the great military engineer James of St George, Master of the Royal Works. Unlike Beaumaris and several other Welsh castles, it is not concentric, since its wall follows the oblong contours of the rock and there is no gatehouse, but the town itself is strongly fortified, and the castle forecourt was defended by two of the great towers. Although the inside of the castle is ruined, the walls are almost intact, and the great round towers still stand to their full height. The entrance is through the old main gate leading into the outer ward, with the old great hall on the right and a narrow gate to the inner ward opposite. The four corner towers of the inner ward held the royal apartments, while beyond this is the east barbican, giving access to the back gate. The castle began to fall into decay relatively early, and in 1628 it was sold to Viscount Conway for as little as £100. At the outbreak of the Civil War it was repaired by John Williams, Archbishop of York, an ardent Royalist, but was taken quite easily by Cromwell's forces, and in 1665 the 3rd Earl of Conway ordered all movables to be shipped to Ireland. Long after the castle's ruin its interest was enhanced by the building of the two bridges which stand side by side alongside it, Telford's of 1817 and Stephenson's of 1848.

☎ Conwy (049 263) 2358

In centre of Conwy S of Conwy estuary

SH 7877 (OS 115)

Open daily: mid Mar to mid Oct 0930-1830, mid Oct to mid Mar 0930-1600 (Su 1400-1600)

⊖ 🅿 WC 🚻 (limited access) 🚌 🐕 ◆ ⚒
𝕏 WHM

Criccieth Castle

Criccieth, Gwynedd

Criccieth Castle stands on a wonderful site – the summit of a headland above Cardigan Bay, offering spectacular views of both the bay and the mountains of Snowdonia. In its original form Criccieth was a Welsh stronghold, probably built early in the 13th century for Llywelyn the Great. The remains of his castle are very broken down, but its plan – a curtain wall with two or three towers – is clear. After the defeat and death of Llywelyn's grandson, Llywelyn ap Gruffydd, the victorious Edward I began building new castles or converting old ones as part of a programme for holding down Wales once and for all. Criccieth, which could be supplied by sea, was one of the conversions. From 1283 a new, characteristically 'Edwardian' curtain wall was built within the Welsh walls, creating an inner bailey or ward protected by a powerful twin-towered gatehouse. The east side of the castle was protected by a single curtain wall (the English wall simply being super-imposed on the Welsh one), strengthened by building the rectangular Leyburn tower, set diagonally in the curtain wall. Edward I's military foresight was demonstrated in 1294, when Criccieth and other coastal castles were cut off by the rebellious Welsh under the leadership of Madoc: the garrison was successfully provisioned by English ships. In 1400, however, the coast was blockaded by a French fleet in alliance with Owain Glyndŵr, and Criccieth was starved out. Glyndŵr burned the castle, which consequently passed out of history.

5 m W of Porthmadog

SH 4937 (OS 123)

Open daily am and pm (mid Oct to mid March Su pm only)

⊖ 🅿 WC 🚻 ♣ ◆ ♨ WHM

Dolbadarn Castle

Llanberis, Gwynedd

Looking down on Lake Padarn, Dolbadarn Castle stands on a knoll at the northern end of Llanberis Pass, from which it once controlled the route from Caernarfon into central Wales. It was a native Welsh stronghold, and its history probably goes back further than the earliest surviving masonry, a plain 12th-century wall around the platform-top of the knoll. By the 13th century it was a royal castle; Llywelyn the Great was probably responsible for the most imposing of its surviving features – the great round keep, three storeys and some 40 foot high, which was built in the 1230s or 1240s. At about the same time two rectangular towers whose remains are still visible were added to the curtain wall; and there is evidence that a hall and other rooms once stood on the site. Within a few years of Llywelyn's death the precarious unity of Wales was shattered; in 1292 Dolbadarn fell to the Earl of Pembroke. The English preferred castles that could be supplied by sea; Dolbadarn was partly dismantled and its timbers taken away for use in building Caernarfon Castle.

9½ m SE of Caernarfon on A4086

SH 5859 (OS 115)

Open throughout year at all reasonable times

⊖ 🅿 🚻 D ♣ ★

Harlech Castle

Harlech, Gwynedd

One of the nine fortresses planned by Edward I to consolidate his conquest of North Wales, Harlech was built on a rocky hill above the shore-line of Tremadoc Bay in the 1280s under the supervision of the King's master mason, James of St George. It is a good example of a concentric castle, with two rectangles of fortifications forming an inner and a middle bailey. As originally planned, the castle could be maintained from the sea; an outer bailey wall encloses the precipitous steps to sea-level on the northern and western sides. To the south and east a moat was hacked out of the rock; the eastern side was the most vulnerable to attack, and here the defences were strongest, with a drawbridge at either end of the moat and the outer one protected by a barbican. The middle bailey forms a terrace round the inner bailey and has much lower walls, so an attacker would come under fire from both sets of battlements. During the Wars of the Roses (1455-85) the castle surrendered to the Yorkists only after a seven-year siege; the song 'men of Harlech' celebrates the bravery of the garrison. The castle's active history came to an end after the Civil War. It was the last Royalist stronghold in Wales. Though neither blown up nor battered after its surrender, it fell into decay and ruin. Today some foundations of the domestic buildings are visible in the inner bailey. The high curtain wall has round towers projecting boldly at each corner, and a powerful gatehouse astride the east wall.

☎ Harlech (0766) 552

In centre of Harlech, E of A496

SH 5731 (OS 124)

Open daily throughout year: mid Mar to mid Oct 0930-1830; mid Oct to mid Mar 0930-1600 (Su 1400-1600). Closed 24-26 Dec and 1 Jan

⊖ Ⓟ 🛏 ♣ ▰ ◆ ⚒ WHM

Penrhyn Castle

Bangor, Gwynedd

This great Victorian mock-medieval building was the result of a large fortune made by Richard Pennant from developing the slate quarries above Bethesda. George Hay Dawkins Pennant inherited both fortune and estate in 1808, and decided to rebuild the existing 'Gothick' house, designed by James Wyatt, as a huge Norman castle. His architect was Thomas Hopper, who was given responsibility for every detail as well as unlimited funds, and building began in 1825. The Norman style had to be rather freely interpreted, but Hopper succeeded in producing a fine Norman-looking building without sacrificing modern comfort, and he clearly enjoyed the challenge. The interiors, though a little overpowering, are undoubtedly spectacular, with arches and columns everywhere, and much elaborate carving and plaster-work. The front door leads into a low, vaulted corridor and thence to the vast great hall, a room more like a cathedral than a castle, rising up the whole height of the building, and lit by softly glowing stained-glass windows. The library has more Norman arches and ornament everywhere, and both rooms contain massive furniture designed by Hopper. Two of the tables in the hall are of carved slate, and there is a slate four-poster bed in one of the bedrooms in the keep. Another of the bedrooms contains a very large collection of dolls and toys. The main staircase is one of the strangest features of any interior in the country, with a profusion of nightmarish writhing ornament.

☎ Bangor (0248) 353084/353356

2 m S of Bangor on A5 turn NE

SH 6071 (OS 115)

Open Apr to late Oct daily exc T 1200-1700 (July and Aug 1100-1700)

⊖ 🅿 WC 🚽 (limited access) 🍴 ♣ 🚻 🎪 ◆ ⚘ (braille guide available) ● NT

Eastnor Castle

Ledbury, Herefordshire and Worcestershire

The massive, dramatic pile of Eastnor Castle was built between 1812 and 1815 for Lord Somers, whose family had owned the manor for 200 years but who now found his ancestral seat unworthy. The architect was Robert Smirke, who was later to design the British Museum. Eastnor is his early experiment in the Gothic style, and is sombrely medieval both outside and in. Only about half of Smirke's interiors remain, as extensive alterations were done in the later 19th century, notably by A. W. N. Pugin, but the great hall, an immense room 60 foot high, is his design, though the embellishments, the coloured marbles and painted walls, were done by George Fox in the 1860s. The dining room is also Smirke's, and has all its original furniture, but the drawing room, with its Gothic-style fan vault, is largely the work of Pugin, who was commissioned to redecorate it in 1849. He designed all the furniture as well as the great iron chandelier and the sumptuous chimneypiece. There are some fine Gobelin tapestries in this room, while most of the other rooms reflect the Italian taste of the 3rd Earl. In the library, which was designed by Fox, there is a set of bookcases and two chimneypieces carved in Verona. The frescos in the staircase hall, brought from Carlton House Terrace, are by G. F. Watts.

☎ Ledbury (0531) 2302/2304

7 m SW of Great Malvern on A449 turn SE onto A438 for 2½ m

SO 7336 (OS 150)

Open Easter and May Bank Hol M; June to Sept, Su also W and Th in July and Aug 1415-1730

🅿 WC 🚻 D (on lead) ♠ 🐾 🛏 ◆ ⚘
🏃 (by appt)

124

Goodrich Castle

Goodrich, Ross-on-Wye, Herefordshire and Worcestershire

A magnificent ruin, perched on a spur of rock above the right bank of the Wye, Goodrich Castle once controlled the ford across the river. A certain Godric Mappestone seems to have been the first builder here, and 'Godric's Castle' is mentioned as early as 1101-2; the great rock-cut ditch that protects the site may well follow the lines of the original defences. However, the earliest surviving building is the small mid-12th-century keep. It was surrounded by a square curtain wall in about 1500, but only the east wall of this is now standing. The greater part of Goodrich is a rectangular Edwardian castle of about 1300 which surrounds the older keep. It has impressive round towers on three corners and a gatehouse on the fourth; the well-preserved barbican protecting the entrance was built a decade or so later. The courtyard holds the remains of the great hall, solar and kitchens. In the 14th century Goodrich Castle passed to the Talbot family, who became Earls of Shrewsbury, and it was theirs until the line died out in 1616. It then passed to the Earls of Kent, who held it until 1740. Goodrich saw a good deal of action during the Civil War. In 1643 the Earl of Stafford seized it on behalf of Parliament, but he withdrew in the face of superior Royalist forces, and the castle was successfully held for the King by Sir Henry Lingon even after Charles I himself had surrendered. When Lingon capitulated, Goodrich was slighted by Parliament.

☎ Monmouth (0600) 890538

6 m NE of Monmouth on A40, turn E

SO 5719 (OS 162)

Open daily am and pm (Su pm only, Oct to Mar)

🅿 WC 🚻 D (on lead, grounds only) ♣ ◆ ✳ EH

Powis Castle

Welshpool, Powys

Powis Castle, continuously inhabited since medieval times, began as a stronghold of Welsh princes, and was built between 1200 and 1300. In 1587 it was bought by Sir Edward Herbert, who added the long gallery and did a great deal of remodelling; in the late 17th century a state bedroom was added, and further alterations were made in the 18th century. Most of the 18th-century work was lost, however, when the architect G. F. Bodley remodelled the interiors in the 1900s in the 'Jacobean' style. In 1784 the Herbert family married into the Clive family; the 2nd Lord Clive (son of Clive of India) was created Earl of Powis in 1804, and his son changed his name to Herbert. This alliance was financially important for the Herberts, and it also brought to Powis a fine collection of books, paintings and furniture as well as a collection of Indian works of art unequalled outside London. The interior of the castle is also interesting for its variety of architectural styles. Notable interiors are the Restoration-period state bedroom with silvered furniture and 17th-century Brussels tapestries; the lovely Elizabethan long gallery with its plaster ceiling and painted panelling; and the ballroom, originally built in the late 18th century to serve as a ballroom as well as a picture gallery, but altered in the 19th century. The dining room, which looks Elizabethan, is in fact the work of Bodley, as is the oak drawing room, though traces of the Elizabethan decoration survive in both. The late 17th-century formal gardens are among the finest in Britain, and there is a huge deer park.

☎ Welshpool (0938) 4336

1 m S of Welshpool on A483 turn W for ½ m

SJ 2106 (OS 126)

Open mid Apr to end June, Sept, Oct (closed M, T) 1200-1700; July and Aug (closed M) 1100-1800

⊖ (1 mile; exc Su) 🅿 WC 🔤 (limited access)
🚻 ♿ 🎁 🍴 ◆ ⚜ ● NT

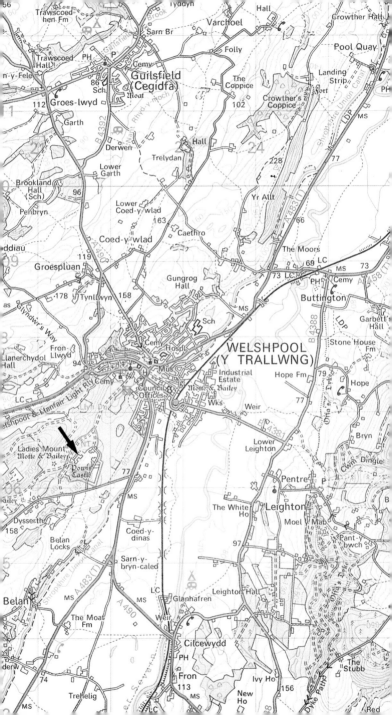

Tretower Castle

Tretower, Powys

Despite its ruinous condition, Tretower Castle is interesting and unusual, as
its main feature is a round keep closely girt by a wall that in fact originated as
a shell keep. The first low motte and bailey, with timber superstructures,
were created in about 1100 by a Norman knight named Picard, who had
taken part in the invasion of the Usk Valley under Bernard de Neufmarché.
In the mid-12th century Picard's son Roger put up an irregularly shaped shell
keep and various domestic buildings, also of stone, inside it; these were
particularly attractively decorated. However, they were largely demolished
by a later Roger Picard to make way for the keep, possibly in response to the
revolt of 1233, when the castle was briefly captured by the Welsh. The keep
still rises to almost its original height, far above the rim of the shell keep. A
massive stone wall was built round the bailey at about the same time, though
only one of its three towers is now standing. By 1300, however, the lords of
Tretower may well have moved out of the castle to Tretower Court, which
stands close to the entrance and is a much visited attraction in its own right
as a manor house. The castle continued to be used, at least in periods of
disturbance. It was taken by rebels in 1322, but in 1404 Sir James Berkeley
succeeded in holding out against an attack by the formidable Owain
Glyndŵr. In the 15th century the Vaughan family concentrated on improv-
ing Tretower Court, whose civilised amenities made the castle obsolete.

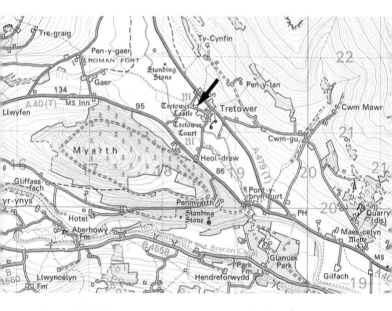

☎ Brecon (0874) 730279

3½ m NW of Crickhowell off A40

SO 1821 (OS 161)

Open daily am and pm; Su pm only

⊖ 🅿 WC 🖻 🛱 ♠ 🛱 ◆ ⚹ 🕴 (audio) WHM

Ludlow Castle

Ludlow, Shropshire

Ludlow Castle, perched on its rocky promontory over the river Teme, is one of the great Welsh border castles, and its extensive remains span the entire medieval period. It was begun about 1085 by Roger de Lacy, but the lovely round Norman chapel, one of the earliest castle chapels in the country, was built in the 1130s by a rival claimant, Sir Joyce de Dinan, who temporarily ousted the Lacys from their home. The outer defences were constructed about 1180, the round towers added a century later, and most of the other buildings within the enclosure – the great hall, great chamber, service rooms and so on – were built in the 14th century and embellished in the Tudor period. After the Lacy line died out in 1240 the castle was held by the villainous Roger Mortimer and five generations of his descendants, becoming royal property in 1461 when one of the line was crowned as Edward IV. The 'Princes' tower is so named because his two young sons lived here before their final imprisonment and death in the Tower of London, and 'Arthur's tower' takes its name from Henry VIII's elder brother, who died here in 1507. The castle then became the increasingly sumptuous residence of the Lords President of the Council of Wales, and extensive rebuilding, including the gatehouse on the north side (1581), was carried out by one of the holders of this office, Sir Henry Sidney, father of Sir Philip. In 1634, the castle had a last glorious fling with the performance of Milton's masque *Comus*, to celebrate the Earl of Bridgwater's presidency of Wales and the Marches.

☎ Ludlow (0584) 3947

In W outskirts of Ludlow

SO 5074 (OS 138)

Open mid Feb to mid Nov daily 1030-1600 (1800 May to Sept)

⊖ ♿ (limited access) D ◆

Stokesay Castle

Craven Arms, Shropshire

Despite its name, Stokesay is not a castle but a fortified manor house, picturesque and an authentic and unique medieval survival. Say was the name of the family who originally owned it, and Stoke means 'dairy farm', but of the de Says' early-13th-century house only the moat (once filled with water) and the base of the north tower remain. In 1281 it was bought by a wealthy wool merchant, Lawrence de Ludlow, who built the hall and solar and the top storey of the north tower, adding the battlemented south tower ten years later when he was given permission to fortify. The only addition since then was the Elizabethan gatehouse, built some time between 1570 and 1620. In 1620 Stokesay was bought by Dame Elizabeth Craven, mother of the ardent Royalist Lord Craven, but it was not built to resist cannon, and surrendered to Cromwell's troops in 1645. It was then leased to the Baldwyn family, and from 1728 to farmers, the hall becoming a coopers' workshop. In 1869 Lord Craven sold it to the grandfather of the present owners, who began its careful restoration. The rooms are empty, but are very atmospheric, particularly the great hall with its timber roof, central hearth and shuttered lower windows. The upper room has a fine 14th-century fireplace; the solar has oak panelling and a Flemish overmantel probably brought here in the 17th century. The south tower, once reached only by a drawbridge, is an irregular polygon of three storeys, with a staircase rising within the thickness of the walls, single lancet windows and garderobes.

☎ Craven Arms (058 82) 2544

10 m NW of Ludlow on A49 turn W

SO 4381 (OS 137)

Open Mar and Oct daily exc T 1000-1700; Apr to end Sept daily exc T 1000-1800; Nov S and Su 1000-dusk

⊖ P WC ♿ (limited access) 🍴 ♣ ♥ ♒ EH

Central England

Bolsover Castle

Bolsover, Derbyshire

Dramatically situated on a ridge rising steeply out of a modern industrial landscape, Bolsover is a fantastic ruin that stirs the imagination – appropriately so, for it is a very early example of a type of building that was in itself a creation of fantasy: the sham medieval castle. The site has a history that goes back to Norman times; William the Conqueror gave it to William Peveril (the builder of Peveril Castle in Derbyshire), and he or his successors put up a castle on it. This has vanished without trace; it seems likely that the present structure stands on the foundations of its medieval predecessor. This keep or 'Little Castle' was built for Sir Charles Cavendish from about 1612, when the age of the true castle was obviously over. It is really a solid, four-square mansion, equipped with crenellations, turrets and many fanciful details redolent of the 'Arthurian' fantasies of the Elizabethans and Jacobeans; the vaulted interior, with its splendid canopied fireplaces, is equally effective as an evocation of an imaginary past. The keep was designed by Robert Smythson, now recognised as the outstanding architect of his time. The roofless set of buildings running along the ridge is the work of Smythson's son John, from about 1620 onwards. The most striking is the long gallery, with eccentric Baroque decorative features.

☎ Bolsover (0246) 823349

In town centre

SK 4770 (OS 120)

Open daily am and pm

♿ 🅿 WC ♿ (limited access) 🚻 D (on lead, grounds only) ◆ ♨ EH

Peveril Castle

Castleton, Derbyshire

The first castle on this steep, craggy site was built by William Peveril, bailiff of the royal manors in the area. William the Conqueror had appointed him and given him the land; evidently Peveril was a trusted lieutenant of the King, as Derbyshire was a particularly important county, rich in deposits of lead. Peveril's castle was erected quite soon after the Conquest (it is mentioned in Domesday Book, 1086) and, unusually, was from the beginning made of stone, not wood. The 11th-century curtain wall, much repaired over the centuries, still stands on the vulnerable northern side of the site; the remaining stretches of wall are early 12th century. The Peveril estates were confiscated in 1155, and in 1176 Henry II put up a keep – now the main visual feature here – at the highest point of the site. The keep is very small and plain, but it stands almost to its original height, and its ashlar (cut stone) facing has survived in part. Peveril had all the standard features of the rectangular keep, including a first-floor entrance leading to the hall. Henry II often stayed at the castle in spite of its small size. In the early 13th century more comfortable accommodation was provided by a large hall put up in the north-west corner of the bailey. Henry III and Edward III were guests here, but it seems to have gone into a rapid decline in the 14th century.

☎ Hope Valley (0433) 20613

20 m W of Sheffield, on A625

SK 1482 (OS 110)

Open daily am and pm

♿ 🅿 WC 🚻 D (on lead, grounds only) ♠ ◆ ♨

Ashby de la Zouch Castle

Ashby de la Zouch, Leicestershire

This originated as a manor house and was fortified at a very late date by an ambitious nobleman. In the 12th century the Zouch family built a stone hall and solar here which were reconstructed on a larger scale in the 14th century; most of the surviving domestic remains date from this period. The Earl of Ormonde owned Ashby de la Zouch until 1461, when he fought on the losing (Lancastrian) side at the battle of Towton and was beheaded. The Yorkist King Edward IV gave Ashby to his Lord Chamberlain, William, Lord Hastings, who was granted a royal licence to crenellate in 1474. Hastings built a 90-foot-high tower house just south of the existing buildings, and surrounded the entire complex with a high curtain wall. Thus Ashby – unlike Kirby Muxloe – was finished when in 1483 Hastings was suddenly arrested and executed on a charge of treason by Richard III. Considering how late it was built, 'Hastings Tower' is a surprisingly orthodox and serious piece of castle architecture. It is a rectangle with four storeys (storeroom, kitchen, hall and, at the top, a private apartment for the lord); a square east wing, as high as the tower itself, has seven storeys. The most unusual feature is the entrance, on the ground floor rather than the first floor. During the Civil War the castle was defended with spirit by the Royalist Colonel Henry Hastings; in 1648 it was disabled with gunpowder on the orders of Parliament – hence the present ruined but majestic appearance of the tower.

On E outskirts of town

SK 3616 (OS 128)

Open am and pm daily (Su pm only)

⊖ 🅿 ♿ (limited access) 🚻 D (on lead, grounds only) ♣ ♦ ✄

Belvoir Castle

Grantham, Leicestershire

The battlements of Belvoir (pronounced 'beaver') are all too obviously the product of early 19th-century 'Gothick' fantasy – to a large extent that of Elizabeth, 5th Duchess of Rutland, aided by the family's domestic chaplain and some help from the more professionally qualified James Wyatt, from 1801 onwards. The core of their romantic castle, which was equipped with the civilised comforts expected by Regency nobility, is a medieval fortress raised soon after the Conquest, and later ruined in the Wars of the Roses. A second castle was demolished by the Parliamentarians in 1649, but rebuilding began during Cromwell's lifetime. About a century later, this in turn was demolished to make way for something grander, which is the castle we see today. The family of de Ros held Belvoir from 1247, and it passed by marriage to the Manners family in the reign of Henry VII. Raised to the earldom of Rutland (1526) and then to the dukedom (1703), the Manners can claim one of their members – under the title of Marquis of Granby (d. 1770) – as perhaps the most popular soldier ever to be honoured by English pubs. The entrance and guardroom contain a small arsenal of old firearms, and the military note is reinforced by the regimental museum of the 17th/21st Lancers. The rest of the interior is decorated in a variety of 19th-century revival styles, and contains, apart from Dutch and Flemish paintings and English portraits, a set of the five sacraments by Poussin and a series of Gobelin tapestries with a rose-pink ground with illustrations of some adventures of Don Quixote.

☎ Grantham (0476) 870262

4½ m SW of Grantham on A607 turn N to Denton and Belvoir

SK 8133 (OS 130)

Open mid Mar to late Sept T, W, Th, S 1200-1800, Su 1200-1900

⊖ (limited; 1 m) 🅿 WC ♿ (by appt) 🚻 (by appt) ♣ 🍴 🍵 ◆ ⚹ 𝕏 (by appt) ● 🌲 🔥

Kirby Muxloe Castle

Kirby Muxloe, Leicestershire

Kirby Muxloe was begun in 1480, unusually late for a castle, and also unusually, it was built of brick. The building, an ambitious project begun for Lord Hastings, was never completed: Lord Hastings, a rich and respected nobleman, was a supporter of the Yorkist King Edward IV, and in 1483 he was executed by Richard III for suspected treason. All that remains now is the gatehouse and one corner tower standing within the broad moat; the building records, which still survive, indicate that the roofs of the towers were never built, although they may have been thatched to give some protection from the weather. Like other castles built at about this time, Kirby Muxloe seems to have been intended more as a fortified manor house than a serious fortress, and the use of the red brick with black-and-white patterning instead of stone may show a preoccupation with aesthetic rather than military values. However, the military aspect was not entirely neglected: the building records show that the gatehouse would have had machicolations (arched openings through which boiling oil and so on was poured), and there are references to murder holes, which probably mean the openings for cannon in the walls of the gatehouse. The plan of the building is typical of a 15th-century castle: a rectangular outer wall with corner towers, towers in the middle of three sides, and the gatehouse on the fourth side. The main living quarters were built against the walls on the inside.

☎ Leicester (0533) 386886

5½ m W of Leicester on A47 turn NW onto B5380 turn N at Kirby Muxloe for 1 m

SK 5204 (OS 140)

Open throughout year; Mar to Oct 0930-1830, Su 1400-1830; Oct to Mar 0930-1600, Su 1400-1600

🅿 🅰 🚻 D (on lead, grounds only) ♣ ◆ ⚘ EH

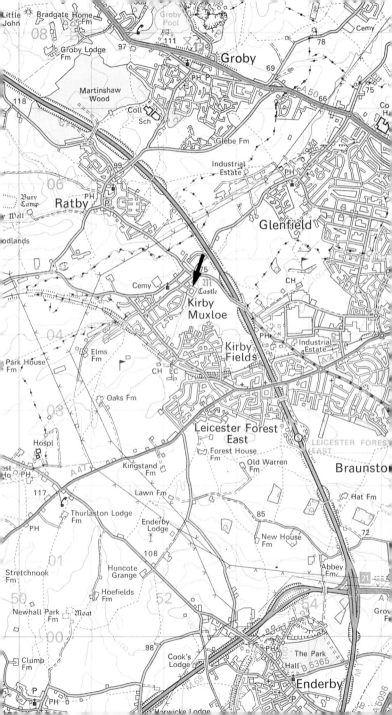

Rockingham Castle

Rockingham, Northamptonshire

The site, a high hill overlooking Rockingham Forest, was a Saxon stronghold of long standing, but William I built the castle, and it was enlarged by subsequent kings, notably Edward I, who made many improvements. By 1530 it had become decayed, and was leased to Edward Watson, ancestor of the present owner, who set about converting it into a comfortable Tudor residence, a task which took him thirty years. His grandson, Sir Lewis Watson, who bought the castle from James I, rebuilt the gallery wing in 1631, but the whole building was so badly damaged in the Civil War that he spent the rest of his life restoring it, a process completed by his son. By 1669 all was complete, though some remodelling was done by Anthony Salvin in 1850, including the addition of a tower. The visitor enters through the servants' hall, past the delightful cobbled 'street', with its bakehouses and breweries, and through the kitchen. The great hall, which was once much larger, was given a lower ceiling by Edward Watson and divided in two to make a hall and parlour (now the panel room). The hall, which is now used as the main dining room, contains an iron-bound chest believed to have been left by King John, another with the painted arms of Henry V, and some interesting 16th-century paintings. The panel room displays a fine collection of Post-Impressionist and 20th-century paintings. The finest room of all is the 17th-century long gallery, which contains some good 18th-century furniture and fine paintings by Angelica Kauffmann, Reynolds and Zoffany.

☎ Rockingham (0536) 770240

3¼ m NW of Corby on A6003 turn S just before Rockingham

SP 8691 (OS 141)

Open Easter Su to end Sept Su, Th, Bank Hol M and following T, also T in Aug 1400-1800

🅿 WC 🍴 (by appt at other times) D (gardens only) 🌳 🦽 🍴 ◆ ✳ 𝄞 (parties only) ●

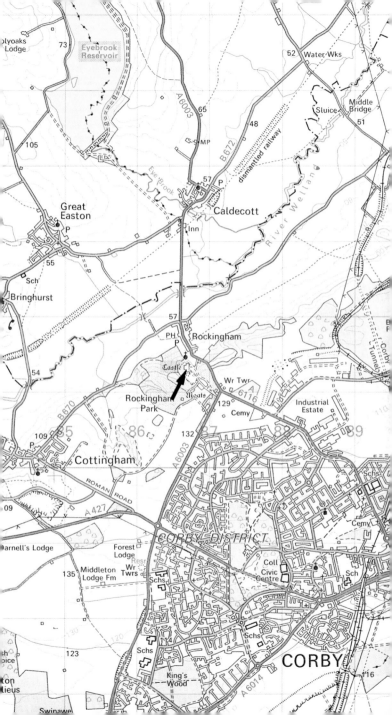

Broughton Castle

Broughton, near Banbury, Oxfordshire

More by courtesy a castle than by virtue of its moat, Broughton is a fine example of a late medieval mansion enhanced by Tudor architects and happily unspoiled by later alterations. In fact, the spendthrift Regency owner, the 15th baron of Saye and Sele, could not afford to keep it up, and so Broughton Castle was spared the enthusiastic 'restoration' imposed on so many country houses in the 19th century. The buildings as left in 1554 (at the start of Mary's reign), gracefully blend the Middle Ages with the English Renaissance in the continuity of their warm yellow stone. The interior was finished in 1599. One can therefore see, all in one house, the 14th-century carved corbel-heads in the groined passage, the private chapel with its untouched altar stone, the exuberant Elizabethan plasterwork ceiling in the white room, and the splendid Jacobean panelling of the oak room. There are also two important chimneypieces: the English-made marble one of not later than 1551, and the stone-and-stucco one in the Fontainebleau style. The only major legacy of the 18th century are the 'Gothick' ceiling pendants in the great hall which, although fanciful, do not offend the bare 14th-century masonry below them. The Fiennes family, whose title of Lords of Saye & Sele is borne today by the 21st Baron, had strong Puritan and Parliamentary associations, and the house was the scene of important meetings of like-minded politicians in the 17th century.

☎ Banbury (0295) 62624

3 m SW of Banbury on B4035

SP 4138 (OS 151)

Open mid May to mid Sept W, Su, Bank Hol M also Th in Jul and Aug 1400-1700

🅿 WC 🚻 (also at other times by appt) ❀ ♣ 🍴 🎪 ◆ ❀ 🎷 ● (not in house)

Tamworth Castle

Staffordshire

Now pleasantly surrounded by a park on the edge of the town, the castle stands on the northern side of the Tame, from which it once controlled the river crossing. Eight centuries of English history are well represented at Tamworth. The Normans constructed the motte in the 11th century, and a certain amount of herringbone pattern masonry survives from about that time. The present shell keep, a striking and well-preserved feature, was built in the later 12th century. Then, probably not long afterwards, a rectangular tower was fitted into the keep wall, rising above it to allow archers to fire down at besieging troops. During the more settled post-medieval centuries, Tamworth continued to be lived in, notably by the Ferrars family, who undertook extensive building and rebuilding in the castle courtyard. The medieval structures were swept away, but as Tamworth was one of the few castles to escape serious damage during the Civil War the Ferrars' buildings are well preserved and, together with still later additions, fill out the small courtyard in a rather engaging fashion. The hall is Jacobean, with fine panelling and carved chimneypieces, and large windows on to the courtyard; other buildings are of the 17th to early 19th centuries. The castle is used as a museum of local history and has interesting collections of Anglo-Saxon coins, costumes and other items.

☎ Tamworth (0827) 64222 ext 389

In town centre

SK 2003 (OS 139)

Open M-Th, S am and pm; Su pm only (exc Christmas)

⊖ 🅿 WC 日 ♣ ⊼ ◆ ⱬ 🗡 (by appt) 🜨

Tutbury Castle

Tutbury, Staffordshire

This castle, looking down on the Dove valley, is worth visiting for the views it offers, and also for its rich historical associations; on their own, the actual remains are bound to seem somewhat disappointing. Tutbury was an early post-Conquest motte-and-bailey castle, but the oldest surviving remains are of a 12th-century free-standing chapel in the bailey; everything else is 14th century or later. The medieval shell keep has entirely disappeared; in its place stands an edifice whose superficially 'medieval' nature is the product of an entirely different and whimsical outlook – a small sham ('folly') keep put up in the 1760s. The other substantial remains are the 14th-century gate-house and the two 15th-century towers, which may have been designed to function as self-sufficient units, on the lines of pele towers. Tutbury belonged to the Ferrers family until 1265, when it passed to the Earls (later Dukes) of Lancaster, to whom it still belongs. In 1399 the Duke of Lancaster, Henry Bolingbroke, became king as Henry IV and carried out an extensive pro-gramme of rebuilding; but by the 16th century the castle was badly neglected – as Mary, Queen of Scots, discovered when she was imprisoned there. Tutbury was damaged, effectively beyond repair, in the Civil War.

☎ Burton on Trent (0283) 812129

3 m NW of Burton on Trent on A50

SK 2029 (OS 128)

Open daily Apr to Oct 1000-1800

⊖ 🅿 WC 🕭 日 D ♣ ⊽ ⊼ ◆ ⱬ 🗡 🜨

141

Kenilworth Castle

Kenilworth, Warwickshire

Kenilworth Castle, proud and romantic, was built in the 12th century by Geoffrey de Clinton, Treasurer to Henry I, and was appropriated for the Crown by Henry II. In 1266 it was held by the son of the rebel Simon de Montfort and was the scene of a famous siege by Henry III. In those days its water-defences consisted of a vast lake 100 acres in area, and the building was virtually impregnable. The garrison held out for six months and only surrendered in the end because they were starving. The oldest part of the castle is the great Norman keep with its square corner turrets, built about 1180; the outer walls date from about 1205, and the group of buildings to the west and south of the keep was erected by John of Gaunt, the castle's most illustrious owner, who completely remodelled it in the 1370s. He spent a great deal of money on turning it into a palatial residence, and although all his buildings are now ruins, the remains of the great hall, with its lovely decorated oriel widows, give some idea of its past magnificence. The last of the builders of Kenilworth was Robert Dudley, Earl of Leicester, Elizabeth I's favourite. The buildings next to John of Gaunt's, still known as the Leicester Buildings, are his work, as is the gatehouse (now a private residence) and the stable block with its ornamented timberwork. In 1575 Elizabeth I was entertained here in a magnificent round of festivities lasting nineteen days and costing, it is estimated, £1,000 per day. These are vividly depicted in Walter Scott's novel *Kenilworth*.

☎ Kenilworth (0926) 52078

In W outskirts of Kenilworth off B4103

SP 2772 (OS 140)

Open daily throughout year; Mar to Oct 0930-1830, Oct to Mar 0930-1600 (Su 1400-1600)

⊖ 🅿 WC ♿ 🚻 D (on lead, grounds only) ♣ ◆ ♨ EH

Warwick Castle

Warwick, Warwickshire

On a sandstone bluff above the river Avon the castle is an impressive survivor, continuing in use with but few breaks for more than nine centuries. The site was fortified against the Danes by the Saxons in the 10th century, and the first castle was erected there by the Normans in 1068. The original motte has survived, and on it fragments of an octagonal shell keep. Today the castle is mainly a 14th-century reconstruction, with later alterations, that mark the change from medieval fortress to great house. The north curtain wall, with its two fine towers, and the splendid barbican and gatehouse constitute a late masterpiece of castle building. Caesar's Tower is particularly impressive. At the river end of the north curtain, it rises nearly 150 foot from the base of a massive plinth; its size and lobed shape, the machicolations and double-tiered battlements, show the last refinement in building techniques. The interior consists of a dungeon and three vaulted storeys for prisoners, and two upper storeys providing a guardroom and a store for arms and ammunition. James I granted the castle to Sir Fulke Greville in 1604. It was then in a ruinous condition, and he spent £20,000 – a fortune in those days – on the house and grounds. The Grevilles were to remain at Warwick until it was sold in 1978 to Madame Tussaud's. The state apartments remain much as the Grevilles left them, and contain a fine collection of paintings, arms and armour and other interesting items.

☎ Warwick (0926) 495421

In centre of Warwick

SP 2864 (OS 151)

Open daily throughout year; Mar to end Oct 1000-1730; Nov to end Feb 1000-1630

⊖ P WC 🚻 ♿ ⛘ ⛱ ◆ ⚒ (also in foreign languages) 🏹 ● (no flash)

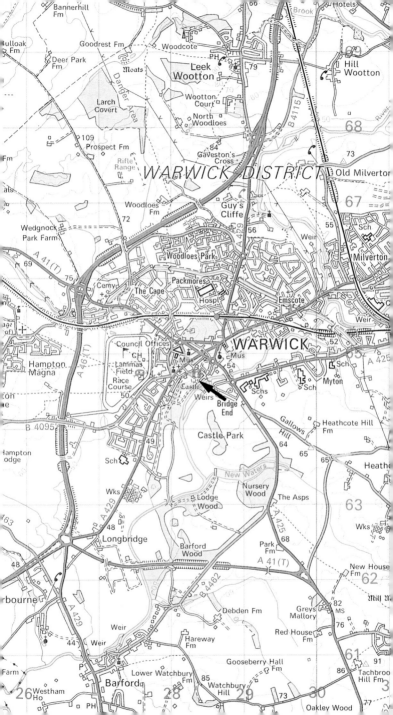

Dudley Castle

Dudley, West Midlands

The earthworks of Dudley Castle now form part of a 40-acre zoo, and the site exhibits an unusual mixture of antique, exotic and juvenile features, with battlements, lemurs and a miniature steam railway all competing for attention. Dudley seems to have had a castle soon after the Norman Conquest, when William Fitz Ansculf was its lord. In 1173 this, or a later structure, was demolished by Henry II. Roger de Somery was granted a royal licence in 1264 and may have built on the site, but the most important remains date from the lifetime of Sir John de Somery; he was a particularly unsavoury 'robber baron' whose depredations on the local countryside were such that he probably needed a place of refuge from pursuit and retaliation. At any rate, in about 1300 he built a large tower house at the top of the Norman motte – an early example of this type of building, never common in southern and midland England. This one was two storeys high and oblong in shape, with massive round towers at the corners and an entrance with a portcullis. It contained a hall and other 14-century mod cons, all of which were duplicated in buildings that Sir John had put up inside the bailey – an indication, perhaps, that the villainous knight liked to keep a healthy distance between himself and his equally villainous retainers. Dudley Castle was slighted by Parliament after the Civil War, and its domestic buildings were badly damaged by a fire in 1750.

☎ Dudley (0384) 52401

In centre of Dudley off A459

SO 9490 (OS 139)

Open daily exc 25 Dec 0900-1600, Su 1000-1600

♿ 🅿 WC ♿ 🚻 ♣ ▭ ◆ ☼

Eastern Counties

Kingston upon Hull

HUMBERSIDE

Grimsby

Lincoln Castle
Lincoln

LINCOLNSHIRE

Tattershall Castle

Castle Rising

Kings Lynn

NORFOLK

Caister Castle

Norwich Castle
Norwich

Burgh Castle
Great Yarmouth

Oxburgh Hall

LEICESTER-SHIRE

Peterborough
Longthorpe Tower

NORTHAMPTON-SHIRE

CAMBRIDGESHIRE

Wingfield Castle

Bury St Edmunds

Framlingham Castle

Cambridge

SUFFOLK

Orford Castle

BEDS

Ipswich

Hedingham Castle

Luton

HERTFORD-SHIRE

Colchester Castle
Colchester

Berkhamsted Castle

Harlow

ESSEX

BUCKS

Chelmsford

Watford

Hadleigh Castle

GREATER LONDON

Southend-on-Sea

BERKS

Gillingham

SURREY

KENT   Canterbury

Longthorpe Tower

Peterborough, Cambridgeshire

Fortified towers have often been converted into comfortable residences by the addition of a hall and other rooms (as, for example, at Sizergh in Cumbria). But at Longthorpe the procedure was reversed. The late 13th-century hall came first; but it was evidently felt to be vulnerable, and a three-storey tower was built on to it in about 1300 by Robert de Thorpe. The defensive function of the tower is confirmed by the fact that it can only be entered from the hall, not from outside. The most remarkable feature of Longthorpe is the first-floor Great Chamber as decorated for Robert de Thorpe, who may be the same person as the builder, or perhaps a son of the same name. Almost all English wall paintings of the Middle Ages have perished, thanks to time, improvers and – in the case of churches – the iconoclastic zeal of Oliver Cromwell's soldiers. Longthorpe's walls, crowded with fresh and lovely images dating back to about 1330, thus have a special value; there is certainly nothing to match them in any secular building in Britain. The activities of the local Home Guard during the Second World War loosened the plasterwork of the Great Chamber, and shortly after the war the long-concealed paintings were noticed and carefully uncovered. The subjects include a Nativity, King David playing the harp, Saints Anthony and Paul, and allegories such as the Wheel of the Five Senses and the Wheel of Life; and there are also musicians, flowers, heraldic and other devices, and large figures of birds.

☎ Peterborough (0733) 268482

2 m SW of Peterborough on A47

TL 1698 (OS 142)

Open 15 Mar to 15 Oct T, Su 1400-1830, W-S and Bank Hol M 0930-1830; also open some days Oct to Mar

♿ 🅿 (limited) EH

Colchester Castle

Colchester, Essex

This mighty Norman keep has many resemblances to the White Tower at the Tower of London, and may well have been designed and built by the same master mason. The site was an historic one, since Colchester had been a British stronghold before the Roman conquest. Characteristically, the Romans advertised their domination by building a temple to the Emperor Claudius in the city, renamed Camulodunum; the British, rebelling under the leadership of Boudicca (Boadicea), burned it down; the Normans, in their economical way, built a keep on the temple foundations, using many of the Roman bricks. It was conceived on a grander scale than the White Tower, measuring about 170 by 145 foot; but only two storeys were completed. The original entrance was on the first floor (north side), as usual, but it was later transferred to the ground floor (south side), presumably as part of a general rearrangement of functions occasioned by the abandonment of further building. Colchester Castle was probably built for Eudo, William the Conqueror's steward, in about 1080. It later became a royal castle and was hotly contested during the civil war that broke out towards the end of King John's reign. Now, as the Colchester and Essex Museum, the castle contains an excellent collection of antiquities.

☎ Colchester (0206) 712490

In town centre, N of High St

TL 9925 (OS 168)

Open Apr to Sept M-S 1000-1700, Su 1430-1730; Oct to Mar M-F 1000-1700, S 1000-1600; closed Su

⊖ P WC ☒ (limited access) ⊟ (by appt) ♠ ◆ ⚹ ✗ (limited times)

Hadleigh Castle

near Leigh-on-Sea, Essex

The romantic aura of Hadleigh Castle owes a good deal to the fact that its ruins were painted by the great 19th-century artist John Constable. The first known building on the site was the 13th-century castle begun by Hubert de Burgh, who as chief justiciar of England had been the dominant figure in the country for a decade and a half. De Burgh was granted a royal licence in 1231, but his years of power ended abruptly in 1232; Hadleigh passed to the Crown, and it may have been Henry III who actually completed the castle. It was rebuilt by Edward III from 1359, when the possibility of a French attack made it advisable to guard the Thames estuary more closely, and the only substantial remains date from this time. These consist of two of the towers set at the corners of the curtain wall, and some parts of the wall itself; the towers are three storeys high, round, and projected very boldly from the wall, enabling those inside them to catch the attackers in a crossfire. The castle was Crown property until 1551, when, during the troubled reign of the boy King Edward VI, it was bought by Lord Rich, one of the most astute opportunists of the Tudor period. Hadleigh seems to have become ruinous by the 17th century. At some time a landslip carried away the southern part of the bailey; the barbican and domestic buildings have also disappeared.

6 m W of Southend-on-Sea, on A13, turn S

TQ 8186 (OS 178)

Open at any reasonable time

⊖ (¾ mile) ☒ (hilly) ⊟ ♠ ★ ⚹ EH

Hedingham Castle

Castle Hedingham, near Halstead, Essex

Hedingham Castle was built by Aubrey de Vere, 1st Earl of Oxford, in about 1140, and the magnificent and well-preserved keep is a monument to his once-illustrious family. It stands alone in the grassy enclosure which was the inner bailey, once also containing the hall, chapel and other principal castle buildings; the original outer bailey is now occupied by a red-brick Queen Anne house (not open to the public). The stone great tower still has all its exterior walls, though two of its corner towers are gone. Access is at first-floor level via a flight of steps and a forebuilding, of which only the lower walls remain. A fine doorway with Norman chevron ornamentation leads into the single room which fills the whole of the first floor, with walls some 12 feet thick. A spiral staircase leads to the second-floor banqueting hall, the most splendid room in the keep, with a timbered ceiling supported by a great central arch 28 feet wide. The smaller arches and the windows are richly decorated with chevron moulding in different patterns. This room would have been used for entertaining, giving audience and so on, and 12 feet above floor level a gallery runs right round the room, tunnelled within the thickness of the walls and with its own set of windows, where minstrels or troubadours played during a banquet. The lovely Tudor bridge spanning the dry moat on the castle's eastern approach was built in 1496 and is the only survivor of several buildings put up by the 13th Earl of Oxford, an important supporter of the Lancastrians and Tudors in the Wars of the Roses.

☎ Halstead (0787) 60804/60261

3½ m N of Halstead turn NE onto B1058 and N at Castle Hedingham

TL 7835 (OS 155)

Open Easter weekend and May to end Oct daily 1000-1700; parties throughout year by appt

♿ (limited) P WC 🖃 ♣ 🍽 ⛱ ◆ ☙ ⚲

Berkhamsted Castle

Berkhamsted, Hertfordshire

This once large castle has been thoroughly plundered for building materials to use elsewhere, and its most impressive surviving features are the earthworks. The motte, which stands 45 foot high, carries the remains of a shell keep and is surrounded by a moat. Beyond it lies the bailey, parts of whose surrounding curtain wall are still in place, rising to about 15 foot. An outer moat encircles the bailey. Beyond the wall, to the north and east, there is another large earthwork, with levelled platforms and bastions whose function is uncertain. William the Conqueror's half-brother, Robert of Mortain, put up a timber castle at Berkhamsted soon after the Conquest; but his son William forfeited it in 1104 after rebelling against Henry I. The earliest building in stone probably dates from 1155-65, when Thomas Becket held the castle as Henry II's Chancellor (that is, before he became Archbishop of Canterbury and quarrelled with the King). In 1216 Berkhamsted was besieged by Prince Louis of France, who was allied with the rebellious English barons against King John. The castle held out for only a fortnight against a continuous bombardment of stones from Louis' siege engines, which may well have stood on the mysterious earth platforms described above. In 1336 Edward III gave Berkhamsted to the Black Prince; it had many distinguished residents, including the captive King John of France, Catherine of Aragon, Anne Boleyn, Jane Seymour and Princess (later Queen) Elizabeth.

Near town centre on A41

SP 9908 (OS 166)

Open at any reasonable time

⊖ 🅿 ♿ 🚻 D (on lead, grounds only) ♣ ★ ♨ EH

Lincoln Castle

Castle Hill, Lincoln, Lincolnshire

The first reference to Lincoln Castle occurs as early as 1068, only two years after the Norman Conquest, when 166 houses were demolished to make way for it. It stands to the west of the cathedral, and the two structures dominate the city visually as they once dominated it in life. The castle is large – over six acres within the walls, and more than as much again within the ramparts and ditches. Its oldest parts consist of a curtain wall and towers enclosing two mottes – this last being an unusual feature, also found at Lewes in East Sussex. The castle is entered from the cathedral side by the imposing eastern gatehouse, whose pointed-arch frontage covers a Norman tunnel-vault leading into the bailey; the western gatehouse is plain Norman work. The tower on the smaller, westernmost motte is a 12th-century shell keep known as the Lucy Tower; it is oval in shape (actually 15-sided), and in places still reaches a height of 20 foot. The motte in the south-east angle of the bailey carries the Observatory Tower, which is Norman with 14th-century additions. Lincoln Castle's military role only came to an end during the Civil War, when it was surrendered to Parliament (1644).

☎ Lincoln (0522) 25951

In city centre

SK 9771 (OS 121)

Open Apr to Oct M-S 1000-1800, Su 1100-1800; Nov to Mar M-S 1000-1600

⊖ 🅿 WC ♿ 🚻 ♣ ◆ ♨ 🎋 (by appt)

Tattershall Castle

Tattershall, Lincolnshire

The huge red-brick keep, perched on the highest point for many miles around, is all that remains of Tattershall Castle, and it is entirely thanks to Lord Curzon (1859-1925) that anything remains at all. He bought the ruin in 1911, when it had already been sold to speculators and the carved stone chimneypieces were on the way to America, and in the following years he carried out extensive restoration work including tracing and reinstating the chimneypieces. The original castle was built in 1231, but almost nothing now remains, and the keep itself is part of the new building campaign carried out by Ralph Cromwell, Lord Treasurer of England, in 1450. The plan followed that of castles built in earlier times, but although certainly fortified, it was clearly more of a country house than a fortress: for example, the windows are relatively large – and thus vulnerable – and there is a decorative roof gallery which serves no functional purpose at all. Cromwell's new tower, which was linked to the old hall by a first-floor passage, contained the state rooms, each storey having one large chamber, with smaller rooms and passages in the turrets. Lord Curzon, as well as replacing the chimneypieces, restored the top two storeys, constructed new floors and replaced tracery in the lower windows, but otherwise the tower is just as it was when built, and provides an excellent example of a 15th-century fortified house. Lord Cromwell had no children, and the castle passed through various hands before being finally abandoned – it was a ruin by about 1700.

☎ Conningsby (0526) 42543

15 m S of Horncastle on A153 at Tattershall

TF 2157 (OS 122)

Open Apr Oct M-S 1100-1830, Su 1300-1830; Nov to Mar M-S 1200-1800, Su 1300-1800 (sunset if earlier)

⊖ (exc Su) ▣ WC 🚻 (limited access) 🚻
D (on lead, grounds only) ♣ ◆ ⚘ NT

Burgh Castle

near Great Yarmouth, Norfolk

This is one of the Saxon Shore forts, a chain of defensive positions constructed along the east and south coasts of England by the Romans, who were increasingly troubled by marauding Germanic sea-raiders. Burgh – Roman Gariannonum – dates from the 3rd century AD and probably defended a nearby dockyard. It seems to have been functioning as late as AD 407, only a few years before the last imperial troops evacuated Britain. The Anglo-Saxons took over the site, and excavations have revealed what are probably the cells and little church of a monastic settlement, confirming the tradition that the 7th-century East Anglian king, Sigeberht, gave the land here to the Irish monk St Fursey. His settlement, along with many others, was destroyed when the Danes descended on East Anglia in 869. The next occupants seem to have been Normans who, just after the Conquest, threw up a large motte in the south-west corner of the fort; but all evidence of this was obliterated by 1839. It is still the Romans who dominate the place. The fort covers six acres; three walls of the rectangular fort survive, in parts standing at the original height (about 15 foot); the west wall has disappeared. The main gate was set in the middle of the long east wall (about 640 foot). At the corners and along the walls are bastions for the Romans' 'artillery' – catapults, and the large crossbow-like ballistae.

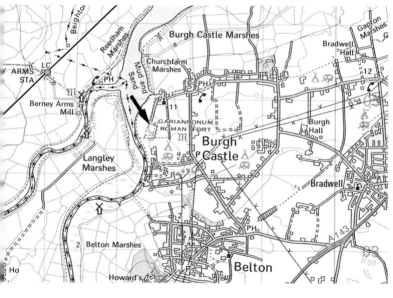

3 m SE of Great Yarmouth off A143

TG 4704 (OS 134)

Open at any reasonable time.

P ★ EH

Caister Castle

Caister-on-Sea, Norfolk

Caister is a spectacular ruin, with a single round tower rising some 90 foot above the River Bure and an accompanying stair turret almost 100 foot high. The builder was Sir John Fastolf, who is known to have been the original of Shakespeare's fat, comically cowardly knight, Sir John Falstaff. In reality Fastolf was a tough character who made his fortune in the French wars and built Caister out of the proceeds. It was one of the earliest English brick castles, built between 1432 and 1435, and was even more unusual in being defended by an elaborate system of moats; as a travelled man, Fastolf may have been influenced by the contemporary German *Wasserburg* (water-castle). The main castle at Caister consisted of a rectangular building round a courtyard; it had gatehouses in the east and west walls, and the tall, slender tower in the west corner. There was a forecourt to the east of the main block; its equivalent on the west side, which had access to a canal linked to the Bure, has been replaced by later buildings. In 1469 the Duke of Norfolk claimed Caister and successfully laid siege to it – supported (according to the Pastons) by 3000 men against their 30. The Pastons later regained Caister and lived there until 1599. It is now mainly ruinous, but it is still possible to climb the great tower, and the hall has been converted into a well-known motor museum.

Wymondham (057 284) 251

m W of Caister-on-Sea on A1064, turn S

G 5012 (OS 134)

Open mid May to end Sept daily exc S 1030-1700

Castle Rising

Castle Rising, Norfolk

Castle Rising stands in a large area of grassy banks and ditches which form an unusually well-preserved example of Norman earthwork fortifications. The huge keep in the centre, which rivals Norwich in size and splendour, was built about 1138 by William de Albini, Earl of Lincoln, who had in the same year married Queen Alice, the widow of Henry I. The magnificent rooms in the keep proudly proclaimed to the world the owner's new wealth and position, and are impressive even in ruins (roof and floors have gone), and the forebuilding, which rises almost as high as the tower and has survived more or less complete, has a very fine staircase and the remains of decorative interlacing arches. The tower itself is rectangular and squat, with horizontal dimensions greater than its height. It is 50 feet high, though it would originally have been several feet higher with its parapet and the roof to the corner turrets, and its length and width are approximately 78 by 68 feet. The other castle buildings are the remains of a Norman church built before the keep, and a Norman gatehouse built at about the same time, a rectangular tower with a room above the entrance passage. For some years Castle Rising was the home of Edward III's mother Isabella, who in collusion with her lover Roger Mortimer had caused the murder of Edward II in 1327 and virtually ruled England. Edward III seized power in 1330, Mortimer was executed and Isabella forced into 'retirement'.

☎ Castle Rising (055 387) 330

5½ m NE of King's Lynn on A149 turn W

TF 6624 (OS 132)

Open daily 15 Mar to 15 Oct 0930-1830; 16 Oct to 14 Mar W-Su 0930-1600

♿ (limited) 🅿 WC ♿ (limited access) 🚻 D ♦

♦ ♨ EH

Norwich Castle

Castle Meadow, Norwich, Norfolk

Though long ago sorn of everything but its keep, Norwich Castle dominates the city. It is a large rectangular block about 76 foot high and 95 by 90 foot in area. It has been restored and adapted for non-military uses so often that only its shape can be regarded as fully authentic; but it also seems clear that the external decoration, though renewed, faithfully follows the original. This is in fact the most remarkable feature of the castle; the walls of this severe military block are, most unusually, covered with a carved pattern of black arcading – that is, lines of low-relief round arches, arranged in tiers; as a result Norwich makes an oddly ecclesiastical impression. There was an earlier castle on the site, erected a few years after the Norman Conquest. The present building dates from the 12th century, and was faced with Caen stone specially imported from Normandy; this was highly valued because it was easy to work but extremely durable. During the Middle Ages Norwich had a particularly turbulent history, changing hands several times during wars and rebellions. Its last historic moment was in 1549, after the rebellion of the Norfolk peasantry had been crushed by German mercenaries at Mousehold Heath. It is now part of a museum complex.

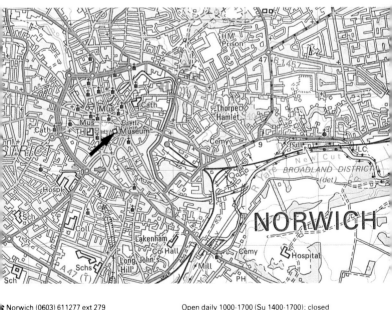

Norwich (0603) 611277 ext 279

city centre

G 2308 (OS 134)

Open daily 1000-1700 (Su 1400-1700); closed
Christmas, New Year and Good Fri

⊖ P WC 🚻 (limited access) 🚻 ♦ 🍴 ◆ ⚔ 𝄞
● (no tripods)

Oxburgh Hall

Oxborough, near King's Lynn, Norfolk

At first sight more of a castle than a house, Oxburgh was begun by S
Edmund Bedingfeld in 1482, just before the Wars of the Roses came to a
end. The house, with its wide moat and great central fortified gatehouse, h
all the features of a medieval castle, but it was clearly intended primarily as
dwelling – the large windows would have had no place in a real castle, ar
the machicolations on the south side are sealed by stone. The Bedingfe
family, who still live here, have made various changes over the generation
not all of them good. In 1775 Sir Richard Bedingfeld pulled down the Tud
great hall and great chamber; in the 18th and 19th centuries respectively tw
low towers were built; and in 1880 external corridors were built round th
courtyard. The oldest interiors are the King's and Queen's rooms in th
gatehouse tower which, although their furnishings are 17th century, hav
not been altered since the 15th century. The spiral staircase that links them
also of the 15th century, and is a masterpiece of intricate bricklaying. Th
rooms seen by visitors are Sir Richard's saloon of 1778 and three roon
decorated in the Victorian Gothic style, richly patterned and with decorate
ceilings. Pugin was possibly responsible for these; the fireplace in the libra
and the small chapel in the grounds are his work. Both staircases are hu
with 17th-century embossed Spanish leather, and one of the upstairs roon
contains Oxburgh's greatest single treasure, a set of bed-hangings and
coverlet embroidered by Mary Queen of Scots and Bess of Hardwick.

☎ Gooderstone (036 621) 258

9½ m SW of Swaffham on road to Cockley Cley
and Oxborough

TF 7401 (OS 143)

Open May to Sept M, T, W, S, Su 1330-1730; Apr
and Oct S, Su 1330-1730, Bank Hol M 1100-1730

🅿 WC ♿ (ground floor only)
♣ 🍴 ♦ ✼ ● (not in house) NT

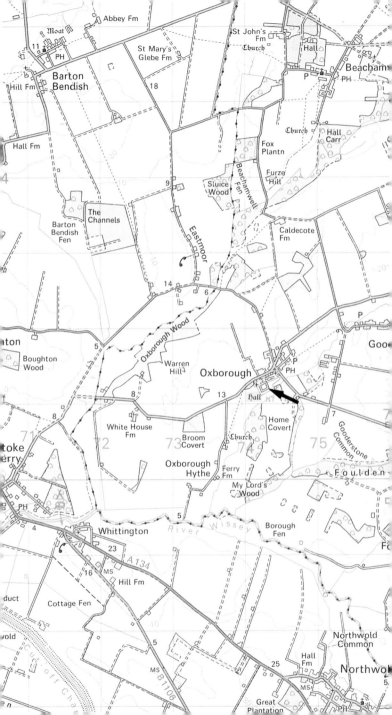

Framlingham Castle

Framlingham, Suffolk

The great curtain walls of this late 12th-century castle, all that remains present a fine sight. The castle was built by Roger Bigod, 2nd Earl of Norfolk on the site of his father's castle. It was built without a keep, its defences being a series of towers and a gatehouse linked by a ring of walls, approached by drawbridge over a moat (the present bridge is 16th century). The Bigod family were rebels against royal authority and, although the castle was besieged and taken by King John in 1216, they were not finally crushed until the reign of Edward I, when their estates were received by the Crown and the castle became the seat of the Mowbrays, followed by the Howards, the new Earls of Norfolk. From time to time it was forfeit to the Crown, and on one such occasion (1553) Princess Mary was staying here when the Earl of Arundel arrived to tell her she had become Queen of England. The Earls of Norfolk made little use of Framlingham as they had more appealing properties elsewhere, and it played no part in the Civil War. The demolition of the domestic buildings which once stood inside the walls was due to other and more peaceful causes. In 1636 it was bequeathed to Pembroke College, Oxford, with the proviso that a poorhouse was built here, and 'all the Castle, saving the stone building, be pulled down'. The poorhouse still stands, the south wing, dated 1636, being the home of the curator, while the rest is empty. The ground floor is open to the public, and there is a wall-walk round the castle walls.

☎ Framlingham (0728) 723330

In centre of Framlingham in Christchurch Park

TM 2863 (OS 156)

Open daily throughout year; 15 Mar to 15 Oct 0930-1830; 16 Oct to 14 Mar 0930-1600 (Su 1400-1600)

♿ (limited) 🅿 WC ♿ (limited access)
🍴 D ♣ ◆ ♨ 𝙭 (by appt) EH

Orford Castle

Orford, Suffolk

At Orford only the keep has survived; but it is a splendid one. It was built for Henry II by his 'ingeniator' (designer), Alnoth, Keeper of the King's Houses. The keep was erected first, in 1165-67, followed by a curtain wall with towers in 1167-73. Orford was a powerful, modern castle, designed to assert royal authority in a part of the country where there were all too many over-mighty barons. The keep was built on a revolutionary principle that was new to England. It was designed not as a rectangle, with jutting right-angled corners, but as a polygon, with so many faces (18 of them) that it was virtually a circle; on the inside the wall is in fact circular. This represented the most advanced military thinking: the new design widened the defender's field of vision, and made things harder for the besieger's sappers, whose technique was to undermine one corner of an enemy castle. Orford has three equidistant rectangular turrets that run the length of the keep and rise some 20 foot above it; and also a protective forebuilding covering the entrance to the keep, which was on the first floor. The main block consists of a basement (divided into storeroom and dungeon) and two storeys, both of which evidently served as halls; the turrets have six lower storeys, including a kitchen on both the ground and the first floor of the west turret. Orford remained a royal castle, seemingly kept in good repair, until 1336, when Edward III gave it to Robert de Ufford; it was in private hands until 1962.

☎ Orford (039 45) 4727

8 m E of Woodbridge, on B1084

TM 4149 (OS 169)

Open 15 Mar to 15 Oct M-S 0930-1830, Su 1400-1830; 16 Oct to 14 Mar M-W, S 0930-1630, Th, F 1300-1600, Su 1400-1600

⊖ P WC 🔊 (limited access) 🚻 D ♣ ◆ ☖ EH

Wingfield Castle

Wingfield, Suffolk

In medieval times Wingfield was the home of one of England's most powerful families, the de la Poles, Earls and Dukes of Suffolk, and in 1384 Michael de la Pole, Lord Chancellor, was given licence to crenellate and fortify his manor house. The de la Poles intermarried with the Wingfields, another prestigious old family, soon after, and the castle remained in the same family until 1510, when it came to Anne, daughter of Edward IV and wife of Lord Thomas Howard. The greater part of the house we see today dates from this period, when the old fortified house was transformed into a more comfortable Tudor residence. Parts of the fortifications were dismantled, and the old manor house was replaced by the Tudor house constructed about 1540 within the remaining fortifications. Most of the great medieval outer walls and towers still remain, however, and the bridge to the entrance gateway still bears the grooves of the former gate, drawbridge and portcullis. The two main towers, dating from about 1384, rise to nearly 60 feet above the moat, with the corner towers only slightly lower, and the south-facing battlement wall is over four feet thick. The visitor can explore the gatehouse towers and the barbican room which straddles the entrance, and there is access to the top of one of the towers, which gives a fine view of the countryside. The courtyard, entered through the lovely arched gatehouse, is now an attractive garden with an impressive backdrop of medieval and Tudor flint and brickwork.

☎ Stradbrooke (037 984) 393

6 m S of Harleston on B1116 turn W at Fressingfield

TM 2277 (OS 156)

Open Easter to end Oct S, Su, Bank Hol M 1400-1800; parties by appt at other times

🅿 WC 🚻 (limited access) 🚻 (reduced rates S, Su) ♣ 🍴 🏕 ◆ ✳

The North

Dundee

TAYSIDE

FIFE

Edinburgh

LOTHIAN

BORDERS

DUMFRIES
&
GALLOWAY

Berwick-upon-Tweed

Norham Castle

Lindisfarne Castle

Bamburgh Castle

Dunstanburgh Castle

Alnwick Castle

Warkworth Castle

Callaly Castle

NORTHUMBERLAND

Naworth Castle

Carlisle Castle

Carlisle

Brougham Castle

CUMBRIA

Appleby Castle

Brough Castle

Hardknott Castle

Muncaster Castle

Kendal Castle

Sizergh Castle

Dalton Castle

Lancaster Castle

Lancaster

Clitheroe Castle

LANCASHIRE

GREATER MAN

Manchester

MERSEYSIDE

Liverpool

Tynemouth Castle

Newcastle Castle

TYNE & WEAR

Newcastle-upon-Tyne

Durham Castle

DURHAM

Raby Castle

CLEVELAND

Middlesbrough

Barnard Castle

Bowes Castle

Richmond Castle

Bolton Castle

Middleham Castle

Scarborough Castle

Pickering Castle

Helmsley Castle

NORTH YORKSHIRE

Knaresborough Castle

York Castle

Skipton Castle

York

HUMBERSIDE

Kingston upon Hull

Leeds

WEST YORKS

Pontefract Castle

Conisbrough Castle

SOUTH YORKSHIR

Sheffield

CHESHIRE

DERBYSHIRE

CLWYD

Stoke-on-Trent

NOTTS

LINCOLNSHIRE

Nottingham

SHROPSHIRE

STAFFORDSHIRE

POWYS

LEICESTERSHIRE

Appleby Castle

Appleby, Cumbria

Appleby, the county town of a once separate Westmorland, is situated within a loop of the river Eden; the castle stands at the neck of the loop, at one end of the broad main street. Its early history is obscure. It began in the 11th century as a motte-and-bailey castle, with impressive ditches and earthworks that still survive. At some point in the 12th century the motte was flattened and a fine square keep was built on it – probably, but not certainly, after the castle had been captured in 1174 by the Scots King William the Lion. The keep – Caesar's Tower – is the principal remain at Appleby, in excellent condition and accessible right to the top, from which there are splendid views of the town and surrounding countryside. The lower portion is well-provided with windows; mysteriously, the upper part (probably added in about 1300) has none. Appleby Castle was slighted after the rebellion of the Northern earls against Queen Elizabeth in 1569, and again after the Civil War. It was restored by Lady Anne Clifford, who also did so much for Brough, Brougham and Skipton Castles. Parts of the medieval curtain wall and other ruinous features survive at Appleby, and the domestic buildings on the eastern side of the castle incorporate much 14th-century stonework. Appleby Castle is now a Rare Breeds Survival Trust Centre where the Gloucester Old Spot pig and other exotic animals and birds may be admired.

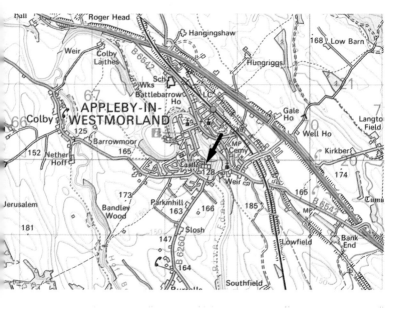

☎ Appleby (0930) 51402)

In town centre

NY 6819 (OS 91)

Open May to Sept daily 1030-1700

⊖ P WC ♿ 🚻 (by appt) D (on lead, grounds only) 🍴 🍽 🪑 ◆ ☼ ⚘ ⚘

Brough Castle

Brough, Cumbria

A noble ruin overlooking Swindale Beck, Brough Castle stands on an ancient site. The Romans built the fort of Verterae here to guard the roads across the Pennines; their earthworks are still visible. Brough Castle was erected on the northern third of the area occupied by the fort. It was begun by William Rufus in the 1090s but largely destroyed by King William the Lion of Scotland in 1174; the only 11th-century survival is a stretch of the north wall with masonry in the herringbone pattern. In the 13th century the castle came into the possession of the Clifford family, passed through various vicissitudes, decayed and was restored, until in 1521 it was gutted by fire. It was restored in the 1660s by Lady Anne Clifford, who seems to have had a passion for castles; at a time when they were very obviously becoming obsolete, she put new life into a whole chain of Clifford castles including Appleby and Brougham. After her death in 1676 Brough steadily decayed, and as with other abandoned castles its decline was hastened by plundering of the stonework for other building purposes. By 1923, when it passed to the Ministry of Works, it had reached its present condition. However, it is still a substantial and interesting structure. The 13th- and 14th-century walls are an imposing sight, and the round south-east tower provides a good example of Lady Anne Clifford's restoration work (the base is 14th century). Of the buildings inside the walls, the late 12th-century keep, though gutted, is much the best preserved.

☎ Brough (093 04) 219

In village centre, near junction of A66 and A685

NY 7914 (OS 91)

Open daily am and pm (Su pm only)

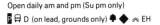 D (on lead, grounds only) ♣ ◆ ﹌ EH

Brougham Castle

Brougham, Cumbria

Cunningly situated so that it controlled the road and river junctions around Penrith, Brougham was not the first military settlement in the area: just to the south-east, the Romans established a large fort whose remains can still be seen. The medieval castle was built in the late 12th century, during the reign of Henry II, and was much altered from the 13th century, when the Clifford family became its owners. It had become ruinous by the early 17th century, but its decline was halted for a time by the formidable Lady Anne Clifford, who restored a number of Northern castles before her death in 1676; a 17th-century inscription on the outer gatehouse records her activities at Brougham. The oldest part is the four-storey keep, mainly dating from the 12th century; the original entrance was on the first floor, up a flight of steps, but in about 1300 a passage was cut to give direct access into the ground floor. With her strong romantic feeling for castles, Lady Anne Clifford named the keep the Pagan Tower. The inner gatehouse was built in the late 13th century; then, from about 1300, the Cliffords added the top floor of the keep, the three-storey outer gatehouse, and the strong tower in the south-west corner of the curtain wall. A passageway was built to link the two gate-houses. At Brougham there are also the remains of a great chamber, built to the east of the keep in the early 13th century, of an early 14th-century great hall and kitchen to the south of the great chamber and of a late 14th-century chapel and other buildings.

☎ Penrith (0768) 62488)

1 m S of Penrith on A66, turn E onto B6262

NY 5328 (OS 90)

Open daily am and pm (March to Oct Su pm only)

♿ 🅿 ♿ (limited access) 🚻 D (on lead, grounds only) ♣ ◆ ⚲ EH

Carlisle Castle

Carlisle, Cumbria

Standing guard for centuries over the wild North, Carlisle Castle has had a long and turbulent history. It is situated inside the city, on a bluff rising above the river Eden. William Rufus put up a stockade here in the late 11th century, and King David of Scotland is said to have done some building on the site when Cumberland and Westmorland briefly came under Scottish control. However, the earliest surviving building, the keep, was erected in about 1160 by Henry II of England; it stands in the south-west corner of the triangular inner bailey. The outer and inner baileys were added soon afterwards, and the castle became a formidable stronghold that withstood Scottish armies on a number of occasions, capitulating only once. In 1568 Mary, Queen of Scots, was imprisoned at Carlisle Castle for two months after her flight into England. Royalist forces were twice besieged, and forced to surrender, during the Civil War; and the castle was still of some military significance during the 1745 Jacobite rebellion. Bonnie Prince Charlie's men captured it on their march south, and after the Prince's retreat a Highland garrison tried unsuccessfully to hold it against the Duke of Cumberland. During its long active history the castle was repaired and altered many times. The best known of its many interesting features are the small medieval cells on the second floor, their walls covered with graffiti scratched by prisoners. A 19th-century building in the castle houses the regimental museum of the Border Regiment.

☎ Carlisle (0228) 31777

In N outskirts of Carlisle

NY 3956 (OS 85)

Open daily am and pm (Su pm only)

♿ P WC ♿ (limited access) 🚻 D (on lead, grounds only) ♦ 🐾 ♦ ⚰ ⚔ EH

Dalton Castle

Dalton-in-Furness, Cumbria

Dalton Castle, or Dalton Tower, stands in the main street of Dalton-in-Furness, a little town that was once the capital of the Furness peninsula. It is a pele tower, doubtless intended as a place of refuge from marauding Scots, and was probably built by the monks of Furness Abbey at some time in the 14th century. By 1545, following the Dissolution of the Monasteries by Henry VIII, the neglected tower 'was in great ruin and decay'. Dalton Castle was repaired, and for a time served as the prison for the Furness area. From 1660 it was the property of the Dukes of Buccleuch, who as lords of the manor used it as their courthouse. In 1965 Dalton Castle became a National Trust property. It is still a sturdy, unpretentious little building, an unbroken rectangle with 5-foot-thick walls that rise to a parapet 44 by 30 foot in area. It has three storeys, the upper floors being reached by a spiral staircase set in the west wall. There is little authentic medieval detail: the windows are mainly 19th century (although at least one in the top storey is original) and the armour on display belongs to the 16th and 17th centuries.

In centre of Dalton-in-Furness

SD 2374 (OS 96)

Open daily throughout year at all reasonable times

♿ 🚻

Hardknott Castle

Cumbria

Despite the medieval-sounding name, the remains at Hardknott are not those of a castle but of a Roman fort built in the 1st century AD. Its strategic value is evident, since it stands on a spur of Hard Knott mountain, looking down on the western end of Hardknott Pass; from there it could control all traffic along the Roman road from Ravenglass on the coast to Ambleside near the head of Lake Windermere. The fort was built of stone and covered about three acres; it formed a rough square with a central gate in each of the four walls. Though little more than the fort's foundations survive, it is well worth a visit for its spectacular setting – and indeed the difficult mountain road still makes a trip to Hardknott something of an expedition. What Roman legionaries thought of their remote, damp, misty, mountainous posting was almost certainly unfit for publication. But even here the Roman military pattern and the Roman way of life were firmly imposed on the landscape, in a fashion reminiscent of the British Raj in India. Excavation has revealed the standard features present in Roman forts all over the Empire, including a bath block just beyond the walls, fully equipped with a cold plunge and cold, warm, hot and extra-hot rooms in which the garrison could relax or reinvigorate themselves. To the north-east of the fort a large levelled area of ground testifies to the important function assigned to drill in maintaining the troops' morale in a far-flung colonial station.

4 m W of Ambleside, turn W to Little Langdale for 10 m

NY 2102 (OS 90)

Open daily throughout year at all reasonable times

🅿 🚻 D (on lead, grounds only) ♣ ★ ♨

Kendal Castle

Kendal, Cumbria

Although Kendal Castle has few claims to historical importance, its ruins are undoubtedly a fine romantic sight, visible from most parts of the town; it is only a few minutes' walk from the centre of Kendal to the top of Castle Hill, a grassy mound now used for the recreation of human and bovine browsers. The first lord of Kendal after the Norman Conquest, Ivo de Taillebois, probably put up a castle at Castle Howe, on the other side of the river Kent; the present castle seems to have been built by Roger Fitz Reinfred in the reign of Henry II. The mound is natural, not man-made, but the Norman moat, ramparts and ditch are easily identified; by contrast, the broken remains of the walls and towers are dramatic but uninformative, and only the husks of two vaulted basements hint at the existence of domestic quarters. Nor is the castle's history well documented. Medieval Cumbria was a turbulent area, and from time to time Kendal suffered severely from the depredations of Scottish raiders; but oddly enough there are no records of actions against the castle. It passed to the Parr family in the 14th century, and is said to have been the birthplace of Catherine Parr, who became the sixth wife of Henry VIII and managed to outlive that axe-happy monarch. By 1586 the antiquarian William Camden noted that the castle was 'ready to drop down with age'.

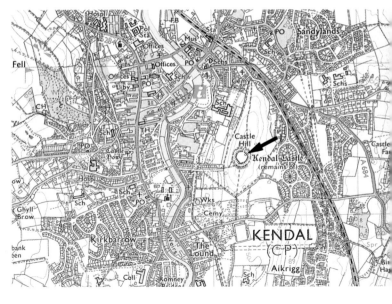

☎ Kendal (0539) 25758

In town centre on River Kent

SD 5292 (OS 97)

Open daily am and pm

Muncaster Castle

Ravenglass, Cumbria

Muncaster Castle, which guards the entrance to Eskdale, is ancient in origin; the lands were granted to Alan de Penitone in 1208. The original castle was built about 50 years later and enlarged by the addition of a pele tower in 1325. However, although the present house incorporates the medieval tower, it is almost entirely the creation of Anthony Salvin, who rebuilt it in the 1860s for the 4th Lord Muncaster. Salvin specialised in restoring castles, and the pink granite building harmonises well with the heather-clad hills and the rhododendrons for which the gardens are famous. The interiors are mainly Victorian, but there is some excellent 17th-century furniture and many good paintings. The house is full of treasures collected over the generations, including Flemish woodcarvings, tapestries and silver. One of the most interesting rooms is the large octagonal library with its coved ceiling. Standing over the site of the medieval kitchens, it dates from about 1780, but was altered by Salvin, who also changed the exterior so that it cannot be seen as an octagon from the outside. The drawing room, with a lovely barrel ceiling decorated with plasterwork by Italian craftsmen, contains one of the finest collections of family portraits in the country. Upstairs is a magnificent Elizabethan bed in the west bedroom, with carved and inlaid scenic panels, and the curtains are hand-painted silk. The carved fireplace is Tudor, as is the one in the tapestry room, and the King's bedroom has 16th-century carved panelling.

☎ Ravenglass (065 77) 614 203

18 m S of Whitehaven on A595

SD 0996 (OS 96)

Open Good Fri to end Sept daily exc M, May 9, 10 but inc Bank Hols) 1330-1630; other times by appt

P WC ♿ (by appt) ♨ D (grounds only) ♠ ♥ ♫ ◆ ✿ ⚹ ⚔ (by appt) ● ⚘ ⚮

Naworth Castle

Brampton, Cumbria

Naworth stands on a good defensive site beside the river Irthing, with the ground falling away steeply on three sides. The first stone fortress there was built after 1335, when Edward III granted Ranulph de Dacre a licence to crenellate his house; Dacre added a tower and a walled enclosure. Although the Dacres were a powerful family, Naworth was neglected until the time of Thomas, Lord Dacre, a warrior who distinguished himself at the battle of Flodden (1513) and remained much concerned with the defence of the North. Lord Thomas rebuilt and heightened Ranulph's tower (now called the Dacre Tower) and gave Naworth essentially its present form. This consists of an irregular quadrangle with towers at each end of the main façade, on the most vulnerable side; the rectangular Dacre Tower projects right out from the walls, extending the façade. In front of it stand once-formidable outer defences that include a moat and a gatehouse. The most notable of the courtyard buildings is the very large Great Hall, measuring 78 by 24 foot. By 1588 Naworth was again 'in very great decay in all parts', and a second restoration was undertaken by Lord William Howard, who had married a Dacre heiress in 1604. He converted the tower into luxurious private apartments, fitted with a superb 14th-century ceiling taken from Kirkoswald Castle. Fortunately this survived the disastrous fire of 1844, though much else was lost. However, Naworth's owner, the Earl of Carlisle, called in the architect Anthony Salvin, who restored the original with great fidelity.

☎ Brampton (069 77) 2692

12 m E of Carlisle on A69 turn N

NY 5662 (OS 86)

Open Easter Su and M to end Sept W, Su, Bank Hol M and S in July and Aug 1400-1700

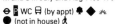
● (not in house)

Sizergh Castle

near Kendal, Cumbria

The layout of Sizergh encapsulates the medieval history of northern England. The building has belonged to the Strickland family since 1239, but the earliest surviving part is a pele tower – one of the many towers built as places of refuge on both sides of the Border in medieval times, when Anglo-Scottish wars were frequent and private sorties endemic. The tower at Sizergh was one of the largest, measuring 60 by 40 foot in plan; the ground floor walls were almost 10 foot thick. Two attached turrets run all the way up the tower and rise above it. The tower dates from 1340, but at some later time – probably in the 15th century – the Stricklands felt prosperous or secure enough to add a great hall. Finally, in the Elizabethan period, two wings were built on to the hall, completing a 'stately home' that could bear comparison with houses in the more settled south and Midlands. Significantly, many architectural details and alterations at Sizergh belong to the expansive Elizabethan period, as do many of its treasures. At the main entrance the visitor is met by a carved wooden screen of the 1550s, and upstairs, on the first floor, there is a wealth of superb Elizabethan woodwork – panelling, ceilings, and above all fine carved chimneypieces, all made between 1563 and 1575. As well as interesting furnishings and works of art, there is a museum on the top floor of the tower; its contents include relics of Bonnie Prince Charlie. The rock garden outside Sizergh Castle is a modern addition, laid out in the 1920s.

☎ Sizergh (0448) 60285

3½ m S of Kendal on A6, A591, turn W

SD 4987 (OS 97)

Open Apr to end Oct M, W, Th pm

♿ P WC ⊟ (by appt, not on Bank Hols) ♠ ⊼ ◆
♨ ● (no flash, video, tripods) NT (gardens only)

Barnard Castle

County Durham

The ruins of Barnard Castle stand on the steep, cliff-like left bank of the river Tees, surrounded by the little town that has grown up round it. The land was given by William II to Guy de Baliol, and it was probably Guy's son Bernard who raised the first motte-and-bailey castle here – Bernard's, or Barnard's, Castle. The Baliols made their mark on British history, albeit briefly: Guy's great-grandson John de Baliol founded Balliol College, Oxford, and John's son (also a John) was King of Scotland for a few years. However, the most dramatic moment in the castle's history occurred long afterwards, in 1569, when Elizabeth's steward, Sir George Bowes, held out for eleven days against the rebellious Earls of Westmorland and Northumberland. After this, Barnard quickly became ruinous. In its heyday, its most unusual feature was that it had four wards or baileys, though now only the town ward and inner ward have much to show. The inner ward was the heart of the castle, and the great hall and other domestic buildings stood against its west curtain wall, above the cliffs; their windows can still be seen in the wall. The best-preserved part of Barnard Castle is the Baliol or round tower, a building dating from about 1250 that straddles the curtain wall of the inner ward. Much of the town ward's curtain wall also survives, along with remains of towers and the still substantial Brackenbury's Tower, a rectangular structure (named after a Lieutenant of the Tower under Richard III) which is said to have been used as a prison.

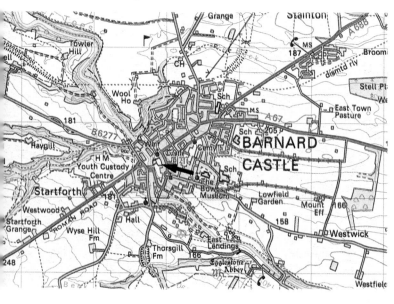

☎ Staindrop (0833) 38212

In centre of Barnard Castle town

NZ 0516 (OS 92)

Open daily am and pm (Sept to Mar Su pm only)

⊖ P ⬙ ⊟ D (on lead, grounds only) ♠ ◆ ⚶ EH

174

Bowes Castle

Bowes, County Durham

Bowes is a desolate spot, but of sufficient strategic importance to have been subjected to frequent military occupation. It was the site of a Roman fort at least as far back as the early 3rd century AD: Bowes – Lavatrae – guarded a fork in the east–west road across the North, and also a ford in the river Greta. As elsewhere, Roman soldiers relieved the bleakness of a northern tour of duty by indulging in the pleasures offered by the baths (which were in fact more like turkish baths or sauna than an ordinary bath); traces of a substantial bathhouse have been identified just outside the fort. The Normans reused a corner of the Roman site, and much of the Romans' own masonry, when putting up Bowes Castle, which stands just to the south of the little town of the same name. Much of the Normans' work has now disappeared, including the bailey walls. Some traces of the moat have been identified, but the only significant remains are those of the keep. This is a ruin, but a massive and most impressive one, about 50 foot high and about 80 by 60 foot in plan. It was built for Henry II between 1171 and 1187 by a royal servant referred to in Henry's records as Richard the Engineer. It is conventional in design, with a forebuilding protecting the east side entrance, which was, as usual, on the first floor of the building. This was where the great hall stood, interconnecting with the kitchen conveniently adjacent; the hall was lit by quite large windows and provided with a fireplace.

In village centre, 5 m SW of Barnard Castle on A67   Open at any reasonable time

NY 9913 (OS 92)   ⊖ 🚻 ★ EH

Durham Castle

Durham, Co. Durham

Durham Castle stands beside the cathedral on high ground above the river; both were begun about the same time, in the 11th century. The stronghold was given to the Bishop of Durham and became a palace of the prince bishops who, in return for the absolute power they held over their territory, were expected to produce an army, when necessary, to counter any threat from the Scots moving south. Little remains of the Norman building except for the chapel, but the castle still follows the original Norman pattern. In the 19th century the last of the prince bishops, William van Mildert, gave it to the newly founded University of Durham, and it is now a postgraduate college. The keep, which was extensively restored in 1831, is not open to the public, but the buildings of the various bishops can be visited. These were constantly altered and modernised by their successive owners, and display a variety of architectural styles, the common factor being a superlative standard of workmanship. Each bishop left his mark on his particular building or improvement by carving his personal coat-of-arms into the stone – on walls, over doorways or wherever else they would fit. A 17th-century porch in the courtyard leads to a screens passage with the kitchen on one side and the great hall on the other. The hall has 19th-century panelling and stained glass but its walls are 14th century, and parts of the undercroft are Norman. Two of the castle's best features are the black staircase, with its lovely carved wooden tracery, and the Norman chapel.

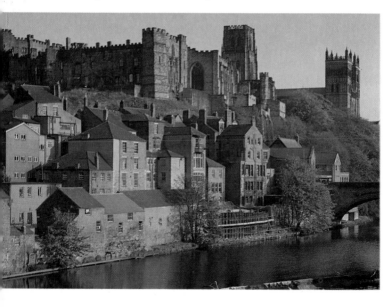

☎ Durham (0385) 65481

In centre of Durham

NZ 2742 (OS 88)

Open Apr, July to Sept M-S 1000-1200, 1400-1630; other months M, W, S 1400-1630

⊖ 🅿 WC 🚻 (by appt in summer) 🍽 (book evening meal in summer) ◆ ⚹ 🖋 (compulsory)

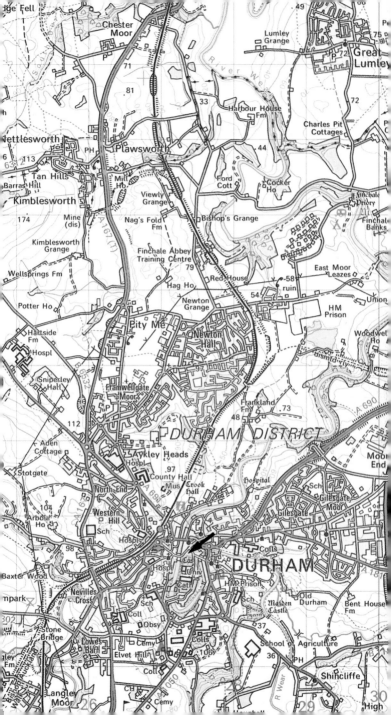

Raby Castle

Staindrop, Darlington, Co. Durham

Raby Castle, with its great, long, battlemented front and its encircling protective walls, readily evokes the spirit of medieval England. It is first recorded as belonging to King Canute, and was evidently fortified some time before Lord Neville was granted a licence to crenellate in 1378, as the oldest parts of today's building date from the 12th century. The power of the Neville family was destroyed after the 'Rising of the North' in 1569 against Elizabeth I, and Raby was acquired by Sir Henry Vane, whose family still own it. Although it still gives the appearance of a 14th-century castle most of the buildings have been turned into something more like a country house. The most complete medieval parts are on the west side, where a drawbridge once led across the moat to the Neville gateway and the inner court. Some of the walls here are 20 feet thick. A good deal of alteration was done in the 1780s by Carr of York, and much of his work was in turn altered by William Burn in the 1840s, so the interiors are a mixture of late 18th-century and mid 19th-century revival styles. The great, Gothic-style entrance hall with its pointed vault and dark red pillars is Carr's work, while the octagonal drawing room with its gilded 'Jacobean' strapwork, silk-hung walls and vast mirrors is the most impressive of Burn's rooms. The house contains a good collection of paintings and furniture as well as some fine Meissen porcelain and the statue of a naked and manacled slave girl by Hiram Powers, which caused a sensation when it was first exhibited in 1851.

☎ Staindrop (0833) 60202
6 m SW of West Auckland on A688 turn W at Maltkiln Cotts
NZ 1221 (OS 92)

Open Easter weekend; early May, June W, Su; July to Sept daily exc S (also Bank Hols) 1300-1700

⚑ WC ♿ (limited access) ⊟ (by appt) D (grounds only) ♣ ▆ ⊼ ◆ ⚹ ⚔ (parties only) ●

Clitheroe Castle

Clitheroe, Lancashire

This castle stands not on a motte but on a knoll of natural rock, looking down on the little town of Clitheroe. After the battle of Hastings the land was granted to Roger de Poitou, an immensely energetic military man who consolidated the Norman grip on wide areas of Lancashire and Cumbria. But although there are early 12th-century references to a castle on the site, the present Clitheroe Castle was probably built in the 1180s by Roger de Lacy, Lord of Pontefract. It is an attractively neat sight. The keep is one of the smallest known (a mere 35 foot square), a fact that must have made for cramped accommodation and, presumably, limited military impact. It follows the normal pattern in having a first-floor entrance; from there a spiral staircase leads to the upper floor and (via one of the turrets) to the battlements. The surrounding curtain wall was appropriately compact, running close to the keep on three sides; part of the wall survives. It opened out to the south-west, taking in a small bailey (now partly occupied by houses that mostly date from much later). From the de Lacys, Clitheroe passed by marriage to Thomas of Lancaster, who led the baronial opposition to Edward II and paid for it with his head. After this it remained a royal castle down to the 17th century. Despite its apparent harmlessness, it was slighted by Parliamentary troops in 1649.

☎ Clitheroe (0200) 24635

In centre of Clitheroe

SD 7441 (OS 103)

Open Easter to end Oct daily 1400-1630

⊖ 🅿 WC 🖫 D ♣ 🗗 ★ ◆ ⚕ ⚗

Lancaster Castle

Lancaster, Lancashire

This castle stands just outside the town centre and looks down on the river Lune. It occupies part of a site on which the Romans built a fort, Longoricum, at least as early as the 2nd century AD. After the Norman Conquest, Roger de Poitou was granted extensive lands in the North, and built the keep at Lancaster in about 1100. The castle and fief of Lancaster remained important throughout the Middle Ages, and Lancaster eventually became a dukedom. In 1399 the exiled Henry Bolingbroke succeeded in asserting his right to Lancaster and went on to usurp the throne as King Henry IV; his Lancastrian dynasty was later involved in a bitter struggle with the alternative Yorkist line. But despite its historical associations, Lancaster Castle is now a mainly 19th-century structure, having been adapted to function as a shire hall and prison. Some of Roger's keep survives, with alterations by John of Gaunt (Henry IV's father) and the Elizabethan owners, but the most impressive feature is the powerful gatehouse; it was built, or at least given its present appearance, by John of Gaunt, and carries the arms of Henry IV and the Prince of Wales (later Henry V). The shire hall, lined with coats of arms, is an early 19th-century pseudo-medieval building.

☎ Lancaster (0524) 64998

In town centre

SD 4762 (OS 97)

Open Easter to late Sept daily am and pm (only some parts open when court is in session)

⊖ WC 🖫 (by appt) ◆ ⚕ 🗡 (compulsory) ●

Alnwick Castle

Alnwick, Northumberland

The seat of the Percy family since Norman times, Alnwick still reflects the plan of the original Norman castle, though it has twice been restructured in modern times. It began as a large, centrally placed motte surrounded by two baileys that enclose 5 acres. During the first half of the 12th century a stone shell keep was erected on the motte, and stone curtain walls round the baileys replaced the original timber structures. In the 14th century the defensive power of the keep was increased by the addition of semi-circular towers, and the gatehouse was strengthened. Several towers were also built on the curtain wall, and a new gateway was erected to guard the entrance to the eastern bailey. A splendid gatehouse and barbican to the western bailey incorporated many of the features of Edward I's powerful fortifications in Wales. The castle, the dominent stronghold of the Scottish border, remained unchanged – except by neglect – for the next 400 years. In the 18th century the keep of the decaying castle was turned by Robert Adam and other craftsmen into a comfortable pseudo-Gothic mansion. In the second half of the 19th century the 4th Duke of Northumberland began another major reconstruction when, under Anthony Salvin, the present palatial apartments were created. There is a riot of Victorian extravagance in the guard chamber, the magnificent library, which houses 16,000 volumes, and the sumptuous drawing room. The apartments contain notable paintings, fine furniture, Meissen china and items of historical interest.

☎ Alnwick (0665) 602207

In N outskirts of Alnwick

NU 1813 (OS 81)

Open May to end Sept daily exc S 1300-1700 and Bank Hol S

♿ 🅿 WC 🚻 (by appt) ♣ ◆ ✸ ● (not in castle)

Bamburgh Castle

Bamburgh, Northumberland

Bamburgh Castle, crouched on its rocky outcrop on the Northumberland coast, blends into its bleak but beautiful landscape as if it grew there. However, although it was an important stronghold from at least Saxon times, what we see today is almost entirely Victorian. The Saxon castle was besieged by William II at the end of the 11th century, and deserted by its lord, Robert de Mowbray, 3rd Earl of Northumberland, whose wife Matilda surrendered only when he was recaptured and threatened with death. The new Norman castle, built over the next hundred years, was more or less complete by the reign of Henry III (1207-72), who made important additions to it, including the double-towered east gate. The age of the great fortified castles was over by the 15th century, and by Tudor times Bamburgh was decayed and ruinous. Early in the 18th century Lord Crewe, Bishop of Durham, bought it for the Crown, and it came under the trusteeship of the remarkable Dr John Sharp, Archdeacon of Northumberland, who spent a great deal of his own money on restorations. In 1894 it was bought by Lord Armstrong, the arms manufacturer, and the present building is largely the result of his extensive restorations, completed in 1903. The interior is a splendid display of Victorian medievalism, the centrepiece being the great king's hall with its fine hammerbeam roof. The guardroom at the bottom of the keep contains an important collection of weapons and armour as well as some good tapestries and porcelain.

☎ Bamburgh (066 84) 208

16 m N of Alnwick on A1 turn E onto B1341

NU 1835 (OS 75)

Open Apr to end Oct daily 1300-1700(1630 in Oct)

♿ 🅿 WC 🍴 ♣ 🍽 ⛺ ◆ ☂ 🔫 ● (not in castle)

Callaly Castle

Whittingham, Alnwick, Northumberland

Although the house does not even slightly resemble a castle, it is – unlike many other houses which have 'dressed' for the part in order to take the name – technically by writ of 1416 a fortified place. Embedded within the stately 18th-century accretions there are still the massive walls of a 15th-century pele tower. This was a type of defensive domestic structure that had space below to drive the cattle in for safety and rooms above for the family and its dependents when the alarm was raised that reivers (rustlers) were out roving. The south front of 1676 is now the oldest visible part and the other two main building periods are Queen-Anne (east and south-east fronts, 1707) and Georgian (central front, 1727, and ballroom front, 1750). The façade is a copy of the 1676 south front. The Claverings, who were established here from 1271 until 1877, retained their Catholic faith and maintained a priest in the house as domestic chaplain right through the penal period. Inside, Callaly Castle is well furnished and contains a particular fine stuccoed drawing room of 1757, possibly by James Paine. A priest's hole has been discovered in the chimney. Among the items of interest in the house are a marble horse's head with bronze bridle from the site of the temple of Artemis at Ephesus, and four out of a set of six oval Gobelins tapestries with scenes from the life of the French king Henri IV, dated 1787.

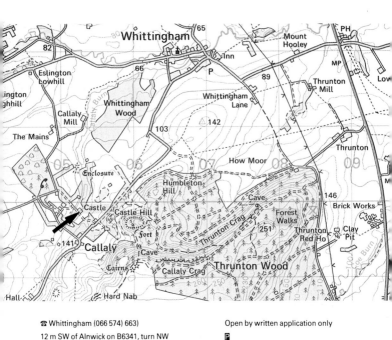

☎ Whittingham (066 574) 663)

12 m SW of Alnwick on B6341, turn NW

NU 0509 (OS 81)

Open by written application only

🅿

184

Dunstanburgh Castle

Embleton, near Craster, Northumberland

Dunstanburgh is one of the most spectacular of all English castle ruins, accessible only on foot along the wild and lovely Northumbrian coastline. There is plenty to see – the gatehouse-keep with its broken towers pointing to the sky, and long stretches of curtain wall interrupted by towers and turrets. The castle was built in 1313-16 by Thomas, Earl of Lancaster, and may well have been intended as an impregnable place of refuge, suitable for dangerous times (Thomas was the leader of the baronial opposition to Edward II). Strongly defended, and with the sea protecting it on the north and east, Dunstanburgh was further strengthened by a ditch dug from an inlet in the south, right around to Embleton bay on the north, which effectively converted it into an island fortress. Unfortunately for Thomas, he was never able to reach the shelter of Dunstanburgh. Defeated and captured at the battle of Boroughbridge in 1322, he was executed in or near another of his castles, Pontefract. In the 1390s Dunstanburgh was strengthened by John of Gaunt, Duke of Lancaster, on whose orders the gatehouse was converted into a keep. It withstood the Scots easily enough, and during the Wars of the Roses remained a Lancastrian stronghold even when the Yorkists were in the ascendant elsewhere; but in 1462, and again in 1464, it was forced to surrender. The damage done was never properly made good, and from that time onwards Dunstanburgh steadily fell into decay.

☎ Embleton (066 576) 631
On coast, 12 m N of Alnwick
NU 2522 (OS 75)

Open daily am and pm (Oct to Apr Su pm only)
🚻 D (on lead, grounds only) ♣ ◆ ⅍ EH

Lindisfarne Castle

Holy Island, Berwick-upon-Tweed, Northumberland

The great crag on Holy Island, suitable though it was as a castle site, was surprisingly not fortified until 1542, when gunposts were set up to defend the harbour against the marauding Scots. The castle was completed by 1550, built from the stone of the ruined priory situated conveniently nearby, but the expected attack never came. There was just one dramatic incident in 1725, when the garrison had shrunk to seven men, and the castle was seized by Jacobite supporters, but they were speedily ejected and the castle went back to sleep. In 1819 its guns were removed and it fell into disuse, but in 1901 Edward Hudson, the founder of *Country Life* magazine, bought it and engaged Edwin Lutyens, then the leading country-house architect, who had begun to show a particular skill in romantic reconstructions using traditional materials. Lutyens's task was to make a comfortable house within the ramparts, and the result was a series of small vaulted chambers and rock passages, a slightly odd mixture of the medieval and the cosy. The views from most of the curiously shaped rooms are superb, and the rooms themselves contain some fine furniture chosen by Lutyens and Hudson, mainly 17th-century English and Flemish oak. One piece, the oval dining table, was designed by Lutyens. The castle is certainly romantic, but it seems that not everyone found it comfortable, and some of Mr Hudson's house guests complained of the intolerable cold.

☎ Berwick (0289) 89244

13 m SE of Berwick-upon-Tweed on A1 turn E at West Mains Inn to Holy Island

NU 1341 (OS 75)

Open Apr (1-16 W, S, Su) to end Sept daily exc F (but inc Good Fri) 1100-1700; Oct S, Su 1400-1700

♿ (limited) 🅿 🏠 ♿ ⊼ ✕ ● (no flash) NT

Norham Castle

near Berwick, Northumberland

Norham, overlooking the river Tweed, guarded England's border with Scotland and was therefore in the front line during the repeated Anglo Scottish quarrels – border raids and declared and undeclared wars – that for centuries plagued the North. It was part of the Palatinate of Durham, a semi independent principality ruled by the bishops of Durham. One of these Ranulf Flambard, built the first castle at Norham from about 1121, probably of timber. It was twice captured by the Scots in the first twenty years of its existence, and this is no doubt why, in 1157, Bishop Hugh de Puiset began constructing a stone keep and two baileys on the site. From this time onwards Norham had an exceptionally good defensive record. It withstood a forty-day siege in 1215, twice baffled Robert the Bruce's protracted attempts to capture it, and only succumbed in 1328, when the Scots took the castle by storm. It saw a good deal of action during the Wars of the Roses, but was unable to resist the artillery brought up by the Scots during the war of 1513 which was said to have included the famous 'Mons Meg', now at Edinburgh Castle. Much repair work was done immediately afterwards and gunports were installed, but Norham's military career proved to be over, and the castle steadily deteriorated from the middle of the 16th century. Thanks to its various vicissitudes, Norham was patched, rebuilt and added to over the centuries, and most of the more substantial present-day remains date from the 16th century.

☎ (028 982) 329

5 m SW of Berwick-upon-Tweed on A698, turn W

NT 9047 (OS 74)

Standard English Heritage opening hours

♿ (limited access) 🚻 D (on lead, grounds only)

♣ ◆ ♨ EH

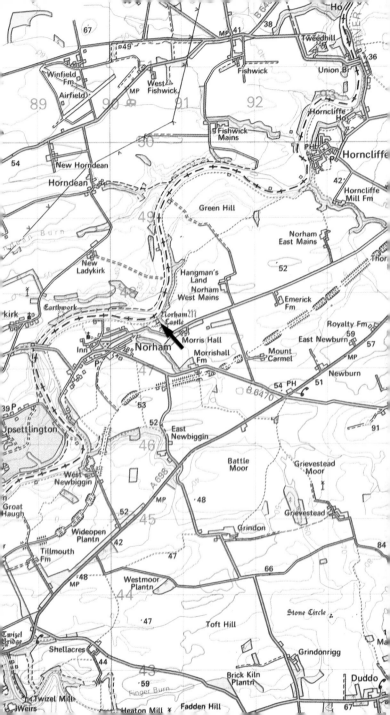

Warkworth Castle

Warkworth, Northumberland

Warkworth presents a fine and dramatic sight, perched on its mound above the town and overlooking the winding River Coquet on the other side. Though small, it has played a major part in England's history. There was almost certainly a Saxon stronghold on the site, and the basic layout of today's castle was established as early as the 12th century. King John stayed here in 1214, by which time it had become an important military base complete with walls, gatehouse, hall and chapel, and in 1332 his great-great-grandson Edward III sold it to Henry, 2nd Lord Percy of Alnwick. The Percy lords improved, enlarged and strengthened it, turning the keep into a small palace and building the tower known as the 'Grey Mare's Tail'. The 'lion tower', which covers the entrance to the hall, is named after the Percy lion carved on the central boss of its vault. The 3rd Lord Percy, a renowned soldier, was created Earl of Northumberland by Richard II, and he and his son Harry 'Hotspur' first supported and then conspired against Henry IV. The conspiracy was hatched within the castle walls, and in 1405 Henry besieged and took Warkworth, giving it, to his brother John, later Duke of Bedford. In 1416 Henry Percy, son of Hotspur, was pardoned and restored to his lands, and thereafter Percys came and went, making alterations and additions to the castle throughout the 14th and 15th centuries. In 1572 Sir Thomas Percy was beheaded for his part in the 'Rising of the North' against Elizabeth I, and the castle finally declined and fell into decay.

☎ Alnmouth (0665) 711423

10 m SE of Alnwick on A1068

NU 2405 (OS 81)

Open daily throughout year; Mar to Oct 0930-1830
Oct to Mar 0930-1600 (Su 1400-1600)

🅿 WC 🚹 (limited access) 🚻 D (on lead, grounds only) ♣ ◆ ✖ EH

Newcastle Castle

Newcastle upon Tyne, Tyne and Wear

William the Conqueror's son Robert built a New Castle on a bluff overlooking the river Tyne in about 1080, following the example of the Romans, but nothing now remains of Robert's earthwork and timber fortress. Between 1172 and 1177 Henry II built the rectangular keep, which is the main surviving feature of the castle apart from the rather later gatehouse. The same man, a mason or engineer named Maurice, seems to have built both Newcastle and Dover Castles, incorporating certain unusual features: the entrance, for example, is on the second floor, not the first, via stairs in an otherwise conventional forebuilding occupying the entire east side. The keep remains largely intact, though the roof and battlements are modern. Apart from the main rooms on each floor there are a number of rooms and stairways cleverly built into the thickness of the wall. The four corner turrets provide a minor mystery – three are square, but one is, for no apparent reason, multi-angled; the turret may have served as a platform for special machinery, perhaps a catapult or some other form of 'artillery'. Black Gate, added by Henry III from 1247, is a gatehouse linked by walls to the old gatehouse to make a barbican-like fortification for the main entrance. By the mid-14th-century the castle was mainly being used as a prison. Black Gate now has the distinction of being the world's only bagpipe museum.

☎ Newcastle upon Tyne (0632) 327938

In centre of Newcastle off A69

NZ 2564 (OS 88)

Open May to end Oct M-S 0930-1730, Su 1100-1730. Nov to end Apr closes 1630

⊖ ☷ D ♨

Tynemouth Castle

near Newcastle upon Tyne, Tyne and Wear

Tynemouth Castle and Priory, set in the centre of the little Northumbrian seaside resort, is an interesting example of a fortified monastery. The first foundation was destroyed by the Danes in 875. The second (11th-century) foundation was short-lived: the monks quarrelled with Robert de Mowbray, the Earl of Northumberland, who threw them out and in about 1090 invited the monks of St Albans to colonise the site. Tynemouth's history as a 'castle' began in 1296, when Edward I licensed the prior to fortify the monastery; and the fortifications were still regarded as important enough to rebuild in the 1380s. The site was well-suited to the purpose: 'Our house is confined to the top of a high rock, and is surrounded by the sea on every side but one,' wrote one of the monks in a letter back to St Albans; and the sea itself was treacherous, with fearsome rocks – the evilly named Black Middens – ready to wreck unwary marauders. The ruined 14th-century gatehouse is still standing; the rest of the monastery has been reduced to foundations except for the church. After the Dissolution of the Monasteries the gatehouse was converted into a royal castle and integrated into the coastal defence system. It was twice captured in the Civil War period.

7 m E of Newcastle upon Tyne

NZ 3769 (OS 88)

Open daily am and pm (Oct to March Su pm only)

⊖ WC ♿ ☷ D (on lead, grounds only)
♣ ◆ ♨ EH

Bolton Castle

Castle Bolton, North Yorkshire

Bolton Castle, with its massive towers brooding over Wensleydale, is still an awesome sight. It was built for Richard de Scrope, who was granted a licence by King Richard II in 1379 but seems to have started building several years before, employing a mason named John Lewyn. Despite its fearsome appearance, Bolton was typical of the late 14th-century tendency to give as much weight to domestic comfort as to military considerations. Like the minimally later Bodiam, in East Sussex, it is essentially a rectangular multi-roomed house, built round a courtyard and equipped with powerful corner towers; in northern style, these are rectangular, not round as Bodiam. There are turrets halfway along the north and south walls, and the original entrance on the east wall was through an arched passage protected by a portcullis at each end. From the courtyard only four doorways led into any part of the castle, and each of these was also protected by a portcullis. The ground floor was given over to stores, stables and other service functions, while the first and second floors housed the hall, kitchens and many other rooms. However, security was taken seriously: the entire south-east corner of Bolton could be sealed off to create a castle within a castle, complete with its own hall, kitchens and other functions. In 1568-69 Bolton served as a prison for Mary, Queen of Scots. It was slighted by Parliament during the English Civil War, but the present-day castle is well preserved.

☎ Wensleydale (0969) 23408

10 m S of Richmond on A6108, turn SW

SE 0391 (OS 98)

Open T-Su and Bank Hol M am and pm

🅿 WC ⊟ (by appt) D 🐾 ◆ ⚕

Helmsley Castle

Helmsley, North Yorkshire

Huge and ruinous, this castle stands at the edge of the town of Helmsley, on a little spur in the valley of the river Rye. It was once a formidable place, set within two massive rings of banks and ditches; the entrances were protected by barbicans to the north and south, behind which bridges led to strong gateways set in a curtain wall defended by a round tower at each of its angles. In the middle of the east wall lay the keep, built with one round side (that is, D-shaped); it is still the focus of the scene, for although only one (straight) side is now left, this stands to its full height in maimed grandeur, its turrets both intact. Other parts that survive are the square west tower and a range of gutted domestic buildings adjoining it, and also the south barbican. Helmsley may go back to the early 12th century, when Walter d'Espec was the local lord. But the earliest surviving parts – keep, towers, gatehouses and curtain wall – were put up by Robert de Roos in about 1200; the barbicans (and possibly the earthworks) were added in the 13th century, the keep was heightened and a great hall constructed during the 14th century, and in the Tudor period the domestic buildings were refurbished and given glass windows. The castle was slighted during the Civil War, when the keep lost its round side. It was owned by the Dukes of Buckingham until 1689, when the banker Sir Charles Duncombe bought the estate.

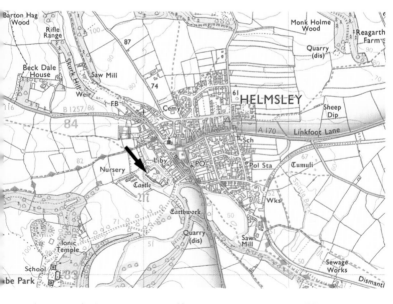

☎ Helmsley (0439) 70442

In town centre, 20 m N of York

SE 6183 (OS 100)

Open daily am and pm (Su pm only, Oct to March)

♿ P 🚻 D (on lead, grounds only) ♣ ♦ ⚒ EH

Knaresborough Castle

Knaresborough, North Yorkshire

The ruins of Knaresborough Castle stand high above the river Nidd. There may have been a castle here soon after the Conquest, when Serlo de Burg became the local lord. However, the most famous – or notorious – occupant of Knaresborough was Sir Hugh de Morville, one of the four assassins of Archbishop Thomas Becket. All the significant remains are much later, dating mainly from the early 14th century. Fragments of the towered curtain wall survive, but easily the most interesting feature is the keep, a rectangular building four storeys high (including the basement) and standing at the point where the inner and outer baileys met. It measures 64 by 52 foot and has two chamfered north corners which make it, properly speaking, an irregular hexagon in plan. The entrance to the keep is in the basement, reached by a set of steps down from the bailey. The ground floor contained the kitchen, but if the first floor was a hall – as we should expect – it must later have been converted to some other use, for there are two large doorways in it that suggest some more martial function. One faces south on to the inner bailey, the other east on to the outer bailey; both doorways now lead nowhere but must once have been linked to the baileys below by bridges of some kind. Like other English castles, Knaresborough was captured by the Parliamentarians during the Civil War and slighted to destroy its military capabilities. The castle grounds are now part of a park, and house the Old Courthouse Museum.

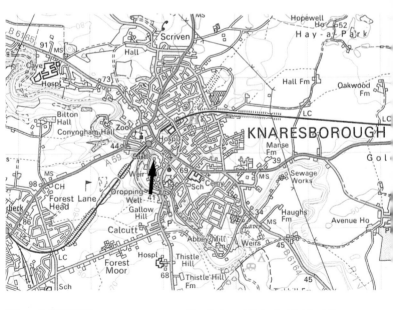

☎ Harrogate (0423) 503340

On W outskirts of Knaresborough

SE 3456 (OS 104)

Open Easter, early Spring Bank Hol, then late Spring Bank Hol to Sept daily am and pm

⊖ P WC ⌖ (limited access) ⊟ (by appt) D (grounds only) ♣ ◆ ⚕ ⚔

Middleham Castle

Middleham, near Leyburn, North Yorkshire

The first castle at Middleham, guarding the road from Richmond to Skipton, was a motte-and-bailey earthwork that stands about 500 yards south-west of the present remains. It was probably built by Alan the Red, a Breton follower of William the Conqueror, who was granted the land in 1069. The first stone castle originated with a keep constructed by Robert Fitz Ralph in about 1170. It was one of the largest in England (105 by 78 foot), and although a roofless and floorless shell it is still the chief feature of the site; the 12th- and 13th-century walls and towers have largely gone, and the outer bailey has been swamped by an expanding Middleham town, leaving the inner bailey and the ruins of some 14th- and 15th-century domestic quarters as the only other significant remains. A doorway on the first floor of the keep indicates that, as was usual, it was entered at that level by stairs enclosed by a forebuilding, though these have long since disappeared. The main living rooms were sited on the first floor. Two turrets contained the garderobes (lavatories). Middleham formed part of the extensive lands of the 'Kingmaker' Earl of Warwick, Richard Neville, until he was killed fighting for the Lancastrians at the battle of Barnet (1571). Via the (Yorkist) Crown it passed to Richard of Gloucester, later the notorious Richard III, and became (Tudor) Crown property after his defeat at Bosworth Field in 1485.

☎ Wensleydale (0969) 23899

In town centre, 24 m NW of Ripon on A6108

SE 1287 (OS 99)

Open daily am and pm (Su pm only)

🚲 ◆ ♨ EH

Pickering Castle

Pickering, North Yorkshire

The ruins of Pickering Castle stand on the edge of the North Yorkshire moors. Although it was a royal castle, its early history is obscure; but there was certainly a stone castle on the present site by the 12th century. The high, steep motte carries a round shell keep of the early 13th century, but this probably replaced or renewed an earlier structure. Not much remains of this, the 'king's tower', though in one place the wall reaches the height of the rampart walk. The buildings that must once have stood inside the keep have long since vanished, but there are a variety of remains in the inner bailey, including the foundations of the early 12th-century hall and the 14th-century new hall built for Thomas of Lancaster. The 12th-century inner bailey wall has an entrance protected on its right hand side by Coleman Tower; this was two storeys high, with the entrance on the first floor, and evidently served as a prison. The wall of the outer bailey, to the south, is much better preserved. It was put up in the 1320s to strengthen the defences of the area after the Scots had invaded and effectively held it to ransom, and is protected by three towers: Rosamund's Tower, equipped with a postern gate (emergency exit), Diate Hill Tower and Mill Tower.

☎ Pickering (0751) 74989

In N outskirts of Pickering

SE 7984 (OS 100)

Open standard English Heritage opening hours, including Su am

⊖ 🅿 ♿ 🚲 D (on lead, grounds only) ♣ ◆ ♨ EH

Richmond Castle

Richmond, North Yorkshire

In spite of its formidable appearance and dramatic cliff-top site above the River Swale, the history of Richmond Castle has been a quiet one, and it never saw military action. Its ruin was due to gradual neglect from the 16th century when, no longer serving any military purpose, it was simply left to decay. However, it is an interesting castle, and has some very early remains. Before the Conquest, the site belonged to Edwin, Earl of Mercia, but it was granted to Alan the Red of Brittany in about 1080, and he was responsible for the early building works, the first of which were the enormously thick curtain walls, triangular in plan to follow the oddly-shaped site. Scolland's hall, the hall block of the castle situated in a corner of the courtyard, was built soon after, and is believed to be the oldest castle hall in Britain. Before the keep itself was built, this would have served a similar purpose, with the ground floor used for storage and possibly as a servants' hall. The hall itself was at first-floor level, approached by a flight of steps, with the solar, or withdrawing room, at the eastern end. Adjoining the building, in an extension of the curtain wall, is the gold tower, which contained garderobes (lavatories). The great keep, Richmond's dominant feature, was added about a century later, possibly by Henry II, and was built as an upwards extension of the existing gatehouse, retaining the fine 11th-century archway. It is extremely well preserved, with all its walls intact, and the top provides a fine view of the town and countryside.

☎ Richmond (0748) 2493

In centre of Richmond on N bank of River Swale

NZ 1700 (OS 92)

Open daily throughout year; Mar to Oct 0930-1830
Nov to Feb 0930-1600 (Su 1400-1600)

♿ WC 🅰 ♿ 🚻 D (on lead, grounds only)
♣ ♦ ♿ EH

Scarborough Castle

Scarborough, North Yorkshire

The advantages of this superb site, on a headland protected by rugged cliffs to the east and north-east, were known long before the Normans arrived. There was an Iron Age settlement here, and remains of a Roman signal station are still in evidence, mingled with those of no less than three medieval chapels of varying dates. Scarborough itself was named from a Viking chief, Scarthi, who built a fortress (burh) on the headland – Scarthi's burh. The first Norman castle was built by William le Gros, Earl of Albermarle and Holderness, in about 1130. Parts of Le Gros' curtain wall can still be seen, but the present keep dates from 1158 onwards; it was badly damaged in the Civil War siege of 1645. During the 13th century the castle was greatly strengthened by the construction of a barbican, a fortified bridge and new curtain walls. The curtain walls are still impressively high and the barbican, with its double-towered entrance and wall towers, is a fortress in itself. Scarborough Castle's history has been dramatic; it includes a siege in which Edward II's unpopular favourite, Piers Gaveston, surrendered on terms to the unruly barons, only to be executed straight away; an attempted coup in 1557 by Thomas Stafford, who seized the castle but failed to raise the country against Queen ('Bloody') Mary; and two long Civil War sieges. The last 'action' was seen when German battleships shelled Scarborough in August 1914.

☎ Scarborough (0723) 72451

To the E of town centre

TA 0589 (OS 101)

Open daily am and pm (Oct to Mar Su pm only)

♿ WC 🅰 🚻 D (on lead, grounds only) ♣ ◆

♨ EH

198

Skipton Castle

Skipton, North Yorkshire

The great round towers of the castle's main gate rise at the end of the sloping high street to dominate the small market town, and the castle itself lies slightly behind. The castle was granted to Robert de Clifford in 1284, and he began a family tenure which was to be unbroken for fourteen generations, rebuilding the castle before his death at Bannockburn in 1314. The Cliffords, at one time castellans of the Castle of York, and builders of Clifford's Tower, were intensely loyal to the Crown and it is fitting that Skipton Castle should have been the last northern stronghold to capitulate to the Parliamentary forces. It held out for three years until December 1645, and was then slighted (had its defences destroyed). Its excellent condition today is largely due to Lady Anne Clifford, the last of the line, who restored it, together with several other castles. A tablet over the entrance records her work, which was completed in 1658. The castle is D-shaped, with six round towers on the curve, and the straight edge along the cliff above the river. The delightful inner courtyard with a yew tree in the centre, known as the conduit court, owes much of its character to a rebuilding carried out about 1500, but on its north side are the original domestic buildings of about 1300, all of which are open to the public. The range of buildings to the right of the castle, now a self-contained residence and not open to the public, was built as an extension to the castle in 1535 on the marriage of Henry Clifford to Eleanor Brandon.

☎ Skipton (0756) 2442

In centre of Skipton

SD 9951 (OS 103)

Open throughout the year M-S 1000-1800, Su 1400-1800 (or dusk if earlier). Closed Good Fri and 25 Dec

⊖ P (nearby) WC ☐ D (on lead) ◆ ⚹ (available in foreign languages) ⚹ (by appt for parties)

York Castle: Clifford's Tower

York, North Yorkshire

This sturdy ruined tower, open to the sky, is a friendly and familiar sight in its present setting (a public park in the city); but its past history was exciting and often grim. It was originally one of two motte-and-bailey castles built by William the Conqueror to control the river Ouse. Both were destroyed by Danish raiders in 1069, and only the timber castle on the present site was rebuilt. In 1190 it burned down – or was burned down – along with the Jews of York, who had taken refuge in it from a mob on the rampage. The present stone structure dates from about 1250 and is really a keep built in a very rare quatrefoil shape (that is, as four overlapping circles). It was a busy royal headquarters during the Scottish wars of the early 14th century, and in 1322, when Edward II defeated the home-grown baronial opposition, Roger de Clifford and other leaders were hanged in chains from the walls; the name Clifford's Tower derives from this event, though it was adopted much later. The castle was bombarded during the Civil War and burned in 1684 before going into a gentle decline. The motte on which it stands was originally surrounded by a moat (now filled in) that separated it from the bailey. There are remains of the bailey wall and two towers at the southern end of the site, behind the 18th-century building that now houses the Castle Museum.

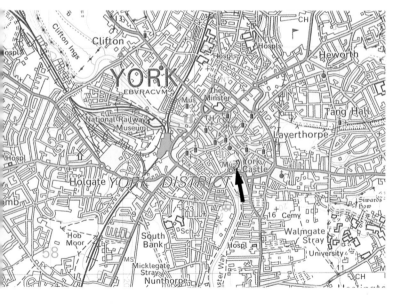

☎ York (0904) 646940

In centre of York

SE 6052 (OS 105)

Open mid Mar to mid Oct daily 0930-1830; mid Oct to mid Mar M-S 0930-1600, Su 1400-1600

⊖ 🅿 🚻 (by appt) ♣ ◆ ♨ EH

Conisbrough Castle

Conisbrough, South Yorkshire

The castle is ruined, but it is still an impressive sight, and the keep itself is an extremely unusual construction. It was built about 1180 by Hamelin Plantagenet, the half-brother of Henry II, at about the same time as the great square keep of Dover Castle was being built, and is one of the first circular keeps in Britain. A further unusual feature is the six massive wedge-shaped buttresses which support it and rise above roof level as turrets. These appear to serve no practical purpose, as all except one, which has a small chapel set into it, are solid, but they must have provided an effective defence as not only does the keep still stand, but the stonework is extremely well preserved. The base of the keep is splayed for extra strength, and the semi-circular bailey surrounding it on three sides is enclosed by a high curtain wall, also splayed at the base and reinforced by solid towers. Inside the walls, the foundations of living quarters can be seen in the grass, but nothing is standing except the keep. Access is at first-floor level via a modern flight of steps, and below is a vaulted basement reached only from above. There were originally four storeys above this, though all the floors have now gone, and they are reached by a stone stairway in the thickness of the walls. The third and fourth storeys were evidently the main living rooms, and the fireplaces can still be seen. The upper room gives into the little chapel, which is partly in the thickness of the wall and partly in the buttress behind it.

☎ Mexborough (0709) 863329

In centre of Conisbrough

SK 5198 (OS 111)

Open daily: Mar to Oct 0930-1830 (Su 1400-1830), Oct to Mar 0930-1600 (Su 1400-1600)

⊖ 🅿 🖾 (limited access) 🚻 D (on lead, grounds only) ♠ ✄ EH

Pontefract Castle

Pontefract, West Yorkshire

Once a very powerful fortress that dominated the town from the east, Pontefract Castle now consists of some rather unimpressive remains in a public park. The keep, known as the Round Tower, was originally quatrefoil in plan and circular inside; it dates from the mid-13th century, and stood at the south-west corner of the 11th-century motte. Other remains include parts of the curtain wall and the postern gate of the Piper Tower (both 12th century), the foundations of the chapel and, beyond the inner bailey, the rectangular Swillington Tower. The outer bailey has been overrun by the town. However, it is not the remains themselves but their historical associations that stir the imagination. The first Pontefract Castle was built by Ilbert de Lacy in the late 11th century. In 1311 it passed to Thomas, Earl of Lancaster, who was the cousin of Edward II and for long periods the most powerful man in the kingdom; eventually Edward shook free of his tutelage, and in 1322 captured him and had him beheaded at Pontefract. Edward was later forced to abdicate and was murdered, a fate that also overtook Richard II; he was imprisoned, and almost certainly killed, at Pontefract Castle, which belonged to the usurping Henry Bolingbroke (Henry IV). The castle's history culminated in the sieges of 1644 and 1648, when it was fiercely contested between Royalists and Parliamentarians. When the Royalists finally surrendered it, Parliament ordered it to be slighted and it was never rebuilt.

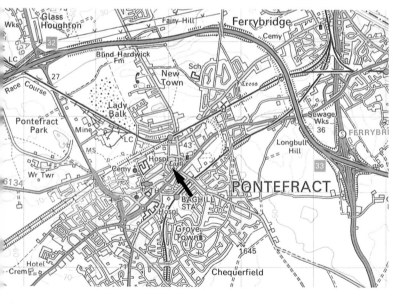

In town centre

SE 4622 (OS 105)

Open daily am and pm; Su pm only

Scotland

Wick

WESTERN
ISLES

Dunrobin Castle

Dunvegan
Castle

HIGHLAND

Cawdor Castle

Inverness

Balvenie Castle

Huntly Castle

GRAMPIAN

Eilean Donan Castle

Urquhart Castle

Kildrummy Castle

Craigievar Castle

Aberdee

Drum Castle

Fort William

Braemar
Castle

Crathes
Castle

Muchalls Cas

Dunnottar Cas

Blair Castle

Edzell
Castle

Glamis Castle

TAYSIDE

Dundee

Claypotts Castle

Huntingtower
Castle

Perth

Earlshall Castle

St Andrews Castle

Inveraray
Castle

Doune Castle

Castle
Campbell

Loch Leven
Castle

CENTRAL

Stirling
Castle

Stirling

FIFE

Blackness Castle

Lauriston Castle

Tantallon
Castle

Edinburgh Castle

Rothesay Castle

Edinburgh

Craigmillar Castle

Glasgow

LOTHIAN

Thirlestane
Castle

STRATHCLYDE

Neidpath Castle

Floors Castle

Brodick
Castle

BORDERS

Ayr

Hawick

Culzean Castle

Drumlanrig Castle

Hermitage
Castle

NORTHUMBER
LAND

DUMFRIES

Dumfries

&

Caerlaverock
Castle

Newcastle-
upon-Tyne

GALLOWAY

Threave Castle

Carlisle

CUMBRIA

DURHAM

Floors Castle

Kelso, Borders

Floors – a romantic-baronial transformation act of the Victorian age – is a masterpiece of architectural imagination and space-handling. Everything that the Edinburgh architect W. H. Playfair added to the regular Georgian central block begun in 1721 for the 1st Duke of Roxburghe works admirably – if theatrically. The array of turrets on the wings, with their Tudor caps, even outdo Hampton Court, while their layout to the north gives amplitude to the Vanbrugh-like grandeur of the conception. The underlying 18th-century building (which can be seen as it was in 1809 in a painting in the sitting room) can be sensed in the arrangement of the rooms. Much of the furnishing is of that time, and a fine collection of French pieces and tapestries was brought over from New York by the American bride of the 8th Duke. One object inside which is in keeping with the supposed period of Playfair's exterior is a fine early-16th-century Brussels tapestry of Pentecost. The celebrated Roxburghe library, which the 3rd Duke had assembled, had to be sold in 1813 by the 5th Duke to meet the costs of a lawsuit settled by the House of Lords (there had been rival claimants to the title). The purchasers, all wealthy peers, formed the Roxburghe Club to issue their newly acquired treasures to each other in facsimile form, and in doing so created another kind of collector's item for the future. The gardens, to the west of the castle, are notable for carnations.

☎ Kelso (0573) 23333

1 m NW of Kelso on A6089

NT 7134 (OS 74)

Open Easter Su, M and early May to late Sept Su-Th, also F in July and Aug 1030-1730

P WC ♿ D (on lead, grounds only)
(by appt)

Hermitage Castle

Liddlesdale, Borders

This large and well-preserved castle stands on a low bluff looking down on Hermitage Water. In its day it was fiercely fought over between Scots and English, and played a significant part in the turbulent internal politics of Scotland. There was a castle here in 1296, and fragments of its masonry appear to have been incorporated in the centre of the present building. Among the earliest Scottish occupants were the de Soulis, one of whom was so detested that rebellious peasants wrapped him in lead and boiled him alive in a cauldron. In 1338 the castle was captured from the English by Sir William Douglas. Douglas's widow married into the Dacre family, who only held the castle until 1365, but put up the earliest substantial building that survives, an oblong block around a small open courtyard. Then the Douglases returned for well over a century, and during that time gave Hermitage Castle its most important feature – a keep or tower house superimposed on the 14th-century building. In 1492 the Douglases, whom the King distrusted, were compelled to exchange their sensitive Border castle for Bothwell Castle on the Clyde; however, the new occupants, the Earls of Bothwell, proved hardly less troublesome. With the union of the English and Scottish crowns, Hermitage lost its importance and was neglected until the early 19th century, when extensive restoration was undertaken.

21 m S of Hawick on B6399, turn W

Open daily am and pm (Su pm only)

NY 4996 (OS 79)

Neidpath Castle

near Peebles, Borders

About a mile from Peebles stands the massive tower of Neidpath Castle, a fortified house on the banks of the river Tweed. Most of the present tower seems to be no older than the 15th century, but there was probably a fortress here during the 13th and 14th centuries, when Neidpath was owned by a great Border family, the Frasers; their Norman origin is recalled by the symbolic strawberries (in French, *fraises*) carved over the courtyard gateway. The last of the Frasers in the male line was Sir Simon, famous for having defeated the English three times in one day on Roslin Moor in 1302. His daughter married one of the Hays of Yester, and it was Sir William Hay who built most of the present castle in the early 15th century; it was altered and added to in the 17th century, when the attic and rectangular turrets replaced the flat roof surrounded by a parapet. Now Neidpath is essentially a tall, imposing block consisting of five storeys and an attic, and with walls up to 10 foot thick. It is built in an L-shape; some domestic buildings, now ruinous, completed a grouping round a courtyard. In 1650, when Oliver Cromwell's army invaded Scotland, Lord Yester conducted an honourably long defence at Neidpath before capitulating. The house was purchased by the Duke of Queensberry in 1686 for his son, the Earl of March, and has remained in the family ever since, currently being owned by the Lord Wemyss Trust.

☎ Aberlady (087 57) 201

1 m W of Peebles on A72

NT 2340 (OS 73)

Open mid-Apr to mid-Oct daily 1000-1300, 1400-1800 (Su 1300-1800 only)

⊖ (1 mile) 🅿 WC 🚻 🍴 (by appt) 🌿 ● (no flash)

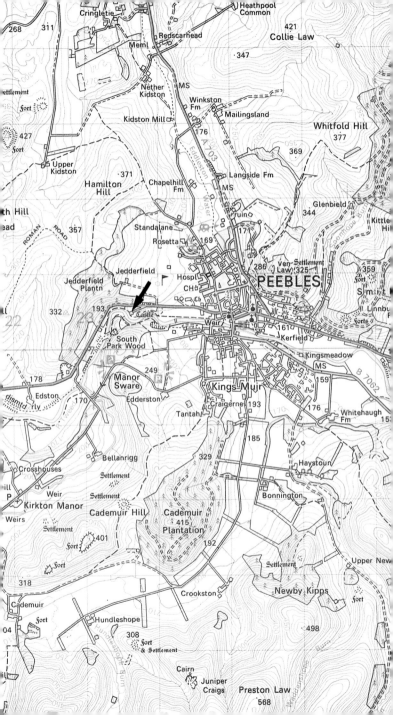

Thirlestane Castle

Lauder, Borders

Thirlestane Castle, home since 1228 of the Maitlands, Earls and Dukes of Lauderdale, is the product of three periods of building, the 1590s, the 1670s and the 1840s. The castle, which was built on the site of an old fort in 1590 by Chancellor Maitland, is an oblong block between four huge corner towers, with smaller stair turrets on the north and south sides. The Renaissance west front, the first work of Sir William Bruce, was built for the Duke of Lauderdale following his marriage to the Countess of Dysart in 1672, and the castle was extensively remodelled inside at the same time. The 19th-century building work, in the Scottish baronial style, extended the west front in both directions, added conical roofs to the towers and raised the central tower, giving the castle its fine turretted silhouette. The building was in a state of serious disrepair when the present owner succeeded in 1972, but a major rescue operation was put under way from 1978 to 1982. The most remarkable feature of the interior is the rich Baroque plasterwork, particularly the ceilings in the 17th-century state rooms. These amazing *tours de force*, with their deeply modelled wreaths and garlands of leaves and flowers hanging suspended just below, were the work of an English plasterer, George Dunsterfield, who worked at Thirlestane continuously for two years from 1674. Most of the furniture made for the house during the 17th-century remodelling was removed to Ham House, which the Duchess had recently inherited, but some good pieces remain.

☎ Lauder (05782) 254/430

3 m E of Lauder on A697

NT 5647 (OS 73)

Open Easter Su, M May, June and Sept W, Th and Su; Jul and Aug daily exc S 1400-1700

🅿 WC 🖶 D ♣ 🍴 🎋 ◆ ⚘ 🕴 ●

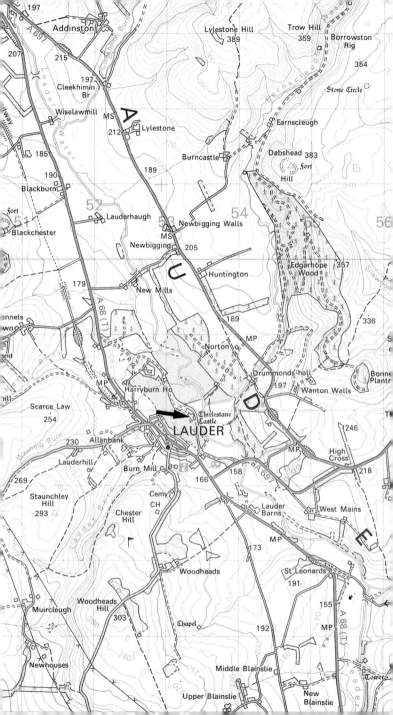

Castle Campbell

Dollar, Central

One of the most spectacularly sited of all British castles, Castle Campbell stands on a spur of the Ochil Hills that rises above the lovely Dollar Glen, offering wonderful views of the Forth Valley. The site passed from the Stewarts to the Campbells of Argyll, and the castle was probably begun by Colin Campbell, who became one of the outstanding political leaders of his time and was rewarded for his services by being created Earl of Argyll. The late 15th-century tower is still the dominant feature of Castle Gloom – or, as the Earl renamed it (by Act of Parliament), Castle Campbell. It was a strong, four-storey fortified house rising some 60 foot to an overhanging parapet. The tower and a range of lower buildings now form a group round a courtyard, bearing witness to the many alterations and additions made over the centuries. They are often luxurious or of very high-quality workmanship, in keeping with the great role the Argyll Campbells continued to play in Scottish history. During the period of the Covenant and English Commonwealth, Castle Campbell was besieged (1645) by supporters of the Royalist Montrose and burned (1654) by the Cromwellian General Monk; but the extent of the damage inflicted seems questionable, since English troops were garrisoned at the castle shortly afterwards. It continued to belong to the Dukes of Argyll until the early 19th century, by which time it was already in an advanced state of decay.

1 m N of Dollar on road to Castleton

NS 9699 (OS 57)

Open Apr to Sept M-S 0930-1900, Su 1400-1900;
Oct to end Mar 0930-1600, Su 1400-1600

Doune Castle

Doune, Central

Great care has been taken to restore the magnificent ruined stronghold of Doune, which stands on the banks of the river Teith and once controlled the main route into the Highlands from Edinburgh and the south. Its principal features are the two large and powerful keeps, the taller of which rises to a height of 95 foot. They are linked by a long, two-storeyed building, forming the north side of a quadrangle; the other sides consist of walls 40 foot high. The castle dates back at least to the late 14th century, when it was the residence of Robert Stewart, Duke of Albany and Regent of Scotland. In 1425 his son was beheaded on the orders of James I, who confiscated Doune. It remained a royal property for over a century, serving variously as a prison and a residence, especially for the widowed queens of Scotland. The Stewarts reoccupied Doune, first as custodians and later (1570) as lords; and not long afterwards they were created Earls of Moray. The castle escaped largely unscathed from the Civil War period and the Jacobite risings, though Bonnie Prince Charlie's men used it for a time to house prisoners of war. Nevertheless Doune was roofless and ruinous by the late 18th century. Restoration began in the 1880s, and a number of interesting apartments may now be inspected. A short distance away another Earl of Moray's works, the Doune Motor Museum, is open to visitors.

SE of Doune off A820

NN 7301 (OS 57)

Open 1st Apr to 30th Sept M-S 0930-1900, Su 1400-1900; 1st Oct to 31st Mar M-W, S 0930-1600, Su 1400-1600

⊖ 🅿 🚽 D (not in house) ♠ ⛩ ◆ ✄

Stirling Castle

Upper Castle Hill, Stirling, Central

Stirling, built on a high and narrow ridge of basalt at the gateway of the Scottish Highlands, was a more important stronghold even than Edinburgh. During the Wars of Independence it was constantly changing hands. The Scots managed to hold it from 1299 to 1304, the year of a great siege by Edward I; the English then held it for ten years, yielding it back to the Scots after their victory at Bannockburn in 1314. The castle that withstood so much was a timber and earthwork construction, which has now entirely disappeared: it was rebuilt in stone, the earliest parts now standing dating from the 15th century. It changed its character too, under the Stuart dynasty, becoming no longer a grim fortress but a splendid royal palace with ornamental gardens. Today's buildings reflect those days of glory. The great hall, built for James III (r. 1460-88) and designed by Robert Cochrane, was one of the first and finest 15th-century Renaissance buildings anywhere in Britain. The curtain wall and towers probably date from the same period; the great palace block with its lovely carved detail was built by James IV (r. 1488-1513) and continued by his son, and James VI rebuilt the royal chapel about 1594. James VI was baptised at Stirling, as was his son, Prince Frederick Henry, but after 1603 the court moved to England and the castle was more or less abandoned, though kept in readiness. It was besieged by General Monk in 1651 and again – ineffectively – by Bonnie Prince Charlie in 1745.

In the centre of Stirling

NS 7994 (OS 57)

Open Apr to end Sept M-S 0930-1800, Su 1030-1730; Oct to end Mar M-S 0930-1700, Su 1230-1620

⊖ P WC ⌂ ♣ ⬤ ☂ ◆ ⚹ Ⱦ

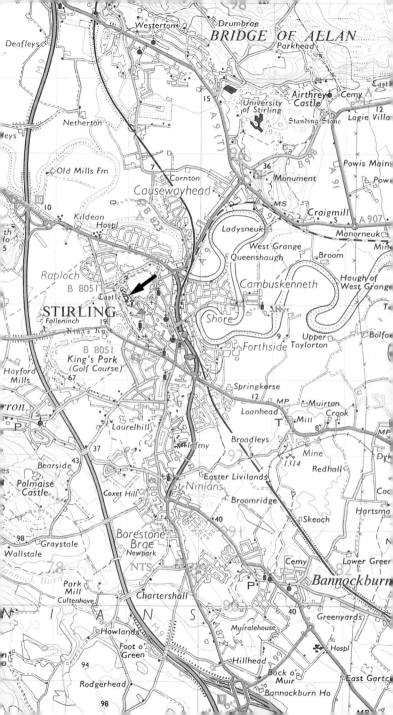

Caerlaverock Castle

Caerlaverock, near Dumfries, Dumfries & Galloway

The extraordinary triangular castle, now a ruin, was the seat of the important Maxwell family for many centuries, and was built towards the end of the 13th century. Its formidable defences have seen much use, and it was besieged by Edward I very early in its history, surrendered and was held by the English for twelve years. After this it deteriorated for a time, but was rebuilt and much strengthened in the 15th century, and the great gatehouse was altered internally to make it residential. Towards the end of the 16th century gunports were put in, and these were put to the test in 1640 when the castle held out for three months against the Covenanters. Lord Nithsdale, the 'philosopher-earl', who held the castle for the King, had earlier been responsible for the last alterations to the building when he put up a three-storey residential block in the Classical Renaissance style inside the walls. Caerlaverock is the only triangular castle in Britain, but its plan is quite simple. It is shaped like a shield, its three huge curtain walls covered by the massive twin-towered gatehouse at one corner and angle towers in the other two. It was surrounded by an inner moat, with earth ramparts around this and then another moat with more ramparts, so that attackers had to cross two bridges before even approaching the heavily defended gatehouse.

12 m SE of Dumfries on B725 at Greenhead

NY 0265 (OS 84)

Open Apr to Sept M-S 0930-1900, Su 1400-1900;
Oct to Mar M-S 0930-1600, Su 1400-1600.
Closed F pm

🚌 D ♣ 🎍 ⚹

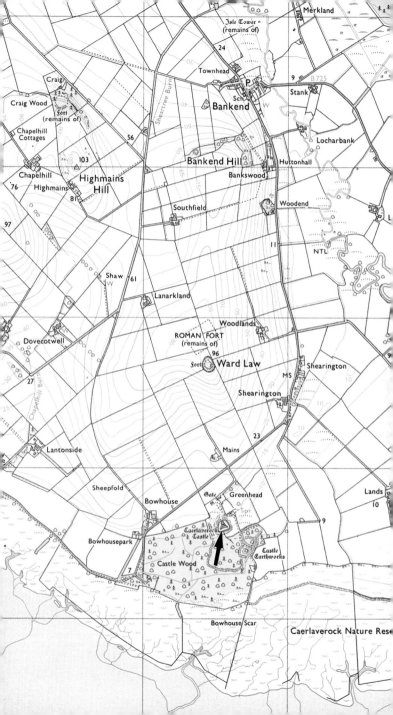

Drumlanrig Castle

near Thornhill, Dumfries & Galloway

The old castle of Drumlanrig in Nithsdale had belonged to the Douglases for over 300 years when, in the reign of Charles II, William Douglas, 3rd Earl of Queensberry, decided to build a new house. The ground plan retained the medieval notion of a moated castle. The new front – especially the flight of steps and the ornate doorway that together form the entrance – boasts Baroque decorative features, but the rest of the house consists of four solid corner towers around a four-sided courtyard, from which newel stairs lead to the upper floors through four narrow turrets. Even the barbizans on the roofs of the turrets have a belligerent air, though the large and pedimented windows below them are designed for essentially peaceful times. The visitor is likely to notice the Douglas badge carved in a variety of places: a winged heart surmounted by a crown. The explanation given for this is that Sir James, the 'Black Douglas', was entrusted with the heart of King Robert the Bruce in a silver casket at his death in 1329 and enjoined to take it on crusade in order to fulfil a royal vow; when he was fatally wounded fighting the Moors in Spain, he hurled it into the enemy with the words, 'Forward, brave heart!' The interior of Drumlanrig Castle is very rich in fine furniture and paintings. In 1810 the title passed to the 3rd Duke of Buccleuch, who possessed many treasures of the late 17th century, including a pair of Louis XIV cabinets, which are displayed here. The paintings – one a Rembrandt of 1655, *An Old Woman Reading* – are well worth the visit.

☎ Thornhill (0848) 30248

3 m N of Thornhill on A76 turn W to Drumlanrig Park

NX 8599 (OS 78)

Open Easter S, Su,M; mid Apr to June daily exc F 1330-1700; Jul and Aug daily exc F 1100-1700

⊖ (limited) 🅿 WC 🚻 (by appt) D (on lead, grounds only) ♣ ♠ 🚻 ◆ ♨ ● (no flash) 🏃 🏃

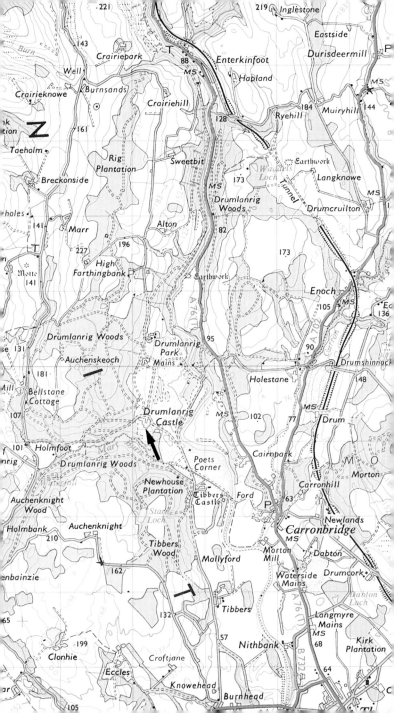

Threave Castle

near Castle Douglas, Dumfries and Galloway

The ruins of Threave Castle stand on a little island in the river Dee, a mile or so west of the town of Castle Douglas; even today the visitor arrives by rowing boat! Threave was a stronghold of the fierce and powerful Black Douglases, Earls of Nithsdale and Lords of Galloway. The castle was begun in the late 14th century by the third Earl of Douglas, Archibald the Grim; something of his nature is indicated by the fact that a granite projection at the front of the building is known as 'the gallows knob', and Archibald himself remarked with Grim humour that it 'never wanted a tassel'. The Douglas castle was a four-storey tower or keep. Under King James II (1437-60) a long and bitter struggle took place between the Crown and the Douglases, who were eventually defeated at the battle of Arkinholm in 1455. Threave became a royal castle, and some time after 1455 it was enclosed by an outer wall with round towers, and – a sign of the times – these were furnished with loopholes so that the place could be defended by firearms. However, it evidently remained important, and was given into the charge of various keepers including the Lords Maxwell, who were hereditary keepers for a time (1473-1526). Threave Castle was dismantled in 1640 after being captured by the Covenanters, but it was still fit for use over a century and a half later, when French prisoners were housed there during the Napoleonic Wars. Nearby Threave House is a National Trust property, housing the School of Practical Gardening; the famous gardens are open to the public.

3 m SW of Castle Douglas on A75, turn N

NX 7362 (OS 83)

Apr to end Oct daily 1000-1700

P WC 🅿 (limited access) 🚻 ♠ ◆ 🐕 ⚸

Earlshall Castle

Leuchars, St Andrews, Fife

The castle, which is believed to take its name from the ancient stronghold of the Earls of Fife nearby, was built in the 16th century as a fortified house rather than a castle. It is roughly on a Z-plan, with a circular tower at one end, and opposite this a platform tower commanding a sea view. This is connected to another tower by a high wall in which there is a fortified gateway bearing the arms of Sir William Bruce of Earlshall, and the third side of the courtyard (the fourth is open) is enclosed by a range of buildings added in the 17th century. The fame of Earlshall today rests on its fine restoration by Robert Lorimer in the 1890s. It was his first job; he was only 26 when he was asked to renovate the castle and create a garden, but it is one of his most successful restorations. Its finest feature is the long gallery with its magnificent coved ceiling painted with armorial devices and fabulous beasts, which Lorimer was able to save only by taking down every single piece of painted woodwork, replacing the missing bits and re-assembling the whole again. The garden, a romantic recreation of the 17th-century formal style, is totally enclosed, its walls shutting out the country beyond, so that house and garden seem to exist in their own world. The topiary work is dramatic and inventive, its highlight being a huge grass chessboard with all its pieces 'carved' in yew. The yew trees were transplanted, already shaped, from an Edinburgh garden, and are still kept in shape and cared for by the present owners of the castle.

☎ Leuchars (033 483) 205

16 m SE of Dundee on A92, E of Leuchars

NO 4621 (OS 54)

Open Easter weekend to end Sept Th-Su 1400-1800; parties by appt at other times

♿ P WC ♨ D (on lead, grounds only) ♣ ☙
⛩ ◆ ⚘ ● (not in castle) ♪

St Andrews Castle

Fife

Although St Andrews Castle is thoroughly ruinous, it has some points of intrinsic interest and is particularly rich in historical associations. It stands on a headland thrusting out into the North Sea, and is protected on the landward side by a deep moat. In its exposed position the castle has suffered from the effects of erosion. The first castle on the site was built by Roger, Bishop of St Andrews, in about 1200. It witnessed much fierce fighting and took many heavy batterings. Rebellious Scottish barons held it between 1332 and 1336 during the troubled period after the death of Robert I (Robert the Bruce); then Sir Andrew Moray captured it for the young King David II, and dismantled it. It was occupied, repaired and ruined again before 1385, when Walter Trail became Bishop of St Andrews and rebuilt it. The last moments of high drama at St Andrews occurred during the Reformation period. In March 1546 George Wishart, father of the Scottish Reformation, was burned in the town at the instigation of Cardinal Beaton, who was himself murdered in revenge two months later at the castle. The Protestants then held St Andrews Castle for more than a year until captured and deported by a French fleet that had been sent to help the Catholic party in Scotland. The most interesting visible features of present-day St Andrews Castle are the lethally cramped and dank 'Bottle Dungeon' (so called from its shape) and the underground tunnels dug by besiegers and besieged in 1547, which are now floodlit and may be visited.

NE of St Andrews, overlooking sea

NO 5116 (OS 59)

Open Apr to end Sept M-S 0930-1900, Su 1400-1900; Oct to end Mar 0930-1600, Su 1400-1600

⊖ 🄿 WC 🚻 D ♠ ⚒

Balvenie Castle

Dufftown, Grampian

One of the earliest stone castles in Scotland, Balvenie is now a substantial ruin, standing above the little town of Dufftown and the river Fiddich, high in the north-eastern 'shoulder' of Scotland. The castle existed in the 13th century, when it belonged to the powerful Comyn family, but almost all the present remains belong to the 15th and 16th centuries. By the early 15th century the property had passed to the turbulent Black Douglas earls, who proceeded to build a courtyard castle measuring 150 by 130 foot and defended by 25-foot-high curtain walls with at least two corner towers. The power of the wild and lawless Douglases was eventually broken, though in almost as lawless a fashion as it had been maintained: in 1452 James II stabbed the eighth Earl, William, in Stirling Castle, and three years later decisively defeated William's brother, James, at the battle of Arkinholm. The Douglas lands were confiscated, and soon afterwards Balvenie was given to the Stewart Earls of Atholl – for an annual rent of one red rose, payable on St John the Baptist's Day. The fourth Earl, John Stewart, demolished the south-east side of the castle and put up the present three-storey house, the Atholl building. In the early 17th century Balvenie was often raided by the Macgregors, and during the Civil War period it was briefly occupied by the Scottish Royalist leader Montrose. Apart from some complicated legal wrangles, its later history was uneventful.

1 m N of Dufftown on A941

NJ 3240 (OS 28)

Open Apr to end Sept M-S 0930-1900, Su 1400-1900; Nov to end Mar M-S 0930-1600, Su 1400-1600

🅰 (limited access) 🚏 D ♣ ♨

Braemar Castle

Braemar, Grampian

There is no mistaking the military function of the place, with its hexagonal, loopholed salients on the 18th-century pattern, its soaring and partly blind walls, its overhanging roof turrets – all suggesting a frontier blockhouse garrisoned to repel marauders at the drop of a flint-lock. And that, very largely, is what it is. Although the site is in the traditionally feud-torn province of Mar, this castle was only begun in 1628 by John Erskine, Earl of Mar, as an operational base for fighting his rivals, the Gordons, the Forbes and, above all, the Farquharsons. It was burned and gutted in the failed Jacobite uprising of 1689 and remained a ruin until after the last Jacobite uprising of 1745. Its reconstruction started in 1748 as an army post to hold down the Highlands, and this is when it acquired the defences it still has today. The French Revolutionary Wars, together with the gradual pacification of the Highlanders, led to the withdrawal of the garrison in 1797 and soon the castle was restored to domestic use – this time by the Farquharsons themselves, whose descendants still live here. The interiors conform to the defensive plans of a fort, with low-ceilinged rooms stacked round the newel staircase which connects the floors. The decoration of the rooms is now entirely domestic, and a number of interesting paintings and relics of Braemar's history are on display. The annual Braemar Highland gathering and games takes place in the castle grounds.

☎ Braemar (033 83) 219

1 m NE of Braemar on A93

NO 1592 (OS 43)

Open May to early Oct daily exc F 1000-1800

⊖ 🅿 WC 🚻 ♣ ♨ 🏸 ● (not in castle)

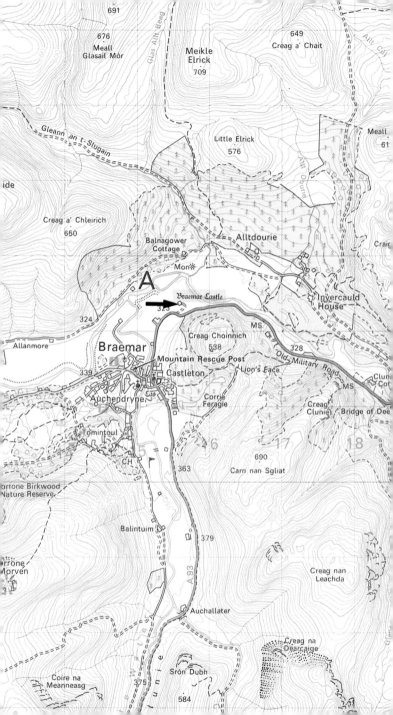

Craigievar Castle

Lumphanan, Grampian

Craigievar is one of the masterworks of Scottish architecture, a fairy-tale castle that represents the culmination of the distinctive Scottish style of fortified-house building. It was built by 'Danzig Willie' – William Forbes, brother of the Bishop of Aberdeen, between 1610 and 1626, and his descendants occupied it until it was taken over by the National Trust for Scotland in 1963. Despite appearances, the plan of Craigievar is a simple one – an L-shape with a square tower fitted into the inner angle made by the two blocks. Its visual impact derives from the way in which the exterior remains quite plain for most of its seven storeys, and then burgeons into a delightful cluster of cone-capped turrets, chimneys and little gables around the balustraded parapet of the tower. The interior in many ways resembles Muchalls Castle and is probably by the same hand, with elaborate moulded plasterwork ceilings and an imposing armorial over the fireplace in the great hall. A coat of arms over the main staircase carries the date 1668 and the admonitory motto of the Forbes family: 'Doe not vaiken sleiping dogs'. Though Craigievar now looks peaceful enough, it was adequately defended in its day: there was and is only one way in, through the tower door, and the building was defended by an enclosing curtain wall which has largely been removed, incidentally making it possible for the spectator to appreciate fully the graceful verticals of Craigievar.

☎ Lumphanan (033 9839 635

7 m S of Alford on A980

NJ 5609 (OS 37)

House open 1st May to end Sept daily 1400-1800; grounds open daily 0900-sunset

♿ F WC 🚻 (by appt) D (in certain areas)
🅿 🏠 ♨ ⚔ ⚓ NTS

Crathes Castle

Banchory, Grampian

This is a well-preserved and hardly spoiled example of the traditional domestic 'castellated' tower of Scotland, of which the finest are at Glamis and Craigievar. Built usually on an L-plan, buildings such as these allowed a family and its retainers to retreat to safety in times of turmoil and brigandage. The lower parts, with a single entrance protected by an iron grille called a 'yett', were made bleakly defensive, but the further up you went, the more convenient the living rooms became (and the more ornament appeared on the exterior). At Crathes, the laird's gallery is on the very top floor, reaching the whole length of one wing. Panelled in oak (unique for Scotland, where pine is normal), it is the showpiece of the castle. Other rooms are impressive in different ways. The great hall is on the first floor – a vaulted chamber with walls that were once plastered and decorated with murals but are now stripped to the bare, rough masonry. The 'green lady's' room is supposed to be haunted, and has brightly coloured but unsophisticated paintings, with texts, all over the rafters and on the undersides of the boards between them, dated 1602. The tower was constructed in 1553-96 by the Burnetts of Leys, who had been granted lands by Robert the Bruce in 1323. The ivory Horn of Leys, granted to the family by the king as a token of tenure, still hangs in the great hall. With the coming of more settled times, a comfortable Queen Anne wing was added, but it does not detract from the sense of a more dangerous age that both the inside and the outside of the tower impart.

☎ Crathes (033 044) 525

2¾ m E of Banchory on A93

NO 7396 (OS 38)

Open Easter to end Sept daily 1100-1800; Oct S, Su 1100-1800; other times by appt

✆ 🅿 WC ♿ (limited access) 🍴 (by appt) D
♣ 🛍 ⛱ ◆ ✹ 𝄢 (by appt) ⚥ ♿ ⚲ NTS

Drum Castle

near Aberdeen, Grampian

A fascinating and effective architectural hybrid, Drum Castle consists of a low quadrangle of mainly 17th-century buildings with a massive, dominating medieval tower at the south-east corner. The rectangular, four-storeyed Tower of Drum, an excellent example of an early, plain Scots tower house, is certainly one of the oldest occupied dwellings in the country. It stands 70 foot high and has walls up to 12 foot thick. It was built in the late 13th century for Alexander III, and guarded the extensive Crown forest land on the north bank of the Dee. On 1 February 1323 – the original charter still exists –Robert the Bruce gave the tower and lands to his armour-bearer and secretary, William de Irwin, as a reward for his loyal service during the wars of independence. Irwins soon became Irvines, and the family owned Drum Castle right down to 1975, when it passed to the National Trust for Scotland. The more secure and prosperous 17th century encouraged a new kind of building, and in 1619 a fine Jacobean house was added to the tower; unlike traditional Scottish buildings, it was horizontal rather than vertical in layout, indicating that timber for roofing was no longer a problem – possibly thanks to the now-flourishing trade between north-east Scotland and the Baltic. A good many 17th- and 18th-century alterations were cancelled in the romantic 19th century, when the medieval arrangements – notably the great vaulted hall of the tower and the enclosed courtyard – were large restored.

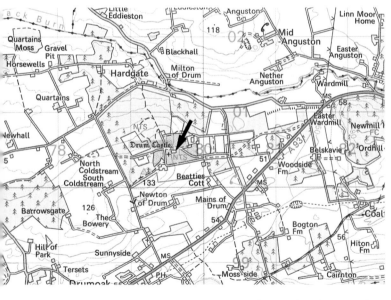

☎ Drumoak (033 08) 204

11 m W of Aberdeen on A93, turn N

NJ 7900 (OS 38)

Castle open May to end Sept daily pm, grounds open all year daily am and pm.

⊖ 🅿 ♣ NTS

Dunnottar Castle

Stonehaven, Grampian

The site of Dunnottar Castle is one of the finest natural strongholds in Britain – the flat summit of a high rock protected on three sides by the North Sea and on the fourth by a deep chasm. No trace now remains of the earliest castle on the spot, though it is known that William Wallace captured it from the English in 1297, the English-backed Edward Baliol took it in 1336, and it was destroyed after falling to the Scots again. The earliest visible remains are those of the parish church, which was razed when Sir William Keith, Earl Marischal of Scotland, built his castle on the rock in 1392. This is the L-shaped four-storey keep, 50 foot high, which dominates the south-west end of the rock; it still stands almost to its full height. Although the keep effectively controls the way in – by a single steep path – in 1575 the defences were strengthened by the addition of a strong gatehouse. In the 16th and 17th centuries no less than four ranges of mainly domestic new buildings were constructed at Dunnottar. In 1645 the castle withstood an attack by the Royalist Montrose, but it was captured (starved out) after an eight-month siege by an English Parliamentary army; meanwhile, Charles II's private papers and the Scottish regalia had been heroically smuggled out. In 1715 the Earl Marischal joined the Old Pretender's rising, bringing with him cannon from Dunnottar. After his failure, in 1719 Dunnottar was slighted.

2 m S of Stonehaven on A92, turn E

NO 8833 (OS 45)

Open throughout year M-S 0900-1800, Su 1400-1700. Closed S Nov-Mar

⊖ (2 miles) 🅿 🚻 D ♣ 🎋

Kildrummy Castle

Kildrummy, Grampian

Few castles can have been built to designs by a saint; Kildrummy is one of them. It is now a magnificent ruin, standing on a ridge above two ravines from which it controlled the road to Strathdon and the Grampians. Kildrummy was designed by St Gilbert de Moravia, who was the royal Treasurer of the North between 1223 and 1245. With a ravine behind it, Kildrummy was built in the form of a great semicircular curtain wall with five projecting round towers; the largest, now called the Snow Tower, served as the keep. The design was modified in the early 14th century, when Edward I of England took over the castle and added a typically 'Edwardian' great gatehouse with two drum towers. The most famous event in the castle's history was the siege of 1306, when Robert the Bruce's youngest brother, Sir Nigel Bruce, held out for weeks against the victorious English. Kildrummy was only captured through the treachery of its blacksmith, who had been promised by the English as much gold as he could carry – and was rewarded by having generous quantities of the molten metal poured down his throat. In the 18th century the Earl of Mar supported the Jacobite rising of 1715, and as a result Kildrummy was slighted.

☎ Kildrummy (033 65) 264/277

15 m S of Huntly on A97

NJ 4516 (OS 37)

Open 1st Apr to 31st Oct daily 1000-1700

🅿 WC ♿ (limited access) 🚻 (by appt) D (on lead) ♣ 🎋 ◆ 🐾 ⚒ ⚔ (by appt) 🧍 🧍 Museum

Muchalls Castle

Stonehaven, Grampian

Muchalls, about ten miles south of Aberdeen and about a mile from the east coast of Scotland, is a sturdy, well-preserved fortified house that is famous for its fireplaces and ceilings. There seems to have been a fortification of some sort here when it was the property of the Frasers, but by 1619 it had passed to the Burnetts of Leys, who built the present castle. Its history is neatly summarised by a panel over the courtyard, which reads: 'This work begun on the east and north be [by] Ar. Burnet of Leyis 1619. Ended be Sir Thomas Burnet of Leyis his sonne 1627.' Muchalls was not the principal residence of Alexander Burnett, who also completed the building of Crathes Castle. Sir Thomas's other main distinction was to have been created a baronet of Nova Scotia, at a time when a baronetcy was a brand new (and eminently purchasable) kind of title. The castle is still very much as the Burnetts made it, an L-shaped building with curtain walls completing the rectangle enclosing the courtyard; the walls have lost their parapet and walkway, but there are still triple loopholes for guns on either side of the gateway. The most striking part of the interior is the great hall, which occupies the first floor of the main east–west block; it has a splendid 17th-century plaster ceiling with heraldic designs and biblical and classical portrait medallions, as well as an enormous fireplace displaying the date 1624 and the royal arms of Scotland.

6 m N of Stonehaven on A92, turn W

NO 8991 (OS 45)

Open May to Sept T and Su 1500-1700

⊖ P WC 🚻 (by appt) ♠ ◆ ⚬
𝄽 (compulsory) ● (permission required)

Cawdor Castle

Nairn, Highlands

This is a good example of an early Scottish tower-house with several interesting features, but its fame – as the home of Macbeth and the scene of King Duncan's murder – is historically unsubstantiated: though Macbeth reigned in Scotland in 1040-57 and was a contemporary of Edward the Confessor, the 1st Thane of the Calders or Cawdors came to the area late in the 13th century. The tower was built on a virgin site as a royal stronghold in about 1370. In the middle of the lower chamber stands an ancient hawthorn trunk, recalling the legend that the 1st Thane was told in a dream to let a donkey laden with gold wander until it lay down at nightfall, and there to build the new tower. It did so under a hawthorn tree, and scientific tests allow this to be that actual tree's trunk. The curtain wall surrounding the tower has been replaced by largely 17th-century buildings on the north and east, away from the burn that defends the western approach. The original entrance can be seen at first-floor level on the east side, but an even stronger entrance was constructed at ground-floor level, with a typical Scottish 'yett' or grille, seized by the 6th Thane from a rival's castle in 1456. A more civilised entrance was made through the 15th Thane's additions in 1663-76. Cawdor Castle is the family seat of the Campbells of Cawdor, and the rooms in the tower and the surrounding houses are comfortably furnished and display a large number of tapestries and interesting family portraits and relics.

☎ Cawdor (066 77) 615

4 m SW of Nairn on B9090 at Cawdor

NH 8449 (OS 27)

Open May to end Sept daily 1000-1730 (last admission 1700); reduced rates for parties over 20

♿ (limited) 🅿 WC ♿ (limited access) 🍴 ♣ ☕ 🍴
◆ ⚲ (available in German) ⚲ ● (no flash)

Dunrobin Castle

Golspie, Highlands

Looking out over the Dornoch Firth eastward into the expanses of the North Sea, the extravagant sham-château of the Dukes of Sutherland presents a challenge to our feelings: it is the expression of the immense wealth and political clout of an English landowner who conducted the 'clearance' of 5,000 Highland tenants from the Sutherland estates. The ancestry of the Earls of Sutherland when created in the first half of the 13th century already reached back into the Celtic past. They held a fort at Dunrobin before 1400, which evolved over the centuries as a typical Scottish castle. So it remained until about 1840. By then the inheritance had, after a complicated family history, passed to the new Dukes of Sutherland. The son of the 1st Duke, who 'cleared' the glens, was the author of the changes at Dunrobin: Barry, who designed the new Houses of Parliament, was brought in to design the palatial structure we see today – in a style imported from the Loire valley with some rugged touches to remind us of the Scottish tradition. The interior was modified in parts by Sir Robert Lorimer after a fire in 1915. The spaciousness and craftsmanship are impressive, and Lorimer's rooms somewhat humanise the scale of the interior. Apart from the usual family portraits, there is an interesting Elizabethan painting of an Irish chief by Michael Wright, a collection of obsolete utensils and a curious museum of game trophies with some carved Pictish stones. Dunrobin Castle is now the home of the Countess of Sutherland in her own right.

☎ Golspie (04083) 3177

1 m NE of Golspie on A9

NC 8501 (OS 17)

Open June to mid Sept M-S 1030-1700, Su 1300-1700; parties at other times by appt (1 day notice)

⊖ (½ mile; limited) 🅿 WC 🚻 D (grounds only)
♣ 🍴 🎋 ◆ ✳ ● (not in castle) ● 🏃

Dunvegan Castle

Dunvegan, Isle of Skye, Highlands

On its commanding rock where Loch Dunvegan opens north-westward to the Little Minch and beyond to the Hebrides, this clan-castle of the MacLeods enshrines their relic-hoard. It cannot matter how gaunt the castle looks from the outside when it contains such treasures as the Fairy Flag, Rory More's mazer, the MacLeod drinking horn, the MacCrimmon pipes and the stays of Flora MacDonald, the Jacobite heroine. Dunvegan has been the headquarters of the chief – the MacLeod of MacLeod – since around 1270, soon after the Scots recovered the Western Isles from the Norwegians. A fort was built here by the clan's first chief, Leod, son of a Viking king of Man. The silken flag with the battle-winning magic seems to have a 7th-century origin in the Near East, and may have been brought back in the 11th century by Harald Haardraade of Norway, who had been in the service of the Byzantine empress. From Leod's time until 1748 the only way in to Dunvegan castle was by steps up from the loch to the sea-gate with its portcullis. The landward side, being more vulnerable to attack, was a sheer wall with scarcely any openings even for windows. When Boswell and Dr Johnson were here in 1773, their hostess, Lady MacLeod, complained to them bitterly about her primitive living conditions, but soon after, General MacLeod began planting trees, and now the surroundings are softened by woods and gardens, while the Victorian extensions within the walls have ensured that the present chief and his family live here in civilised comfort.

☎ Dunvegan (047 022) 206

On Island of Skye, 1½ m NW of Dunvegan on A850

NG 2449 (OS 23)

Open early Apr to mid May and Oct daily exc Su 1400-1700; mid May to end Sept daily exc Su 1030-1700

⊖ 🅿 WC ♿ ⊟ D (grounds only) ♣ ♟ ⚶ ◆ ●

Eilean Donan Castle

Dornie, Wester Ross, Highlands

Eilean Donan, standing guard on a small rocky island at the junction of three lochs, and facing the Isle of Skye, looks just like everyone's dream of a romantic Scottish medieval castle. And so, in many ways, it is, but the building itself dates entirely from the 20th century, as it was rebuilt at enormous expense between 1912 and 1932 by Colonel John Macrae, a direct descendant of the last constable of the castle. The site may have originally been an old Pictish fort, but the castle proper was one of many built in 1220 by Alexander II to protect Scotland from the Norse raiders. It was held for centuries by the Earls of Seaforth (the Macraes were their hereditary constables) and met its doom in 1719 through loyalty to the Jacobite cause. It was garrisoned by Spanish troops supporting the Old Pretender, and they were bombarded by an English man-of-war, HMS *Worcester*, which reduced the castle to rubble. The story goes that the method of reconstructing the castle came to Colonel Macrae in a dream, which seems unlikely, but it is certainly very authentic-looking, with massive rough stonework, bare walls, and the usual collection of Highland Scottish objects – pistols, powderhorns, antlers and tartans.

☎ Dornie (059 985) 202

12 m E of Kyle of Lochalsh on A87 just S of Dornie

NG 8825 (OS 33)

Open Apr to Sept daily 1000-1230 and 1400-1800

P WC ♿ (limited access) ♨ ♣ ♦ ✂ ✗
● (not in castle)

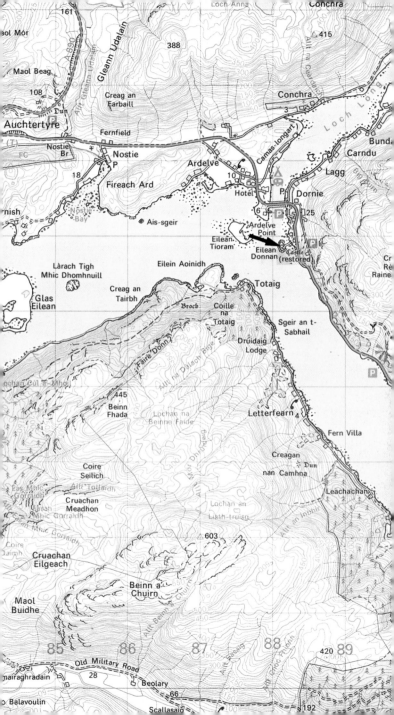

Urquhart Castle

Drumnadrochit, Loch Ness, Highlands

Now a picturesque ruin on a little promontory overlooking Loch Ness, Urquhart Castle has had a long and turbulent history. The site has obvious military advantages, lying astride the Great Glen, the huge geological fault that separates the northern from the central Highlands. There was an Iron Age settlement here, possible a fort. Written records of Urquhart Castle begin only in the 13th century, when it was one of the strongholds held by Alan Durward, Lord Urquhart, the most powerful man in Scotland. It passed to another great family, the Comyns of Badenoch, before becoming involved in the Scottish Wars of Independence against Edward I of England and his successors, when it was taken and retaken several times. By 1346 it was a royal castle, and became involved in the long struggle between the virtually independent Macdonalds and the kings of Scotland. Urquhart Castle was evidently in poor condition by 1509, when James IV gave it to John Grant of Freuchie. The Grants must have built extensively, as most of the present remains date from the 16th century; the most substantial of these are the lower storeys of the great gatehouse, the keep, and the ground floor walls of some domestic apartments. Parts of Urquhart Castle were blown up in the early 1690s, apparently to prevent its use by Jacobite troops, and weather and scavengers completed its ruin.

☎ Drumnadrochit (04562) 551

16 m SW of Inverness

NH 5328 (OS 26)

Open daily am and pm (Su pm only)

⊖ P WC ⓔ (limited access) ⊟ D (on lead)
◆ ✻ ⟨ (by appt)

Blackness Castle

Linlithgow, Lothian

Blackness Castle dominates the village of Blackness, once a flourishing seaport on the south shore of the Firth of Forth. The first record of a castle on the site dates from the 15th century, as does the oldest surviving part. This is the keep or central tower; its turnpike (circular stairway) is a later feature, added when the castle began to be used as a prison. In the 16th century the keep was enclosed by a wall which was later modified and strengthened when massive artillery emplacements were installed. The entrance is notable for its old 'yett', an iron grille of a type once common in northern England and Scotland. In the 15th century Blackness was disputed between the Crichtons (who seem to have been the lawful occupants) and the Douglases. One fascinating but obscure episode occurred in 1452-53, when Sir George Crichton was created Earl of Caithness, only to resign his estates in the following year. Why he did so is a mystery – and his son was so outraged that he seized Blackness and held the Earl a prisoner there until the King forced him to surrender it. After this, Blackness became a royal castle. It was frequently used as a prison, mainly for eminent Scottish offenders, but remained of military significance; the Scots' French allies took it over in 1548, the English General Monk captured it in 1654, and it was still being garrisoned in the 18th century. In the 19th century it was used to store powder and other military supplies, until it became a public monument.

4½ m NE of Linlithgow on A904, turn N onto B9109
NT 0580 (OS 65)

Open Apr to Sept W-S 0930-1900, Su 1400-1900, M 0930-1200; Oct to March closes 1600

P WC 🚻 ♣

Craigmillar Castle

Edinburgh, Lothian

Conveniently situated on a ridge just outside Edinburgh, Craigmillar Castle became a favourite retreat for the kings and queens of Scotland, and was closely concerned in the nation's history. Sir Simon Preston of Gorton bought the land in 1374 and started building the castle, after which the Prestons were the lords of Craigmillar and hosts to royalty for almost three hundred years. The heart of the castle is the massive, plain tower house, L-shaped in plan, with a four-storey main block and a five-storey wing. In the 15th century, curtain walls enclosed the tower in a courtyard. This was a significant strengthening, since the walls were 30 foot high, with sturdy round towers at the corners and some formidable machicolations; there were also emplacements for 'modern' weaponry, i.e. cannon. In the following century Craigmillar was further extended by the creation of a large outer enclosure within walls and a moat. The castle was burned in 1544 by an English punitive expedition under the Earl of Hertford, and it was probably after this that the present east range of buildings was constructed within the courtyard. In 1660 Sir John Gilmour bought the barony of Craigmillar from the Prestons, and in the following year put up the west range of buildings in the outer enclosure. Craigmillar's strongest historical association is with Mary, Queen of Scots, who frequently stayed there.

4 m S of Edinburgh on A68, turn E after Bridge End

NT 2870 (OS 66)

Open Apr to end Sept M-S 0930-1900, Su 1400-1600; Oct to end Mar 0930-1600, Su 1400-1600

 WC 🚻 ♦ ✕ ●

Edinburgh Castle

Edinburgh, Lothian

The castle perches on a rocky promontory nearly 300 foot above the streets of the modern city. The approach is along the ridge through the Old Town to the esplanade, an open space a bow-shot wide in front of the curtain wall, where no building was allowed. Across this the gatehouse and wall rise behind a deep moat. On the other sides the rock falls precipitously from the walls. Today the castle recalls the turbulence of Scottish history. Edwin, King of Northumbria, built a wooden fortress on the rock early in the 7th century and gave the place its name – Edwin's burgh. Though seemingly an impregnable site, the castle was taken and retaken many times by Scots and English. The buildings were demolished after it was captured for Robert the Bruce by his nephew, Randolph, Earl of Moray, in 1313, though the little 11th-century chapel of St Margaret was spared. By 1341 the castle was refortified and again in English hands. During the Civil War it surrendered after twelve days to Oliver Cromwell. The east side of the courtyard is occupied by the palace, mainly a restoration of the early 17th century. To the east of the palace is the great bastion known as Half-Moon Battery, erected in 1573 on the remains of a tower erected by King David II, son of Robert the Bruce, in about 1370. On the south side of the courtyard stands the 16th-century banqueting hall, its outer wall an upward continuation of the precipitous rock.

☎ Edinburgh (031) 225 9846

In centre of Edinburgh at W end of High St

NT 2573 (OS 66)

Open M-S Apr to end Sept 0930-1800 (Su 1100-1750); Oct to end Mar 0930-1700 (Su 1230-1620)

⊖ 🅿 (winter only) WC ♿ (limited access)
🍴 ♦ ◆ ⚘ 🏒 (summer)

Lauriston Castle

Cramond Road South, Davidson's Mains, Edinburgh, Lothian

This fine mansion just outside Edinburgh began as a 16th-century fortified house, though the additions made since the early 19th century are much more extensive than the original building and have reduced it to no more than a south-west corner of the whole. In the 15th century the land belonged to the Louranston family, from whom the name presumably derives. In 1587 it was bought by Sir Archibald Napier of Merchiston (father of John Napier, the inventor of logarithms), who built Lauriston Castle. The castle was essentially a three-storeyed rectangular block with an attic. There are characteristic angle-turrets at the two southern corners; the original entrance was below and between them, on the ground floor. On the north side, the two-storey round stair tower is crowned with a little watch chamber. Some curious features were connected with the hall on the first floor: at one end of it a secret stairway led up to a little chamber cut into the wall; this was equipped with a spy-hole from which the occupant could see what was happening in the hall. Nothing is known of Sir Archibald Napier's life and habits that might explain this carefully contrived outlet for suspiciousness or voyeurism. The most famous of Lauriston's later occupants was John Law, the Scottish financier who founded the Bank of France. Lauriston Castle now contains a collection of mainly 19th-century English and French furniture and antiques.

☎ 031-336 2060

4 m W of Edinburgh on A90, turn N

NT 2076 (OS 66)

Castle open Apr to Oct daily (exc F) 1100-1300, 1400-1700; Nov to March S and Su only, 1400-1600

⊖ 🄿 WC ♿ (grounds only) 🚻 (by appt) ♣ 🎋 ◆ ♨ 🍴 (compulsory) ● (not in castle)

Tantallon Castle

North Berwick, Lothian

Tantallon is one of the most famous and romantic of Scottish castles, ruined yet so substantial and well formed that it gives an impression of indestructibility. The grandeur of the rose-coloured ruins matches that of the site, a rugged cliff top looking out at the North Sea and mighty Bass Rock. It is protected by the sea on two sides, with earthworks and ditches barring other approaches. Once past these and other outworks, the attacker was confronted (as the visitor is today) with a daunting curtain wall flanked by round towers and entered only through a strong gatehouse. Tantallon was the stronghold of the Red Douglases, and probably dates from the late 14th century; its builder may well have been William, the first Earl of Douglas. The Douglases certainly needed a stronghold; their lives were crammed with intrigues, betrayals, rebellions and sieges, broken only by intervals of exile or uncharacteristically law-abiding behaviour. A typical example was the fifth Earl, Archibald 'Bell the Cat' Douglas, who withstood a royal siege at Tantallon one year, and was made Chancellor of Scotland the next. The career of his grandson, the Earl of Angus, was a forty-year epic of office, exile and rebellion (including another siege at Tantallon in 1528) that ended only with his death at Tantallon in 1557. The catle was garrisoned by the Covenanters from 1639, and badly damaged by the English General Monk's artillery in 1651. By the end of the century it had been abandoned altogether.

☎ Edinburgh (031) 556 8400

2½ m E of North Berwick on A198

NT 5985 (OS 67)

Open M-S Apr to end Sept 0930-1900; Oct to end Mar M, T, F, S 0930-1600, Th pm; opens 1400 Su

⊖ ⓟ WC ♿ (limited access) ⊟ D ⊼ ◆ ⁂ ⚹

Brodick Castle

Isle of Arran, Strathclyde

Brodick Castle, on the lovely Isle of Arran, is an austere mansion placed in an intensely romantic setting and enriched by stirring historical associations. A Viking fortress is said to have stood on the site in the days when Norse invaders controlled lands on both sides of the Irish Sea. Later, during Scotland's struggle to maintain independence from England, the castle changed hands several times. In 1306 Robert the Bruce landed on Arran. He seems to have attacked Brodick (then garrisoned by the English) without success. The history of the present building begins with the Hamilton family. In 1503 James, Lord Hamilton, 'so distinguished himself by feats of strength and valour at Holyrood during the rejoicings of the King's marriage' that he was created Earl of Arran on the spot by his cousin James IV. Brodick remained in the family until the 20th century, and although it was too out-of-the-way to be involved in most of the ups and downs of the Hamiltons' fortunes, it was sacked by Henry VIII of England's troops and occupied for a time in the 1650s by a Cromwellian force. The present building is mainly 19th century, but the work was done – by James Gillespie Graham – in a restrained 'Scottish baronial' style in keeping with the 15th- and 16th-century towers at the east end. The comfortable Victorian rooms contain excellent and varied collections of paintings, porcelain and books, and Brodick is renowned for its gardens.

☎ Brodick (0770) 2202

2½ m N of Brodick pierhead

NS 0037 (OS 69)

Castle open Easter to end Sept daily 1300-1700; grounds open all year daily 1000-dusk

♿ P WC 🅿 🚻 D (on lead, grounds only) ♣ ☞ 🍴 ◆ ⚹ 🐕 🧍 NTS

Culzean Castle

Maybole, Strathclyde

The castle, its great towers rising up sheer from the sea, looks from the north side like an archetypal medieval stronghold, but in fact it is an 18th-century 'Gothick' building by Robert Adam. It is the best-known example of Adam's castle style, but he was less at home with the Gothic Revival style than with his own brand of Classicism. The estate had been owned by the Kennedy family since the 14th century, and by the 1690s the old castle had already been turned into a mansion house, but the 10th Earl of Cassilis, who succeeded in 1775, called in Adam, and work began on the first stage, the south front, in 1777. This incorporated the older mansion house, and with the interior decoration of library and dining room was completed by 1782. The next stage was the lower range on the north side, followed by the great round tower on the north front, and finally this was linked to the south front by a huge oval staircase. Some alterations were made during the 19th century to Adam's brewhouse, and an entrance hall was added to the east front. The interiors show Adam at his best, and the great circular saloon and oval staircase are among his most inventive works. As usual, he supervised every detail and designed much of the furniture as well as the carpet in the saloon, and the craftsmanship throughout is superb. The country park, of 560 acres, includes the walled gardens laid out by the 10th Earl and decorated by Adam with picturesque mock-ruins, as well as woodland walks, lakes and picnic places.

☎ Kirkoswald (065 56) 274/260

11 m N of Girvan on A77 turn NW onto A719

NS 2310 (OS 70)

Open Apr to end Sept daily 1000-1800; Oct daily 1200-1700

⊖ P WC ♿ ♨ D (grounds only) ♠ ♣ ☂
◆ ❀ ✄ ⚲ ● ☂ ☗ NTS

Inveraray Castle

Inveraray, Strathclyde

Inveraray is the seat of the Dukes of Argyll, and the fairytale 'Gothick' castle, much admired by Dr Johnson, was built by the 3rd Duke in the 18th century close to the old Campbell stronghold. Not content with this, he also rebuilt the town itself, so that the whole ensemble became a Georgian capital in miniature. The castle was begun in 1744, and the architect was Roger Morris, who had already built Clearwell Castle in Gloucestershire in the Gothick style; the work was supervised by William Adam and his sons John and Robert. In 1877 a fire gutted the upper floors, and the attic storey with dormer windows was added by Anthony Salvin after this. The interior of the castle is quite unlike the exterior. Graceful, light and classical, it was the work of Robert Mylne, who was called in by the 5th Duke in 1772 and redecorated all the main apartments in the most advanced 18th-century style, with delicate plasterwork, tapestries and painted panels. The finest room is the dining room, with a huge central ceiling rose and wall panels of *grisaille* surrounded by painted decoration by Biagio Rebecca. The drawing room, with its coloured and gilded ceiling, was designed for the seven Beauvais tapestries which still hang on the walls, and the saloon, hung with family portraits, has a frieze, doorcase and chimneypiece made by James Adam. All the main rooms contain superb furniture, and there are no less than ten sets of gilded chairs, several of them covered with Beauvais tapestry. The family portraits include works by Gainsborough, Hoppner, Opie and Batoni.

☎ Inveraray (0499) 2203

½ m NW of Inveraray on A819 turn NE

NN 0909 (OS 56)

Open Apr to Oct M-S 1000-1800 (closed 1300-1400 Apr to June, Sept, Oct); Su 1300-1800

♿ (limited) P WC 🚻 (limited access) D (grounds only) 🍴 ♣ 🎁 ⴲ ♨ 𝑘 (by appt) ◆ 𝑘 ●

Rothesay Castle

Island of Bute, Strathclyde

The ruins of Rothesay Castle date from a period when the destiny of the Western Isles was still undecided. The castle stands on the Island of Bute. There may have been a Norse stronghold here in the 11th century, but the first records are of a successful siege by Norsemen in 1230. King Haakon of Norway later took control of Bute, but after the battle of Largs in October 1263 the island became unquestionably Scottish territory. The greater part of Rothesay Castle dates from the 13th century, and in most respects it is typical of its period, with massive 20-foot-high curtain walls and four huge drum towers surrounding a courtyard. However, at Rothesay the courtyard is circular, not rectangular – a design that is unique in Scotland. The best-preserved feature of the castle is the gatehouse tower, which was substantially remodelled in 1520. It is built on an L-plan, like many a tower house or keep, and contained a hall, private room, garderobe (lavatory) and other amenities. Rothesay Castle is surrounded by a wet moat, and had a drawbridge that could be let down from the entrance. It changed hands twice during the Civil War, but the worst damage seems to have been done during the 1685 rebellion, when it was burned. During the 19th century the Marquesses of Bute did much to preserve what remains. The town of Rothsay also has a Bute Museum devoted to local history, natural history and geology.

In centre of Rothesay on Isle of Bute

NS 0864 (OS 63)

Open Apr to end Oct M-S 0930-1900, Su 1400-1900; Nov to end Mar 0930-1600, Su 1400-1600

⊖ P WC ♿ (limited access) D

Blair Castle

Pitlochry, Tayside

The home since the 13th century of the Earls, and then Dukes, of Atholl, the castle at Blair has been extended and several times transformed to reflect the changing needs and taste of the age. The square corner tower – known as Cumming's Tower, after the intruder from Badenoch who built it there while the Earl was away with King Alexander III on crusade (1269) – was all there was of Blair Castle until the 17th century, when a wing in traditional Scottish style was added. It was at this period that the Murray family, who still hold the Atholl title, came into its possession. The campaigns of the Civil War and of the Jacobite risings in 1715 and 1745 – including a siege in 1745, the last on British soil – left the Murrays divided between Stuart and Hanoverian loyalties, but the title was kept by the 2nd Duke, a Whig in his sympathies. He it was who turned Blair into the fine Georgian mansion which hides beneath the 'baronial' exterior of today. The 18th-century sash windows beneath the sham crenellations give this away. Inside there are elegant mouldings and marble fireplaces, and an audacious wooden staircase rising clear through two storeys to the roof. It is hung with 17th- and 18th-century portraits of the Murrays. In 1869, in the Victorian enthusiasm for all that was medieval and Scottish, Blair Castle began to regain the appearance that its name suggests. On the 7th Earl's instructions, it was re-castellated, turretted and generally baronialised–leaving only the urbane windows to betray what it had been before.

☎ Pitlochry (0796) 81 356

1 m NW of Blair Atholl off A9

NN 8666 (OS 43)

Open Easter weekend; Apr Su, M; end Apr to mid Oct M-S 1000-1800, Su 1400-1800

⊖ (1 mile) 🄵 WC 🚻 (by appt) ♣ ♥ 🛏 ◆ ☀

248

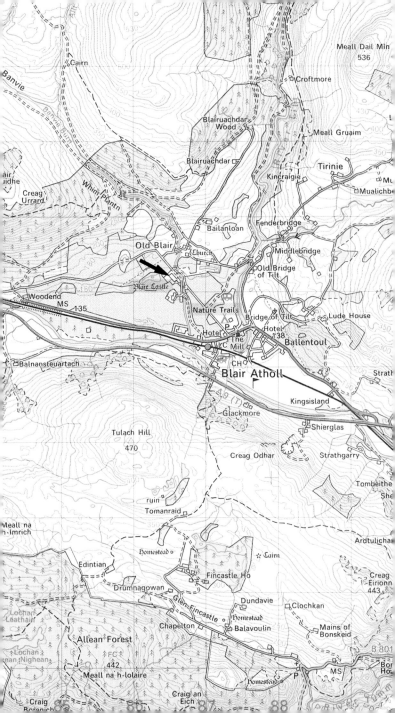

Claypotts Castle

Dundee, Tayside

This castle, just outside Broughty Ferry and the environs of Dundee, is of particular interest to architectural historians as an early example of the Z-plan Scottish tower house. It consists of an oblong central block with a very large round tower built into each of two diagonally opposite corners (north-east and south-west), creating the 'Z' effect. A narrow semi-circular tower is fitted into the angle between the south-west corner tower and the central block. The central block is three storeys high, plus a garret. The towers are a storey higher, culminating in the squared-off watch chambers with gabled roofs that give Claypotts its distinctive appearance. The dates of their construction are carved on the gables – 1569 and 1588 – and help to explain the failure of symmetry in their placing. The builders were the Strachans, who had leased the property from the Abbey of Lindores in 1511 and became proprietors in their own right in 1560, thanks to the sale of church lands after the Scottish Reformation. Although the internal arrangements suggest that comfort and convenience were prime considerations for the Strachans, Claypotts was well equipped to survive at least minor affrays, with a useful parapet walk and loopholes for firearms all the way round the building, not forgetting the kitchen. In the event, its subsequent history was peaceful (though its owners included the ruthless Jacobite leader Claverhouse, 'Bonnie Dundee'), which is why it is still in such excellent condition.

☎ (031) 244 3089
.51 m NW of Broughty Ferry on A92

NO 4531 (OS 54)

Open Apr to Sept M-S 0930-1900, Su 1400-1900
P (limited) WC ♿ (limited access) ⊟
D (on lead) ♣ ⌒ ◆ ⚹ ⚔

Edzell Castle

near Brechin, Tayside

Situated a mile or so outside the lovely village of Edzell, the castle stands in the Grampian foothills, controlling the road to Glenesk and other once important lines of communication. The Stirlings were here from at least the 11th century until 1357, when Edzell passed by marriage to the Lindsays, who became Earls of Crawford. The oldest part of the present castle is the tower house or keep, which was erected in the early 16th century. It now stands four storeys high; both the attic and the parapet have gone. In the late 16th century the 9th Earl of Crawford greatly extended the castle by adding a range of buildings, now very ruinous, which, together with the tower house and a curtain wall, enclosed a courtyard; the inclusion of a large round tower suggests that defence remained a significant consideration. The best-preserved and most original part of Edzell Castle was the last major addition: a large 'pleasance' or walled garden on the southern side of the courtyard, complete with a lodge or summerhouse that is still in excellent condition. The garden's 12-foot-high walls carry an extraordinary series of stone panels illustrating the liberal arts and similar subjects. These were copied from works at Nuremberg seen by Sir David Lindsay, son of the 9th Earl, who was responsible for creating the pleasance in 1604. It is now maintained by the Department of the Environment as a 17th-century garden.

☎ Edzell (035 64) 361

8 m N of Brechin

NO 5869 (OS 44)

Open daily am and pm, Su pm only

♿ 🅿 WC ♿ 🚻 D (on lead, grounds only) ♣ ⌂
◆ ♨

Glamis Castle

Glamis, Tayside

Occupying unusually flat ground for a medieval fortress, Glamis stands 12 miles north of Dundee. Behind the French-influenced extensions of the 17th century, a late 14th-century tower house survives. This type of castle was still strongly fortified, but relatively comfortable. The castle was granted by King Robert II of Scotland to his Keeper of the Privy Seal, Sir John Lyon, in 1372. The site had long been fortified by the Scottish kings, but Sir John Lyon effected a complete reconstruction. A strong, rectangular tower with a small wing on the south side rose four storeys to battlements. The original entrance was at second storey level, and the great hall occupied the third storey. The crypt, the old kitchen and Duncan's Hall on the first floor are the least altered parts of the 14th-century castle. During the 17th century major developments were undertaken: two wings were added to the original tower, and the present main entrance was made at the foot of the tower's corner turret. The height of the original tower was raised and roofed, and the attractive bartizans and cone-topped corner towers built. The Lyon family has remained at Glamis by direct descent since 1372, taking the name of Bowes Lyon in 1767. The castle now has a special interest as one of the childhood homes of Queen Elizabeth, The Queen Mother.

☎ Glamis (030 784) 242

6 m S of Kirriemuir on A928 turn E at Bridgend

NO 3848 (OS 54)

Open May to end Sept daily exc S 1300-1700; Oct to Apr by appt only

⊖ 🅿 WC ♿ (limited access) 🚻 (by appt) D (grounds) ♣ ♥ 🎪 ◆ ⚑ ✂ ● 🏌 🐕 🎿

Huntingtower Castle

near Perth, Tayside

The evolution of this building, like its historical associations, is quite out of the ordinary. The castle – actually a fortified house – stands on a slope running down to the river Almond, about three miles from Perth. It was built by the Ruthvens, a family that appeared in Perthshire during the 12th century and flourished mightily until the end of 16th. Huntingtower Castle originated with a tower house erected in the early 15th century, when it was known as Ruthven Castle. Towards the end of the century the Ruthvens put up a second tower a few feet away; the two buildings could be linked by a wooden bridge from parapet to parapet, but were otherwise quite separate. The idea was evidently to strengthen the defences by having two keeps: if one was about to fall, the occupants could cross to the other and haul in the bridge, leaving the attackers little better off than before. In the late 16th century the space between the towers was filled in with a slightly lower (three-storey) block. The Ruthvens played a great part in 16th-century Scottish politics, and were raised to the earldom of Gowrie in 1581 – only to perpetrate 'the raid of Ruthven', seizing the young James VI at Huntingtower the following year. Finally, in 1600, the third Earl and his brother were killed and posthumously hanged, drawn and quartered for supposedly fomenting 'the Gowrie conspiracy'.

☎ Perth (0738) 27231

3 m W of Perth, off A85

NO 0825 (OS 53)

Open daily am and pm (Su pm only)

♿ WC 🚻 ♿ 𝕏

Loch Leven Castle

Kinross, Tayside

Romantic in setting and historical association, Loch Leven Castle stands on one of the little islands in the loch, which is now a nature reserve. The water level was much higher until the 19th century, so that the castle occupied almost the entire island and boats moored right under its walls. Loch Leven was a royal castle by 1257, when the youthful Alexander III and his queen were abducted from the island and taken to Stirling. It withstood English attacks in the 14th century, when it passed to the Douglas family. The earliest surviving part of the castle, the five-storey tower or keep, dates from the late 14th or early 15th century, though it may incorporate some older masonry; it is the best-preserved feature of the castle, standing to parapet height. Later in the 15th century a curtain wall was constructed that enclosed most of the island. Loch Leven Castle is now remembered above all as a prison from which Mary, Queen of Scots, made a famous escape after being confined following the battle of Carberry Hill in 1567. The laird himself was her jailer, but she won over his young orphan cousin, Willy Douglas, who helped her to get away – to face defeat, flight, a far longer confinement, and ultimately execution.

½ m E of Kinross on island in loch

NO 1301 (OS 58)

Open Apr to end Oct M-S 0930-1900, Su 1400-1900;
Nov to end Mar M-S 0930-1600, Su 1400-1600

♿ ♿ 🚻 D ♦ 🎡 ◆ ♿

Index

Photographic Acknowledgements
Ken Andrew 188, 208, 210, 218, 221, 233, 237, 241, 245, 247, 250, 251; Lord Barnard, Raby Castle/Eddy Ryle Hodges 178; John Bethell 20, 25, 26, 33, 34, 38, 44, 45, 46, 82, 98, 100, 101, 106, 107, 108, 114, 116, 120, 122, 126, 129, 133, 140, 148, 150, 156, 160, 161, 166, 170, 175, 176, 182, 186, 190, 197, 201, 205, 214, 238, 240, 242; Peter Burton 70; Cawdor Castle (Tourism) Ltd 231; W. F. Davidson, 130, 172; Earlshall Castle 219; Eastnor Castle 124; Derek Forss 49; Hamlyn Group/Michael Warren 91; Heart of England Tourist Board, Worcester 146; Michael Holford 144; Geoff Johnson 142; A. F. Kersting 30, 40, 134, 158, 216; S. and O. Mathews 32, 42, 51, 55, 56, 63, 125, 168; Muchalls Castle 230; Ian Muggeridge 84; National Trust, London/John Bethell 72; Chris Orlebar 52; The Photo Source/Colour Library International, London 99, 181; Pilgrim Press Ltd, Derby 252; Rockingham Castle/Norman Hudson & Co. 138; Roxburghe Estates 204; Scottish Tourist Board, Edinburgh 206, 212, 220, 222, 232, 236, 244, 246; Bob and Sheila Thomlinson 58, 165, 173, 185, 211, 224, 234; Judy Todd 29, 37, 48, 65, 66, 80, 86, 102, 111, 113, 118, 193, 198, 226; Unichrome (Bath) Ltd 22; Wales Tourist Board, Cardiff 96, 97, 104, 110; Jeffery Whitelaw 136, 153, 155; Derek Widdicombe 199; Wingfield Castle 162; Woodmansterne/Clive Friend (courtesy of Lord Courtenay, Powderham Castle) 76; Woodmansterne/Jeremy Marks 248; George Young 6-7.